7   **Twilight of Princes**

1713

1720

1736

Newsweek Books New York

Editor Christopher Hibbert

1740   **1742**   **1749**   **1751**

7 Twilight of Princes

1755   1759   1770

ISBN: Clothbound edition 0-88225-070-1
ISBN: Deluxe edition   0-88225-071-x
Library of Congress Catalog Card No. 73-81689

© 1970 and 1974. George Weidenfeld and Nicolson Ltd
First published 1970. Second edition 1974

Printed and bound in Italy by
Arnoldo Mondadori Editore – Verona

1772

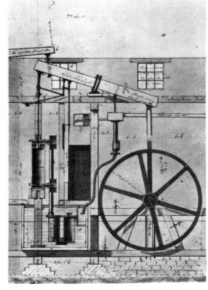

1775

1776

1789

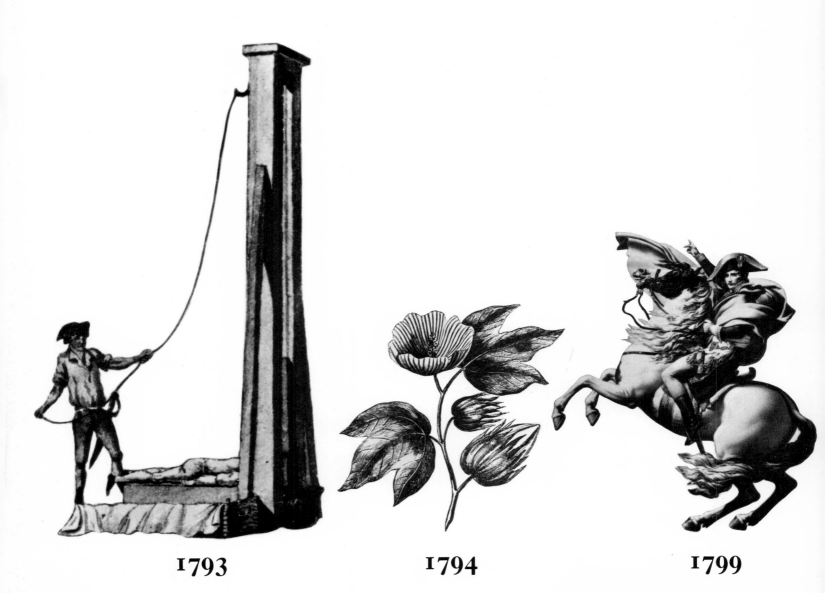

1793   1794   1799

Contents

Introduction

"The eighteenth century lies like a nightmare on the imagination," wrote the English historian Edward Jenks, who was born in the early heyday of the Victorian era. "It is with a sense of relief that we see it disappear before the whirlwind of the French Revolution, in a cloud of full-bottomed wigs, hoops, patches and powder, sedan chairs and preposterous family coaches."

It was a view that an older, even more didactic and severe writer, Thomas Carlyle, shared to the full. In Carlyle's mind the eighteenth century lay "massed up as a disastrous wrecked inanity," useless to dwell upon. Coleridge agreed with him. So did Chateaubriand. Indeed, to many another nineteenth-century mind, the contemplation of the eighteenth century was an experience as painful as it was unconstructive. John Morley and William Lecky might write of those times with tolerance and empathy; but it was the harsher, condemnatory verdict of Cardinal Newman that struck a more responsive note. There was, to be sure, much to condemn.

Before the French Revolution every major European state except Venice was a monarchy, and every monarch except the King of Poland succeeded to his throne by right of birth. It was an Age of Absolutism, in which a sovereign could claim—as Louis XIV is alleged to have claimed—"I am the state"; it was an age in which an autocrat could, in his will, bequeath his country to his sons as though it were his own personal property; it was an age in which a monarch might bestow vast estates and innumerable peasant-slaves upon a favorite—as Catherine the Great did when she retired her violent lover, Count Grigori Orlov, with a fortune of seventeen million rubles, a marble palace and estates staffed by forty-five thousand serfs.

"Kings are absolute lords and have full authority over all people," wrote Louis XIV whose practical example deeply influenced the rulers of eighteenth-century Europe. His opinion was shared by Peter the Great and Frederick the Great, different though their concepts of autocracy were. It was Frederick the Great's belief that "a well-conducted government must have a system as coherent as a system of philosophy, so that finance, police and the army are coordinated to the same end, namely the consolidation of the state and the increase of its power. Such a system can emanate only from a single brain, that of the sovereign." Catherine the Great, who continued Peter's work in modernizing and Westernizing Russia, insisted in her *Instructions to the Commissioners for Composing a New Code of Laws* that while all men were equal before the law, the sovereign was absolute: "The extent of the empire necessitates absolute power in the ruler. Any other form of government would bring it down in ruins."

The effective exercise of absolute power required immense sources of energy and application. Catherine the Great, though she delighted in good food, good conversation and good lovers, would often work for fifteen hours a day, beginning at five o'clock in the morning. Frederick the Great also got up at five, and allowed himself no more than two hours a day for relaxation. "I rise at five in the morning," said King Charles III of the Two Sicilies, who "thought himself the most absolute monarch in Europe" according to the British ambassador. After the death of Maria Theresa of Austria her son, the Emperor Joseph II, threw himself into his work with such avidity that he was able to issue more than six thousand long decrees on all manner of subjects in the ten years before his own death. Louis XIV, whose life appeared to revolve around the choreographic ceremonial of an enervating court, had a real talent and taste for administration: his ministers were forbidden to seal anything without his order or to sign anything without his consent. His successor, Philip, Duke of Orleans, who ruled as Regent after Louis' death, worked all day and—in the opinion of more than one observer—simply wore himself out.

The drive and forcefulness of these absolute despots were decisive in transforming frontiers and upsetting the balance of power. Striding across the years with such vitality they set their firm mark upon the history of their times and by the end of the eighteenth century they had transfigured the map of the world. Some states had grown, others had shrunk and several had altogether been effaced. In Europe, where national frontiers had seemed to be securely fixed by the Treaty of Westphalia which ended the Thirty Years War, public law had been flouted time and again and almost every frontier had been obliterated and redrawn by the Continent's ruling dynasties, until by the end of the century the slow process of transforming the fractured territories of medieval Europe into a relatively small number of powerful, centrally govern-ed states had been finally completed, and Europe's dominant position in the world—foreshadowed by the skill and daring of the early navigators—had been firmly established.

Two new powers, which were later to become the most formidable in all Europe, had emerged with ruthless force. These were Russia, which had pushed southward to the Black Sea and westward to the Baltic; and Prussia, which had been created by the vigor of the House of Hohenzollern. While Russia and Prussia had grown in size and influence, Spain's European empire had disintegrated as Sardinia fell to the House of Savoy, Franche Comté to France, and the Spanish Netherlands to the growing power of Austria. Sweden's power had also been eclipsed. Poland's independence was at an end and her territories had been dismem-bered by her neighbors. Of the great maritime states of Western Europe, Holland's power was in decline through competition with larger countries; England, now known as Great Britain, was creating the strong outlines of a vast overseas empire; and France, which had seen the well-trained armies of the old order halted and turned aside by the massed forces of the Revolution—an event described by Goethe as marking "a new era in the history of the world"—was soon to recover her lost glory under the direction of Napoleon, the epitome of the hungry power of the Revolution and the ultimate victim of its ambition.

Elsewhere in the world the changes wrought by the end of the century were no less dramatic. In India the British had usurped the lost authority of the Moguls; and in North America, having fought France for the control of Canada, they were forced to witness the birth of an independent United States. In Europe the ancient Ottoman Empire had begun to crumble as the Turks had lost Hungary to Austria, the Crimea to Russia and had ceased to be a threat to the Christian world. In the South Pacific a whole new world had been discovered. A foreign dynasty in China had driven the Gurkhas from Tibet, conquered Turkestan, reduced the Burmese to their suzerainty and so greatly extended the frontiers of the Chinese Empire that it was larger than it had ever been in the whole of its long history.

Yet although the absolute monarch of the eighteenth century had played so decisive a part in these upheavals there were unmistakable indications that the long era of the hereditary despot—even of the enlightened despot who thought himself, in the words of Frederick the Great, "the first servant of the state"—was drawing to a close. No future Emperor of China was to govern with such serene confidence as Ch'ien-lung; no future potentate in India was to wield such power as Aurangzeb, the last of the great Moguls; no future King of France was to shine as brightly as the Sun King; and no future King of Sweden was, like

Gustavus Adolphus, to lead victorious armies through the plains of Germany.

Twilight of Princes seems, therefore, an appropriate title for this volume in the series. But it is only one appropriate title. For the Age of Absolutism was also the Age of Reason and the Age of Enlightenment. And to its nineteenth-century critics, it must be said, it was none the less unpalatable for that. To Coleridge the "sandy foundations" of the Enlightenment were as displeasing as the uncontrolled ambitions and excesses of the despots of the *ancien régime*. To Carlyle it was a matter for celebration that the Europe of Voltaire had collapsed in ruins, that Mirabeau and Robespierre had risen to destroy a France which for far too long had been a "despotism tempered by epigrams." For Carlyle did not know what he "should have made of this world" were it not for the French Revolution which had flung aside all the "poisonous trumpery" of the Age of Reason and had trampled it underfoot.

A century later we may look upon that age with more understanding and sympathy. We, too, recognize its faults; but distance enhances its many virtues, its commonsense, its vigor and optimism, its inventiveness and artistic brilliance. Wars were still fought; but they were fought for gain rather than principle and so were sooner ended. Life for the poor was still hard and bitter; but men were being taught to be more tolerant and more humane. It was beginning to be understood that the disciples of Calvin might well turn with profit to the writings of the French *philosophes*, to Diderot's *Encyclopédie*, even to Voltaire's *Candide*. Men were also beginning to believe that cruel punishments, as Sir Samuel Romilly warned the House of Commons in London, had "an inevitable tendency to produce cruelty in the people." In Paris a man who had made an attempt upon the life of Louis xv might still be tortured: his hand was cut off; molten lead and boiling oil were poured into the stump; and four horses were used to tear his body apart. Yet the age of Louis xv was also the age of Cesare Beccaria and of Jeremy Bentham, of Hume and Kant and Wesley, of Mozart and Fragonard. It is the age of the *Twilight of Princes*; but, as the following pages will show, it is also the dawn of hope.

CHRISTOPHER HIBBERT

Twilight of the Sun King

Louis XIV's claim to the Spanish Netherlands was a tenuous one at best—and all Europe was incensed when the French monarch's troops occupied the Spanish Netherlands in 1667. Forty-six years, two inconclusive wars and one inconsequential treaty later, the territorial ambitions of the Sun King were finally curbed and peace was restored to Europe. The treaties signed at Utrecht in 1713 and at Rastatt a year later established a new balance of power among the nations of Western Europe—one that was to last for nearly a century. The militarily humbled French Empire was shorn of several of its overseas possessions; Holland, already weakened, was reduced to second-class status; and Russia, Prussia and England emerged as the dominant European powers. More important, the defeat and subsequent death of Louis XIV ended the Age of Absolutism in continental politics and inaugurated an epoch of enlightened despotism.

Philip V of Spain. After the Treaty of Utrecht he renounced his claim to the French throne.

Opposite Marlborough and his staff at the Battle of Blenheim. This battle ended sixty years of French invincibility—a fact formally acknowledged nine years later by the Treaty of Utrecht.

The treaties concluded at Utrecht in 1713 and at Rastatt in 1714 finally ended the long years of European wars that had resulted from Louis XIV's efforts to extend French hegemony. They also established a new European balance of power that was to survive until the French Revolution.

From the moment Louis XIV took control of the French government in 1661, he was intent on providing France with the best army in Europe—and then using that army, in conjunction with the skilled French diplomatic corps, to make France the most powerful nation on the Continent. Until 1688 it seemed that he would succeed. In 1668 Louis marched into the Spanish Netherlands, using as a pretext Spain's failure to pay the dowry promised him when he married Maria Teresa, daughter of Philip IV. When the Dutch Republic formed a defensive alliance with England and Sweden, Louis made plans to punish the insolent little nation and at the same time destroy the Dutch as trade rivals. In 1672 he invaded the Republic, thus beginning the first of his great wars. The Dutch managed to keep the French army from advancing on the province of Holland by opening the dikes and inundating the land, and by 1678 Spain, England and the Holy Roman Emperor, Leopold I, had joined the Dutch against France. The war ended in stalemate.

The anti-French coalition only temporarily checked the French drive toward supremacy in Europe, however. During the next ten years Louis turned from war to diplomacy and nearly succeeded in making himself master of Europe. He annexed several cities, including Strasbourg, on flimsy legal grounds, and fear of France once more led to the formation of a defensive alliance. Known as the League of Augsburg, that alliance centered around Leopold I and ultimately included most of the German states, Sweden, England, Spain, the Dutch Netherlands and Savoy. From 1688 to 1697 the League—also known as the Grand Alliance—waged a dreary, indecisive, exhausting war with France.

The war ended with the Treaty of Ryswick in 1697, but nothing was really settled.

The threat of French hegemony had not been the only irritant to European stability before 1697. Maritime rivalry between France and Spain on the one hand and England and Holland on the other, and ideological differences between the Catholic and the Protestant countries had also been sources of conflict. Now a further element was added: the question of who would succeed to the Spanish throne. Louis had claimed that throne on behalf of his grandson Philip of Anjou; Leopold I had claimed it for his grandson Charles.

Louis, exhausted by the War of the League of Augsburg, was ready to renounce in part French claims to the Spanish throne, and to put an end to hostilities by coming to terms with the maritime powers. In 1700, however, Charles II of Spain died, bequeathing to Philip of Anjou his great inheritance. Louis accepted on behalf of his grandson, and from that moment onward war was virtually inevitable.

The War of the Spanish Succession was to last ten weary years. Right from the start, the participating powers spent as much time in negotiations as in fighting. The coalition against France was led by a "triumvirate" consisting of England's Duke of Marlborough, Prince Eugene of Savoy and Antonius Heinsius of the Dutch Republic. It was in the interests of all three of them to prolong the war until France was finally forced to surrender. In 1710, however, Marlborough fell into disgrace and the Tories, who took over the English government from the Whigs, were in favor of making a reasonable peace with France. A year later Emperor Joseph I died, leaving his throne to his brother Charles VI, who was also the Austrian pretender to the Spanish throne. England, which felt just as threatened by an alliance between Austria and Spain as by one between France and Spain, withdrew from the war and signed a preliminary treaty with France on October 8, 1711.

The Treaty of Utrecht was finally brought to a

Spanish America. She was allowed to send one "authorized ship" annually to trade in Spanish waters, and she secured a monopoly of the slave trade for the next thirty years.

Holland, on the other hand, derived very little benefit from her efforts, apart from the fact that France renounced all claims to the Low Countries, which came under Austrian rule. Spain had to give up all her European possessions outside the Iberian Peninsula to Austria and to the Duke of Savoy, who had been proclaimed King of Sicily.

Surprisingly, the English reacted unfavorably to the Treaty of Utrecht. The opposition was led by the Whigs, who were critical of the Treaty for several reasons. First, they were bitter because they had lost power scarcely twenty years after the Glorious Revolution of 1688 (which had led to the deposition of the Catholic monarch James II and the accession of William and Mary to the English throne). The Whigs of course had brought about the Revolution and, not surprisingly, they had hoped to reap the benefits from it. They therefore opposed the peace treaties, at least in part, simply because they had been drawn up by their opponents, the Tories. More fundamentally, they felt that the whole spirit of the Glorious Revolution had been betrayed by a peace treaty that had preserved the French monarchy practically intact and that had not interfered with the Spanish overseas possessions. Finally, they pointed out the striking contrast between the ever-growing popularity and influence of English ideas on the Continent and the Tory leaders' meek attitude toward two Catholic monarchs who, for all intents and purposes, had been defeated.

It was quite another story on the Continent, especially in France. Although the failing Louis XIV persisted in his rigid absolutism, French thought and writing was becoming more and more permeated with the subtle influence of English science and rationalism. From the year 1715 on, the regent,

Charles XII of Sweden, whose eventual defeat heralded the arrival of a new power in Europe—Russia.

Right Prussia, led by Frederick William I, built up the finest army in Europe, thus laying the foundations of the German military tradition.

successful conclusion after Philip of Anjou—now Philip V of Spain—had renounced all rights to the French throne on July 8, 1712. Even then Charles VI was reluctant to give up his rights to the Spanish throne and delayed signing the peace treaty until the following year at Rastatt.

Those treaties marked the end of French expansion in Europe; they also represented a great victory for England. Louis XIV was forced to recognize the Protestant succession in England and to expel the Stuart pretender, the son of James II, from French soil. Philip V's renunciation of all rights to the throne of France and the French princes' renunciation of the Spanish succession were declared to be inviolable law. Moreover, Louis XIV ceded to England Hudson Bay and Strait, Acadia, Newfoundland and the island of Saint Christopher in the Lesser Antilles. The port of Dunkerque was to be filled up and its fortifications demolished. Britain received Gibraltar and Minorca from Spain and, far more important, she was granted certain exclusive trading rights with

Philip of Orleans, and his minister Cardinal Dubois adopted a pro-English policy, encouraging more cordial relations between the two countries. (Later on, the Whig minister, Sir Robert Walpole, was to support that entente.) During that period, the intellectual links between the two countries grew much closer. Montesquieu and Voltaire, in particular, were profoundly influenced by English life and literature. The England of John Locke, George Berkeley, Daniel Defoe and Jonathan Swift set the trend for the age of the *philosophes*.

In short, England now represented the country of freedom, the land where the popular press and partisan pamphlets played a decisive role in the political arena. People on the Continent knew all about the political pamphlets written by Swift and Defoe in the course of the fiery polemic that had developed as a result of the Utrecht peace talks. England seemed to be the only country where public opinion was sometimes a decisive factor in influencing governmental decisions. Her economic prosperity seemed to be a fitting recompense for her liberal and enlightened government.

Clearly, that contemporary concept of England was based partly on illusions. The corruption so vividly denounced by Hogarth was completely ignored, while enormous interest was shown in the progress of industry and trade, in the amazing discoveries of Isaac Newton, in the promotion of new ideas by the National Academy of Sciences (the Royal Society), and in the predominant role played by the London Stock Exchange. The Treaty of Utrecht brought England a lasting prestige on the Continent, both with her former enemies and with her former allies. The eighteenth century was dominated by England in the way that the preceding century had been dominated by France and the sixteenth century by Spain.

The Treaty of Utrecht reshuffled the European powers into a new pattern of relationships that was to remain in force for nearly a hundred years. Further, the consequences of the adventurous policy of Charles XII of Sweden in northern Europe, and the victories of Prince Eugene over the Ottomans affected the European balance of power just as much as the Treaty of Utrecht. With the final defeat of Charles XII a new major power appeared on the eastern horizon—Russia, whose Tsar Peter revealed his intention of taking an active part in European affairs from that time on.

Russia's emergence as a major power came at the time of the decline of two other formerly powerful states: Poland, which had been weakened as a result of internal anarchy, and Sweden, which had been reduced by the actions of Charles XII to the status of a second-class nation. The Ottoman Empire was

Left Prince Eugene of Savoy who, together with Marlborough and Heinsius, formed the "triumvirate" against France.

Below left George I, first of the Hanoverians, came to the English throne the year after the Treaty of Utrecht.

Claude, Duke of Villars. The greatest French general of the eighteenth century, who defeated Eugene of Savoy at Denain.

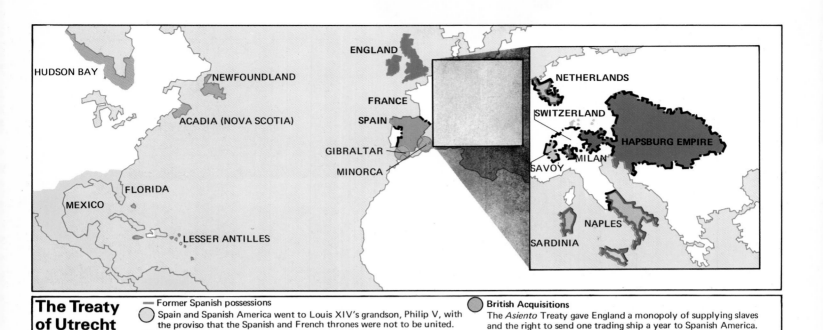

another great power that was in a state of decline during that period. Although it still ruled over vast territories, it no longer constituted a serious menace to the Hapsburg states. Prince Eugene's Austria, on the other hand, had been victorious against both Louis XIV and the Ottoman Sultan and was far more solidly established on the banks of the Danube than it had ever been before.

In Germany, the new kingdom of Prussia was emerging as the heir to the former Swedish territories. The nebulous concept of a loosely knit group of German states, deliberately fostered by the treaties of Westphalia, was in the process of becoming clarified and condensed, while the German people, having recovered from the disasters and ruin of the Thirty Years War, were becoming aware of their identity. At the time, Prussia was still only one of several powerful states within Germany. Saxony and Bavaria were equally powerful German states, but the former was hindered rather than strengthened by the enormous dead weight of Poland, while the latter was growing progressively weaker, without any apparent gains, as a result of its abortive, imperialist ambitions. Prussia, on the other hand, had a history of strong rulers who had developed the Prussian army into the best in the world. That army was the base on which Prussia rose to great power during the reign of Frederick William I (1713-40).

In Italy, the north and central regions were dominated by Austria, while the Republic of Venice was falling into a fatal state of decline. Neither the Papal States nor the Kingdom of Naples were in a position to play a decisive role in the affairs of the country. The newly created Kingdom of Sardinia, on the other hand, had its eyes fixed more and more determinedly on the fertile plains of the Po River in the north. At the same time, it was playing off the

Bourbons of France against the Hapsburgs of Austria —a diplomatic game that had proved most successful up to that time.

Spain, now that her European possessions had been taken away from her, had turned her attention to internal reforms, as well as to the development of her vast overseas empire. Geographically almost as isolated as England from the European Continent, and in possession of a powerful fleet of ships, there was nothing to prevent Spain from becoming a great maritime power. Unfortunately, a nostalgia for her former Italian possessions, combined with the ambitions of Elizabeth Farnese, the second wife of Philip V, diverted Spain from her main course into a fruitless attempt to bring about a revision of the treaties of Utrecht and Rastatt. Elizabeth's ambitious scheme,

16

which was supported by both Charles XII and the Stuart pretender, was to prove disastrous for all.

France was equally split by memories of past glories and concern for the future. She soon recovered from the exhaustion of the long wars, but a violent division of opinion still existed. On the one side were those people who held the traditional anti-Austrian views, dating back to the time of Francis I and Richelieu, and who were now reinforced by supporters of the new enlightened thought; on the other side, the Ultramontane Catholics were hoping for a reconciliation between the Catholic Bourbons and Hapsburgs. The policy of the latter group was to be triumphant with the Family Compact, a series of alliances between the French and Spanish branches of the Bourbons. The former attitude involved

France in the War of the Austrian Succession and reappeared during the French Revolution in the policy of the Girondins, who in 1792 succeeded in having war declared on Austria. Everyone in France was agreed, however, that England was their greatest rival.

While the Continent was busy solving its immediate problems, England had quietly arranged the disputed maritime and colonial affairs to her own advantage. For although the Treaty of Utrecht had placed her in a relatively favorable position in general, it had failed in these areas to give England the decisive victory that the Whigs had hoped for. On the surface, England seemed to be even more divided on the right policy to adopt than the continental powers were, but that dissension was more

The announcement of the Treaty of Utrecht in the streets of The Hague ten days after it was signed.

Left top The allies meeting during the treaty negotiations to discuss peace terms.

Left above The exchange and signing of the treaty.

An engraving of the city of Utrecht produced to celebrate the signing of the treaty on May 12, 1713.

17

apparent than real. The English knew very well that the future of their country lay on the high seas rather than on the European Continent. After the middle of the century they took no further interest in European affairs, except when it was a question of weakening French naval power.

The confrontation of two opposing political views all over Europe was more striking after the Treaty of Utrecht than perhaps at any other time in modern history. On the one side were the traditionalists, who stubbornly persisted in views that very often dated back to the wars of religion. On the other side were the supporters of a new, enlightened policy whose only concern was the reality of the present. Public opinion, when it existed, was equally divided between these two currents of thought.

Cabinet decisions in the eighteenth century, although they did not neglect material interests or ancient traditions, paid little attention to the aspirations of the common people. During the War of the Spanish Succession, the Catalans had demonstrated heroic loyalty toward the Austrian pretender, mainly because they hated the centralist policy of the Castilian government. The people of the German Tyrol showed a similar loyalty toward the Hapsburgs when they were invaded by the Bavarians. Such actions were ignored during the peace talks, however. At that time, the people were still treated like herds of cattle, to be exchanged at the will and convenience of princes and kings, who did not consider the peoples' own wishes on the matter. For example, Sicily was given to the Duke of Savoy, only to be taken away from him a few years later, in exchange for Sardinia; Lorraine was given by Louis xv to his father-in-law, Stanislaus I, ex-king of Poland, as compensation for the loss of the Polish throne. There were numerous similar examples.

John Churchill, first Duke of Marlborough, whose victories over the French at Blenheim, Ramillies, Oudinarde and Malplacquet convinced Louis of his inability to join the thrones of France and Spain.

Right Blenheim Palace, designed by Vanbrugh, was given to Marlborough by a grateful nation after his victory.

It is worth noting, however, that one of the colleagues of the French representative at the Utrecht peace talks, Cardinal de Polignac, was the same Abbé de Saint-Pierre who published, in the very year that the treaty was signed, his *Projet de la Paix Perpétuelle*. That project was considered for many years to be nothing more than a pleasant utopian dream, a revival of the ideas expressed in the *Mémoires* of Sully. Yet by writing his book, as well as by founding, some years later, the *Club de l'Entresol*, the Cardinal was ushering in the new generation of economists and philosophers who believed that the best antidote to war was the general prosperity of the country. Their influence spread far beyond the frontiers of France and England, the most advanced countries of the day. Saint-Pierre drafted a program for "enlightened despotism" which, although it was not directly concerned with the wishes of the people, at least showed an interest in their well-being, since it encouraged the creation of greater prosperity.

Thus the Treaty of Utrecht not only put an end to a series of wars that had proved disastrous to all concerned, it also marked the opening of new perspectives that were totally alien to the spirit of domination reflected in the absolutism of Louis XIV.

JACQUES MADAULE

Above Louis XIV, whose ambition of uniting the thrones of Spain and France was finally frustrated by the Treaty of Utrecht.

Above left Louis XV taking his seat in *Parlement* for the first time, from a contemporary engraving.

Queen Anne with Knights of the Garter. Under Queen Anne's rule, and particularly as a result of the Treaty of Utrecht, Britain's colonial territories increased.

Paper money is used in France

Law's system

For all the elegance of the more fashionable parts of Paris, France at the end of the War of the Spanish Succession was on the verge of financial ruin. The country had rich resources, but its government was without credit and it could raise loans only at enormous cost. The government's financial condition was such that a declaration of national bankruptcy was seriously considered.

Among the distraught advisers of the French regent, Philip, Duke of Orleans, was a Scotsman, John Law (1671–1729), who appeared confident that if a proper fiscal system was adopted, the crisis could be resolved. Law, the adventurous, attractive and keenly intelligent son of an Edinburgh goldsmith, had led a dissolute youth in London and had been forced to flee to Holland in 1694 after killing an opponent in a duel. Since that time he had traveled widely, made an extensive study of the operations of the banks of Europe, lived by gambling and speculation and endeavored to persuade various governments to adopt his schemes. His contention was that finance was a science, resting on fundamental principles and able to support a coherent policy. He assured the regent that France's troubles were entirely due to past financial mismanagement, that trade depended on money and that the solution lay in creating a supply of money to meet its present scarcity —a supply that could not be hoarded and could never become scarce. What Law meant was that paper—or in other words the credit of the state—must henceforth be used for money.

Impressed by Law's confidence and ingenuity, the regent allowed him to found a private bank with the right to issue notes. The bank was immediately successful; its notes combined the advantage of fixity of value with convenience. A decree, issued on April 10, 1717, ordered tax collectors to receive them as payment and to exchange them for coins.

Having successfully established his bank, Law was permitted to set up a commercial company, the *Compagnie de la Louisiane ou d'Occident*, for the purpose of colonizing and exploiting the French regions of North America. In December, 1718, Law's bank became *La Banque Royale*. Its notes were guaranteed in the King's name and became legal tender throughout the kingdom. Branches were opened in five of France's principal towns. Law's company rapidly amalgamated with other commercial interests and under its new name, *La Compagnie des Indes*, it developed a virtual monopoly of French overseas trade. To exploit its opportunities fully, capital was needed—and fifty thousand shares of company stock were therefore issued at five hundred *livres* each. The price of the shares rose rapidly, another issue of fifty thousand shares was made, and two annual dividends of six percent were promised. As a result speculation in the company's stock increased further.

Law now proposed to take over the national debt and to manage it on terms that would be advantageous both to the government and to the *Compagnie des Indes*. The company agreed to lend the bankrupt French government fifteen million *livres* at three percent interest, and financial transactions involving huge sums of money followed. Immense fortunes were made as the price of the stock rose from five hundred to twelve thousand *livres*. As the rage of speculation continued over the succeeding months the price rose to twenty thousand *livres*. Provincial families sold all that they had and came to Paris to play the market. John Law became, in the words of Lady Mary Wortley Montagu, a famous English diarist of the period, "absolute in Paris."

In March, 1720, Law's efforts were crowned with a final accolade of success; the title of Superintendent of Finance was revived and bestowed on the Scotsman. By that time, however, Law's system was already showing signs of decay. It was becoming clear that the prosperity was artificial and that the company would not be able to pay the promised dividend. Men began to sell their shares to invest their profits elsewhere, the price of the shares fell and the worth of Law's paper money depreciated also. By declaring dividends as high as forty percent, the Scot endeavored to stimulate the circulation of the bank's notes, but in May it was declared that their value should be reduced by half. Confusion turned into panic: the police were forced to disperse stockholders in the Paris streets as the bank, the company and the system collapsed in ruins around their founder's head.

John Law's initial success in manipulating credit encouraged the launching of a similar system— called the South Sea Company—in London; one that was soon to collapse no less dramatically and devastatingly than had the *Compagnie des Indes*. But the South Sea Bubble was in a sense an even greater disaster because it involved members of the government in scandalous financial dealings.

England after the Glorious Revolution

During the joint reign of William III and Mary, many of the constitutional problems that had most vexed England during the seventeenth century were at last solved. But many difficulties still remained, the most serious being the succession to the throne and the concomitant danger of a major Jacobite rising. After the death of Mary in 1694, William continued to rule alone, but in March, 1702, he was thrown when his horse tripped over a molehill. The King never recovered, and after his death two days later, the danger of a Jacobite rising was intensified. The Jacobites celebrated his death with toasts to the mole, or "the little gentleman in black velvet." The new monarch, Queen Anne, a dull but worthy woman with an even more worthy and still duller husband, was notable chiefly for her fecundity; she bore seventeen children. All of them, however, were weak and sickly, and all predeceased the Queen.

Anne showed little political talent. During the early years of her reign she left the government largely in the hands of friends of the Duke of Marlborough, but later she fell out with the Duke and Duchess and followed a slightly more independent policy. In practice this proved unwise as Marlborough had sought to avoid the danger of

John Law, France's Superintendent of Finance, who caused a financial crisis similar to England's South Sea Bubble.

to replenish a depleted treasury

Engraving of the statue of Queen Anne erected at Blenheim Palace by the first Duke of Marlborough.

tying the government too closely to one political party.

The early years of Anne's reign were a time of continuing political crisis. In 1710 the Sacheverell affair—when a Tory priest, Dr. Henry Sacheverell (c. 1674–1724), preached a sermon in St. Paul's Cathedral against the 1688 Revolution—shows how politically unstable the country was. When the predominantly Whig House of Commons tried to impeach Sacheverell, the London mob rioted. As a result of this display of popular feeling Sacheverell was only lightly punished, and the display of support for the Tories allowed Queen Anne to get rid of

Marlborough and his friends, with whom she had been quarreling.

The last few years of Anne's reign were quieter. The new Tory administration under Robert Harley (1661–1724), Earl of Oxford, devoted its energies to ending the war in Europe, which was finally achieved at the Treaty of Utrecht. The major problem facing the government was the succession. Both Anne, who did not like her Hanoverian cousins, and Harley, who rightly thought that the Hanoverians would favor the Whig party, toyed with the idea of a Jacobite succession in the person of James Edward. But James' resolute refusal to become an Anglican made negotiations difficult, and before any arrangements could be made Queen Anne died in August, 1714.

The Hanoverian succession

The succession of George 1, the Elector of Hanover and son of Princess Sophia of Hanover, granddaughter of James 1, had an immediate and far-reaching effect on English politics. The fifty-three-year-old King was unable to speak more than a few words of English, and his ministers could speak no German. Communication had to be carried on in Latin, which neither George nor his ministers spoke well, or through interpreters. In addition George was far more interested in his German principality than in his English kingdom. Suspecting the Tories of Jacobitism, George appointed Whig ministers and allowed them virtually a free hand in running the country. Largely as a result of fears of a Jacobite rising, a strongly Whig

The Jacobite defeat at the Battle of Preston, 1715.

parliament was elected in 1715, which gave the newly appointed ministry further support.

The fears of Jacobitism were to be proved well founded almost at once. Jacobitism had not disappeared with James 11's flight from Ireland in 1690. In Scotland the Church was disestablished because of its refusal to abandon the Jacobite succession, and a number of bishops and clergy in England had to be removed for the same offense. There had been occasional outbreaks of military support for the restoration of the Jacobites, but these had been easily suppressed. In 1715 Jacobite fury at the Hanoverian succession led to a more serious rising.

In the wake of the Whig victory in the elections, several leading Tories, including Harley, were arrested. The worst Whig fears— that the Tories were all Jacobites in disguise—seemed to be confirmed when Henry St. John (1678–1751), Viscount Bolingbroke, fled to the court of the Jacobite claimant to the throne, "James 111" (1688–1766), known as the Old Pretender, and became one of his chief advisers. There were widespread but usually

ill-coordinated uprisings, mainly in Scotland. The Earl of Mar (1675–1732) led the largest of these risings, and "James 111," believing that the government would collapse, sailed to join the rebels. But by the end of the year the Jacobites had twice been decisively defeated in battle—at Sherrifmuir and at Preston—and the rising had collapsed. As a result of their support for the Jacobite cause the Tories were regarded with suspicion for the next fifty years.

The newly appointed Whig government was led by Charles, Viscount Townshend (1674–1738), James Stanhope (1673–1721) and Robert Walpole (1676–1745). Although the danger of serious parliamentary opposition from the Tories was almost non-existent after the 1715 rising, the government was open to attack as a result of the corruption of most of its members. In 1720 a major financial and political scandal rocked England, and even threatened for a moment to overthrow the Hanoverian dynasty. This scandal—the South Sea Bubble—made clear once again the dangers of following John Law's ideas.

Dr. Henry Sacheverell, political preacher.

George I, King of England.

DOMINE

IN TE

SPERAVI

Sarga finissima de Inglaterra
de la Nueva Fabrica
Nᵒ Con Yards

RIO DE LONDRES

The South Sea Bubble

In January of 1720, a newly formed English trading corporation known as the South Sea Company issued stock worth £31,000,000—enough to cover England's enormous war debt, which the Company absorbed. Shares of Company stock sold at first for £128 each; by July of the same year the Company's enterprising directors had pushed the value of those shares to £1,000. Generous bribes to high government officials, coupled with equally generous loans to investors (loans that enabled those investors to reinvest their original cash outlays in subsequent issues of Company stock) fed a dangerous inflationary spiral—and led to the Company's inevitable collapse. The bursting of the "South Sea Bubble" toppled the government, bankrupted countless small investors and eventually altered England's financial structure.

At nine o'clock on the evening of September 17, 1720, sixteen of the most important men in England met at the General Post Office in London. Their chairman was James Craggs, England's Postmaster General and a senior member of the government that was led by Stanhope and Sunderland. Craggs was joined by five other ministers: his son James, Secretary of State; William Aislabie, the Chancellor of the Exchequer; the Duke of Kent, who was Lord Privy Seal; and two politicians who had recently joined the ministry (following the settlement of a rift in the Whig party), Robert Walpole and Charles Townshend. The other men present were leading members of the governing bodies of the Bank of England and of the South Sea Company.

The meeting lasted six hours. Its purpose was to consider a way to stave off the impending collapse of the market in South Sea stock. From a modest 128 pounds per share—the asking price at the beginning of the year—that stock had soared to nearly 1,000 pounds per share by July of 1720. On September 1 it had sunk to 775, and on the day of the meeting it was being quoted in Exchange Alley at 520. (By the end of the year it would be back to 155.)

Much the same thing was happening that same autumn in Paris, where the elaborate financial "system" constructed by John Law had expanded to encompass the whole of the French national economy, including its currency. Indeed, the growth of the "South Sea Bubble"—as that stock's inflationary spiral was dubbed—was not an isolated incident in British economic history but rather was part of a wave of speculation that swept over Western Europe in the second decade of the eighteenth century. Its influence was felt in Portugal and Switzerland, Hamburg, Vienna and Amsterdam. Much of the dealing, in fact, was international and competitive; the canton of Berne invested in South Sea stock, and Law, speculating on a fall in price, tried to mount a "bear" operation against it by dumping thousands of shares on the market.

The South Sea Company had been founded in 1711 by Harley's Tory government, which had swept into power by promising to wind up the wars waged by Marlborough and, if possible, to dispose of the legacy of debt that had resulted from them. (The discovery that wars could be fought on credit had enabled Marlborough to finance his victorious campaigns at Blenheim and Malplaquet. It had also left the country deeply in debt.) Harley's scheme was a relatively simple one: he created an impressive-looking trading company with power to issue stock, and then invited the holders of certain government debts to exchange them for stock. In return the Company received an annual payment from the Exchequer that was more or less equivalent to the interest on the debt that the Company had taken over. Although the Company was said to have commercial prospects, the scheme was not much more than a camouflaging of the war debt to make it more acceptable to the squires who formed an important part of Harley's majority in Parliament.

It may well have been John Law's stupendous success in manipulating French credit that encouraged the South Sea Company to launch the scheme that culminated in the extraordinary South Sea Bubble of 1720. The leading member of the group of financiers that controlled the Company was John Blunt, a blustering Baptist who had long been jealous of the financial privileges of the Bank of England. The Bank of England was traditionally Whig, and there was more than a hint of Tory reprisal in Harley's decision—based on Blunt's counsel—to create the rival South Sea Company. In any case, the mainspring of the promotion was the ambition of Blunt and his associates.

Early in 1720 the South Sea Company obtained an act of Parliament under which virtually the whole of the outstanding national debt of 31 million pounds could, at the option of the holders, be converted into South Sea stock. In theory, that act authorized the Company to create one hundred pounds' worth of stock for every one hundred pounds' worth of debt that it took over. In practice, the rate

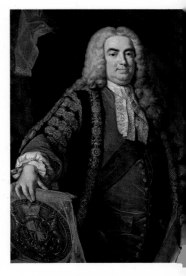

Sir Robert Walpole who gained power in England's House of Commons as a direct result of the South Sea Bubble scandal, and during his period in power created the British premiership.

Opposite The trade label of the South Sea Company.

23

at which debt was exchanged for stock was left to the Company—and it was no secret, from the very beginning of the scheme, that the stock would be issued at a premium. That action would create a stock surplus (because the Company would be able to issue more shares than it needed for the exchange operation) and that surplus—said the promoters—could then be sold for the Company's benefit. The stock's promoters therefore urged debt-holders to exchange their government bonds at a rate that clearly favored the Company. They argued that such a move would actually increase the debt-holders' profits because the Company in which they had become shareholders would have more surplus stock to sell. So great was the confidence of the promoters that they undertook to make the national Exchequer an outright gift of 7 million pounds out of proceeds from the sale of surplus stock. This huge public bribe was necessary to outbid the Bank of England, for the Bank's directors, seeing their privileged position threatened, had also made proposals for taking over the national debt and converting it into Bank stock. Parliament, in fact, held a kind of auction between the two great financial institutions to decide which of them should wield the great, new and ill-understood engine of credit.

In those days the stock exchange, which revolved around Garraway's Coffee House and the little maze of lanes in which it stood, was a smallish affair and largely unregulated. There were already licensed brokers in existence, but the stocks that they quoted were limited—until the South Sea Year—to government issues and to the stocks of the East India Company, the South Sea Company, and the Bank of England and a few issues bearing the names of companies that had survived the great turn-of-the-century enthusiasm for joint stock promotion. Such companies had originally operated under charters entitling them to carry on a specified enterprise, but by 1720 almost all of them had been converted into "shells"—companies that had ceased the activity for which they had been incorporated—by financial syndicates.

The triumph of the South Sea Company in the spring of 1720 had not gone unopposed in Parliament. It had been fought by a determined group of supporters of the Bank of England—notably Robert Walpole—and its path had been eased by large bribes to certain ministers and parliamentarians. Those bribes characteristically took the form of stock in the South Sea Company, nominally transferred to the legislators at market prices and actually delivered free on demand. The value of the bribes was thus, ironically, proportionate to the success of the scheme. Among those probably bribed in this fashion by Blunt and the South Sea Company's cashier, Robert Knight, were Aislabie, the Chancellor of the Exchequer; Charles Stanhope, the Secretary to the Treasury; the two Craggs; and the Earl of Sunderland who, with James Stanhope, was the government's leading minister. Through Aislabie, King George I, who was titular governor of the Company, also benefited—and so did his two mistresses, the Duchess of Kendal and the Countess of Darlington.

At first matters went well enough. The actual conversion began in May at the rate of 375 pounds' worth of debt to secure only 100 pounds' worth of stock, and large quantities of stock were then marketed at vastly inflated prices. (By August, the going rate for a block of stock purchased at 100 pounds in May had risen to the sum of 1000 pounds.) To promote additional speculation the Company interspersed its issues of stock with loans to purchasers of stock, thus constructing a kind of financial pump by which the same limited supply of cash was used over and over again to force the price of stock to ever greater heights.

The South Sea directors had never expected a boom on this scale, and they did their best to damp down competition. They even obtained an act

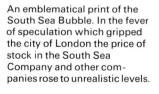

An emblematical print of the South Sea Bubble. In the fever of speculation which gripped the city of London the price of stock in the South Sea Company and other companies rose to unrealistic levels.

against unauthorized joint stock companies. (That piece of legislation, the so-called "Bubble Act," remained on the statute book until 1825 and severely restricted joint stock enterprise throughout the eighteenth century.) Their efforts were to no avail, however, and by September of 1720 it was evident to the entire English financial community that the South Sea Bubble was about to burst. Many factors contributed to the crash; the collapse of Law's financial system in France, the panic induced by the arrival of a fresh epidemic of plague, and the sudden realization that even a guaranteed dividend of fifty

![BUBBLE CARD.]

percent—which the Company's desperate directors promised their stockholders in August—gave the stockholder who had bought at one thousand only five percent on his money. But the chief reason for the slump was that a mountain of short-term credit had been extended during the preceding months of intense speculation—and that credit could not be supported by those who had incurred it.

This was the problem that Craggs and the group at the Post Office confronted on the evening of September 17, 1720. They were unable to solve it, and by the end of the year trade was virtually at a standstill and there was widespread unemployment. A parliamentary inquiry was set in motion and it soon began to dredge up the murky story of the passage of the South Sea Act. Blunt became a willing witness against his fellow directors but not before his colleague Knight—of whom the committee "found it proper to observe that it has appeared to them, throughout their examination, that Mr. Knight, the cashier of the South Sea Company, was principally concerned in their most secret transactions"—was able to abscond to the Netherlands.

During the spring of 1721 the ministry evaporated in a cloud of death and disgrace: Postmaster General Craggs committed suicide; his son, the Secretary of State, died of smallpox; Stanhope, the Prime Minister, burst a blood vessel while defending his government in the House of Lords; and Aislabie, the Chancellor, was expelled from the House of Commons.

The country was in an uproar. "They are *Rogues of Prey*, they are *Stock Jobbers*, they are a *conspiracy of Stock Jobbers*, a name which carries along with it such a detestable deadly image, that it exceeds all humane

Change Alley where dealing in stocks and shares took place.

A satirical "bubble card" showing "headlong fools" plunging into frenzied investment and eventually into the water.

25

The House of Commons in George I's reign, by Tillemans; a number of members of the House were involved in the South Sea Company.

Sir James Craggs, Postmaster General, who kept the House informed of developments during the crisis.

invention to aggravate it," screeched one anonymous publicist, the author of *Cato's Letters*. Soothing that tempest, which had destroyed the government and shaken the Hanoverian settlement itself, was Robert Walpole's supreme achievement. Walpole, who succeeded to the perilous office of First Lord of the Treasury upon the resignation of Sunderland in April, 1721, confronted, opposed and finally defeated the "party of revenge" during the next three months.

The age of Walpole—and of the Pelhams after him—is one of the longest periods of political and economic stability in British history, an era that witnessed the establishing of certain traditions that have survived to this day. The consolidation of power in the House of Commons, the heritage of mistrust of overt collaboration between government and business, and the concept of the importance of a basic continuity in affairs of state—all date from the long period of calm that succeeded the shock of the South Sea Year. So too does the enduring domination of the country's finances by the Bank of England. Sir Gilbert Heathcote, speaking for the Bank at the Post Office meeting, made it a condition of the Bank's collaboration that in the future the South Sea Company's account should be kept by the Bank of England and by no one else. The Bank and the Treasury justified the confidence they demanded. British public finance, from Walpole's time, became the best managed and the soundest in Europe, and its techniques steadily improved. The fact is of incalculable importance for the history of the next two hundred and fifty years.

Walpole achieved domestic stability not through the offices of the Bank of England but by falling back on the landowners, and their interests and prejudices

were to remain uppermost in the minds of British politicians for the next hundred years. It is true that British commerce continued to grow, that London supplanted Amsterdam as the financial capital of Europe, that business families made marriages with the landed gentry and that the importance of trade to the country was everywhere lauded, but business in England never achieved equality of respect with landed wealth. A landed estate remained the ideal security for an Englishman. The former great commercial powers—Florence, Venice, Amsterdam—had been dominated by merchant princes; England lacked them, even in the period of her greatest commercial power.

England's social structure hardened during this period. The absurd inequities of the unreformed House of Commons—to which members were returned on the decision of a single magnate or a tiny caucus of electors—were perpetuated by a series of eighteenth-century decisions concerning the right to vote and the respect paid to landed property. The "Venetian oligarchy" denounced by Disraeli, the system of patronage by which progress in life depended primarily on influence, and the deep conservatism that allowed almost no change in social or constitutional law between 1720 and 1780—all these are marks of this remarkable era of stability. Its saving grace was that it was a diffused not a centralized stability. The rights of individuals and, above all, the rights of corporate bodies—be they local authorities, colleges, charities or guilds—are the stuff and tissue of eighteenth-century English society.

To some extent the period following the South Sea Year can be called stagnant as well as stable. It contrasts vividly with the preceding thirty years, during which the enduring outline of the British constitutional settlement had been established. The conquest of Ireland, the union with Scotland, the Hanoverian succession, the supremacy of Parliament and the shape of ministerial government were all achieved in the generation following the Revolution of 1688. It was a period of greatness and promise, not only in politics but in economics, science and letters. It was an age of new vitality that accompanied Britain's emergence as a great European power. The tendency, unquestionably, was toward political stability, but in another sense the chaotic South Sea Year was a culmination of effervescence.

The succeeding years fell short of the promise of the first twenty of the century. Except in the field of agriculture, technology was slow to find application, despite the earlier progress of scientific theory. For reasons which have never been satisfactorily explained, even the rate of growth of the population decelerated until about 1740, when it resumed a sharper upward trend. It is not unreasonable to attribute some of this slowing down of progress to the recollection of the almost insane burst of optimism which had ended in the disaster of 1720.

That disaster can perhaps best be explained as the impact of new, barely understood financial techniques upon an economy that was still predominantly agricultural. It was in part the penalty that

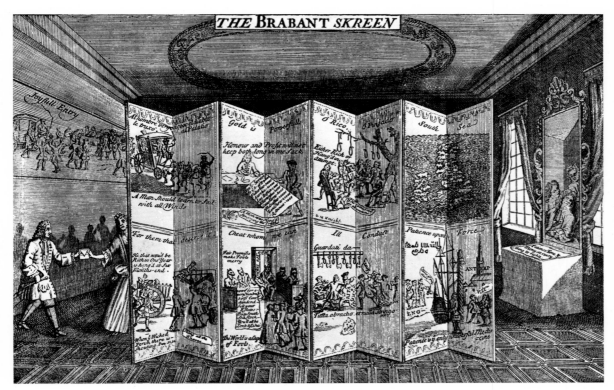

The Brabant Skreen, a satirical print of 1721: on the right behind the screen three directors of the Company are hiding, on the left the South Sea Company Treasurer, Knight, receives a letter from a royal favorite, authorizing him to flee to the Low Countries. The pictures on the screen attack the morality of the directors and the Treasurer. It was thought at the time that royal patronage was used to hush up the crisis, as members of the royal family were involved in the Company and its ruin.

Old Custom House Quay in London during the 1720s; the immense expansion of trade that accompanied the growth of Britain's foreign empire was one of the factors that caused the South Sea Bubble.

England paid for becoming the first nation-state to assume the commercial leadership of Europe. The later period of comparative stagnation—the age of Walpole and the Pelhams—can be seen as one in which the new nation-state, still led by its landed gentry, gradually assimilated its new role in Europe and the world.

The contrast between the aftermaths of the speculation in London and Paris is not insignificant. In Paris, an effort was made to wipe away the memory of Law and his system, and huge piles of paper—representing the era of credit—were publicly burned. Law's real success—for he had succeeded, during his five years of power, in revitalizing the French economy as well as inflating the currency—was lost in an almost religious revulsion for high finance that swept the country. France settled down to a long period of backward-looking despotism that was relieved only by her native sons' essentially critical intellectual brilliance. In England, where many had been ruined (and more cheated of wholly imaginary gains) and an extensive reconstruction of the South Sea Company had been necessary, there was no bankruptcy. In the end, the Company's obligations to its shareholders were honored and South Sea annuities remained a feature of the British national debt until Gladstone abolished them upon becoming Chancellor in 1854. The period of stagnation that followed the slump was an age of digestion rather than decay. The commercial and constitutional vitality of the early years of the century was checked, but not destroyed.   JOHN CARSWELL

Spain and France

When the South Sea Bubble burst, Louis XIV had been dead for five years and his nephew, the Duke of Orleans, was ruling as regent for Louis' five-year-old great-grandson, Louis XV. In defiance of the Treaty of Utrecht, Philip V of Spain—Louis XIV's grandson and the first of the Bourbon kings of Spain—had also claimed the regency. He sought to revive Spain's former glory, lost under the later Hapsburg kings, and refused to allow himself to be bound by the terms of the Treaty of Utrecht. It was still his ambition to unite the crowns of Spain and France. Orleans was able to thwart Philip's ambitions only with the active assistance of Britain and Holland.

Philip's rule in Spain was hampered—as was George I's in England—by his ignorance of the language of his new kingdom. Few Spaniards spoke any foreign language, and almost no Frenchmen spoke Spanish; the troubles of the seventeenth century had driven Spain ever deeper into a self-imposed isolation. Unlike George I, Philip had other problems. The War of the Spanish Succession had been seen as the opportunity to carve up Spain's European empire. The Spanish Netherlands were lost, and Spanish rule in Italy began to collapse. Even more serious, parts of Spain itself had passed into British hands. Philip left the government of Spain largely to Cardinal Giulio Alberoni (1664–1752), an Italian, and later to the Dutchman John Ripperda (1680–1737), while he concentrated on foreign affairs.

Undaunted by internal difficulties, Philip invaded Sardinia

Elizabeth Farnese, Queen of Spain.

and Sicily in 1717 at the insistence of his ambitious second wife, Elizabeth Farnese, who wanted a secure inheritance for her two sons. Philip's seizure of Sicily in 1718 so provoked his enemies that Austria, England, France and Holland set up a quadruple alliance.

That Philip's French hopes continued was shown by his abdication in favor of his son Luis in 1724. Philip hoped that by divesting himself of the crown of Spain he would be regarded as eligible for the throne of France, but the death of Luis in the same year made it necessary for him to resume the throne.

Sweden

Russia's entry into European affairs during the reign of Peter the Great coincided with the beginning of the decline of Swedish power. When Charles XI of Sweden died in 1697, his fourteen-year-old son, a clever, precocious and austere boy, succeeded him as Charles XII. The *Riksdag*, jealous of the power of the regents, offered him full sovereignty in the following year. Charles accepted, and proceeded to attack a coalition that had been formed by Denmark, Poland and Russia to dismember the empire that his father and grandfather had built. Charles first marched on Denmark, whose army had invaded Holstein, landing his troops at Zeeland, a few miles north of Copenhagen, in August, 1700. Two weeks later, by the terms of the Peace of Travendal, Charles gained a large indemnity and a guarantee that Denmark would not make any further hostile moves against Sweden.

Charles then turned his attention to Russia. Against the advice of his generals, he took his army on a week's march through Ingria to attack the Russian fortified camp at Narva. On November 20, 1700, in a heavy snowstorm, his troops overwhelmed a Russian army four times their size in one of the most decisive victories of modern times. Charles captured eighteen generals and 145 cannon. His losses were light—nine hundred men—compared with Russia's losses of more than nine thousand.

Charles could have marched on to St. Petersburg, but, fearful of the enemies who lay undefeated behind him, he turned back to attack Poland. Charles was determined to depose Augustus the

Charles XII of Sweden as a baby.

Strong of Saxony, who had recently secured his election as King of Poland, and to replace him with his own nominee, Stanislas Leszczynski. He entered Warsaw in May of 1702 and on July 2 defeated a large army of Poles and Saxons at Klissow. Three weeks later he captured Cracow. In 1703 he won another important victory at Pultusk and seized the fortress of Thorn. Finally in July, 1704, soon after the King's twenty-second birthday, Stanislas Leszczynski was elected as King of Poland in place of Augustus II.

Supremely confident, impulsive and unstable, Charles seemed totally addicted to the excitement of war. His schemes became ever more ambitious and were ruinous

to the finances of his country. In August, 1707, he again attacked Russia, marching toward Moscow at the head of an army of 44,000 men. Unfortunately for Charles, while he had been "immersed in the Polish bog," Peter the Great had had time to reorganize his armies and to reconquer the lost Baltic provinces.

After a battle on the Warbis River, the Swedes forced Peter's army to retreat. In the appallingly cold winter of 1708—the most bitter winter that Russia had endured for a hundred years—the Swedes pursued the retreating foe across a burned and desolate countryside. By the time they caught up with the Russians on the Vorskla River, the Swedish force had been

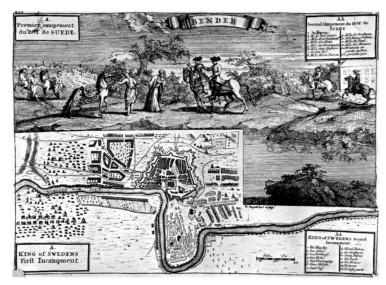

Diagram of Charles XII's encampment in Moldavia.

dominant in the Baltic

reduced to twenty thousand men. At the Battle of Poltava on June 27, 1709, a vastly superior Russian army overwhelmed the Swedes. Charles, who had been wounded on June 7 and was too feverish to lead the battle himself, rode south to seek refuge in Turkey with a small force of cavalry, leaving behind an all-but-annihilated army.

Charles stayed in Turkey for four years and three times persuaded the Sultan to declare war on Russia, each time with inconclusive results. In 1715, after an absence of fourteen years, Charles returned to Sweden. Aided by his powerful minister Baron Gortz—who shared his belief that Sweden was still a great power—Charles raised another army and attacked Norway, hoping to capture enough territory to give him a strong hand in negotiating with his enemies. It was his last campaign; on December 11, 1718, while laying siege to the fortress of Fredriksten, Charles was killed by a stray bullet.

In reality, the fate of Sweden and the Great Northern War had been decided nine years earlier, at Poltava. By the terms of the Treaty of Nystadt in 1721 Sweden lost her empire, Denmark moved into Holstein and Augustus II regained the Polish throne. Russia replaced Sweden as the dominant power in the Baltic region.

Persia and the Afghans

In 1722 the Safavid dynasty of Persia, founded by Shah Ismael two centuries before but increasingly unable of late to control its large empire, came to an end. From about 1690, the Persians' Afghan neighbors to the east began a series of increasingly bold border raids. In 1722 the Afghan general Mir Mahmud laid siege to the Persian capital, Isfahan, and the last of the Safavid shahs, Hussein (1694–1722), surrendered the city and his title. Mahmud became Shah, but he proved to be an unstable ruler. He went mad in 1724, and his assassination in the following year threatened to destroy the unity of the Afghan conquerors. However, his successor, Ashraf (1725–29), was able to gain control of most of the country.

There was still some support for the Safavids, and both the Afghans and the Safavid claimant, Tahmasp

Nadir Shah, the Turcoman chief who defeated the Afghans and sacked Delhi.

II, sought to buy the friendship of Persia's neighbors by offering to give them large areas in return for support. In 1729, with the aid of a Turcoman clan chief, Nadir Shah, Tahmasp became Shah and the Afghans were driven out. But Nadir soon overthrew his nominal ruler and became Shah himself. For nearly twenty years he dominated Persia and the surrounding areas. He forced the Russians to retire from within the borders he claimed, beat the Turks decisively on several occasions, conquered Afghanistan and even occupied Delhi briefly. At the time of his assassination in 1747 he was planning still further wars of conquest.

Nadir's death prevented further Persian advance. He was succeeded by a series of weaklings and children, who reigned only for short periods and presided over the dissolution of Nadir's gains. Afghanistan regained its independence, powerful clan leaders in Persia itself became independent in all but name, and for the rest of the century Persia was a backwater of anarchy, rebellion, civil war and violence.

Japan

The history of Japan in the seventeenth and eighteenth centuries is dominated by its attempts to cut itself off from the rest of the world.

Although Christianity had been held suspect by the government in the sixteenth century it had never been formally banned. In 1614 Ieyasu attempted to suppress Christianity altogether, as he feared that in the event of a Spanish attack Japanese Christians would support their European coreligionists. Despite increasingly energetic persecution over the following decades, however, Christianity refused to die. Indeed, as a result of persecution it became an active agent of social discontent, and a short-lived rebellion in 1677 in the Shimbara peninsula was supported mostly by Christians. The purge of foreign religious influence was followed by an attack on foreign traders and an almost total ban on travel abroad by Japanese citizens.

Neither the isolation, which was only broken by the arrival of Commodore Perry in 1854, nor the social stagnation, which the Tokugawa dynasty of shoguns encouraged, prevented considerable economic growth. The dynasty established itself firmly and remained in power for two and a half centuries after Ieyasu's death in 1616.

China

The stability of Chinese society under the early Manchu emperors is reflected in the length of their reigns; Shun-chih ruled for almost twenty years, from 1644 to 1661, and Sheng Tsu for sixty years, from 1662 to 1722. During their reigns Manchu power was consolidated. Sheng Tsu in particular showed himself ambitious, resourceful and hard-working. In 1673 he was able to suppress the power of the three great feudatories without whose support the Manchu would not have been able to rule. The death of his son Shih-tsung in 1735, led to the succession of yet another able and long-lived ruler, Ch'ien-lung.

Silk weaving, China's most famed and ancient industry. Chinese silk was in great demand in Europe.

Ch'ien-lung Becomes Emperor of China

1736

The first man to place all China truly under imperial rule was not Chinese, but a Manchu— the scion of northern "barbarians" who had conquered China a century earlier. In the reign of Ch'ien-lung, however, China was not only unified but grew prosperous and, despite widespread censorship and book-burning, witnessed a cultural and artistic flowering. Also during Ch'ien-lung's reign, China and the West began making serious contact. The disinterest of the Chinese in the West's avid desire for trade would later have serious repercussions.

During the last two-thirds of the eighteenth century, while Europe and Russia were dominated by Louis XV, Frederick the Great and Catherine the Great, China was ruled by an emperor richer than any of them, controlling a vaster territory and a larger population, who during his sixty-year reign achieved so much that he may be regarded as the greatest Chinese emperor of all time. His name was Hung-li, but he is better known by the title given to his reign, Ch'ien-lung.

Although totally Chinese in outlook, Ch'ien-lung was an alien ruler. His people, the Manchus, "barbarians" from the northeast of China and formerly her vassals, had conquered the mighty Chinese Empire in 1644. His grandfather, Sheng Tsu, the second emperor of the Ch'ing dynasty, which the Manchus established, succeeded in pacifying the country and in laying the foundations for the even greater achievements of his grandson. Sheng Tsu had early noted the intellectual ability of Hung-li and appointed as his tutor the eminent scholar, Fu-min, who was an important influence on the development of Hung-li's knowledge of philosophy, literature, warfare and statesmanship. The old Emperor also accompanied his protégé on the traditional hunts of which the Manchus— until they sank into the decadence of a luxurious court life—were so fond. On one of these hunts he was impressed by the boy's courage, for although aged only about twelve, Hung-li sat calmly upon his pony when a bear leaped out at him.

It was rumored that Sheng Tsu not only appointed his own successor, Shih-tsung (since the heir to the throne was decided by the incumbent and not determined by primogeniture), but also, anticipating Hung-li's brilliance, decreed that he too should eventually succeed. This legend is probably without much foundation; it was also said that, beginning a practice adopted by later rulers, Shih-tsung kept a sealed box in which was written

the name of Hung-li, and that as he lay on his deathbed, the box was opened and Hung-li declared his successor. Shih-tsung ruled for the comparatively short period of twelve years, during which he merely continued the many reforming measures begun by his father. His reign is otherwise an unmemorable interlude between two notable periods in history. He died on October 7, 1735, and Hung-li ascended the throne, although in accordance with the Chinese custom, his reign is dated from the beginning of the following year, 1736, when he also adopted the reign-title, Ch'ien-lung.

Upon succeeding, Ch'ien-lung, aged only twenty-five, inherited two extremely able ministers, O-erh-t'ai and Chang T'ing-yu. From them he learned much statecraft, but after the death of the former in 1745, and the retirement of the latter in 1749, he began an autocratic rule of many years during which all the outstanding achievements of the reign occurred. Ch'ien-lung has been accused of manipulating historiography, and undoubtedly both he and his successors ensured that only the most flattering portraits of themselves were passed on in official writings. It is thus difficult to judge just what sort of man he really was. We can only surmise from the accounts of foreign visitors to his court that he was, by the standards of his time, moral, sincere and broadminded in some matters. But he was also impulsive, intolerant of failure, superstitious and—perhaps his greatest fault— quite unaware of China's place in the world, so that by barring foreign contacts he held back some aspects of his country's progress. He was, however, a true "Renaissance Man" in the breadth of his abilities—a soldier, politician, scholar, artist, poet, historian and statesman, whose personal talents are reflected in the successes of his empire in many different fields.

Ch'ien-lung was a forceful personality and a disciplinarian who maintained his parental authority

A carved jade circular screen on a gilt bronze stand. Ch'ien-lung was a great patron of the arts and a discerning collector.

Opposite Ch'ien-lung in his eighty-fourth year. The greatest emperor of the Manchu dynasty, he forcibly united China and imposed cultural orthodoxy. This watercolor by William Alexander was painted while he was on Lord Macartney's mission to China in 1793.

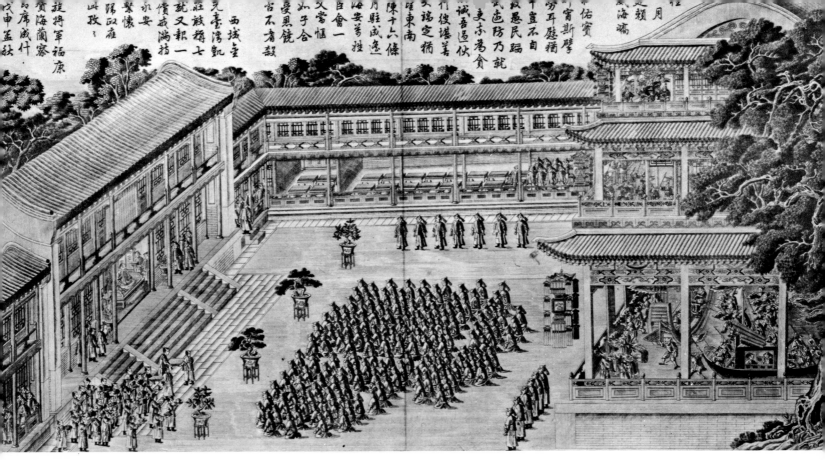

A feast given by the Emperor Ch'ien-lung to General Fu K'ang-an and his officers after their victorious campaign against the rebels in Taiwan. The inscription was written by Ch'ien-lung in 1788.

throughout his life and preserved the respect of his sons and grandsons—no mean achievement in view of the almost traditional interfamily rivalries and intrigues which beset China's imperial houses. He in turn, in customary Chinese fashion, honored his father and particularly his mother, who always accompanied him on his imperial "progresses." The sad tale is told of Ch'ien-lung's capture of Hsiang Fei—"Fragrant Concubine"—the former wife of his enemy, Khozi Khan. His own wife having died eight years before, Ch'ien-lung became enamored of the beautiful Hsiang Fei and had Turkish-style buildings erected in his capital to prevent her becoming homesick. She did not return his love, however, and when the Emperor's mother became angry at the unsuitable and one-sided liaison, the girl was obliged to commit suicide. Ch'ien-lung is reported to have made no protest at this act, and continued to pay daily visits to his mother's apartments up to her death.

He was no nominal ruler. He worked hard and expected the same dedication from his servants. Rising at 4 A.M. he would eat a light breakfast and summon his courtiers who would bring him reports on official business which he would approve by signing in red ink, "Chien Ngon"—"ourself." He would continue to work at affairs of state for at least five hours a day, taking only two meals, neither lasting more than fifteen minutes, and would spend the afternoon in amusement or study. He was an excellent horseman who made the traditional form of Manchu hunting part of an elaborate ritual. He enjoyed the chase at his park at Jehol right up to his eightieth year. He also took an active part in the day-to-day affairs of court life, making an annual sacrifice to the Kitchen God, himself

beating drums and singing a song entitled *The Emperor's Search for Reliable Officials*.

The Manchus were a warlike people, and Ch'ien-lung, for all his cultural aspirations, was no exception. He kept a standing army of 200,000—and was not averse to using it, ostensibly for defense, but frequently also to expand Chinese territory. He was noted for his "Ten Great Campaigns," some of which were different campaigns against the same enemy. The most notable of these took place in the 1750s and were directed against Sungaria (now part of Sinkiang, or the "New Dominion"). During a civil war over a disputed succession, the pretender, Amursana, fled to China, returning with Chinese aid to occupy the territory. He later quarreled with the Chinese and annihilated the occupying garrison. The Manchu soldier, Chao-hui, was sent with a large army and crushed the rebels, drove Amursana out and annexed Sungaria. The Chinese force killed 600,000, many more dying during a smallpox epidemic which swept the country, and others fleeing to Russia. Ch'ien-lung consolidated this huge territorial gain by colonizing it with migrants from other parts of his empire. On the Emperor's behalf, Chao-hui also invaded East Turkestan in 1758–59, defeating two Moslem brothers who opposed Ch'ien-lung. The Emperor gained control over Tibet in 1751 after a brief campaign, and when in 1791 the Gurkhas of Nepal plundered Tibet, he sent a Chinese force of 70,000 over the Himalayas and was by the next year the master of Nepal—the Gurkhas sending tribute to Peking for over a hundred years. Campaigns against the Annamese and Burmese, and rebels of Chin-ch'uan and Taiwan met with similar success. The Chin-ch'uan rebels were mountain dwellers who were flushed from their fortified homes by a cannon bombardment, but not without difficulty. One campaign against them took five years and cost the equivalent of two years total government revenue. Another expensive campaign was launched against the Miao, the non-Chinese indigenous inhabitants of West Hunan, who objected to Chinese attempts forcibly to colonize their ancestral lands. In Ch'ien-lung's least laudable campaign, the Miao were ruthlessly exterminated and for the first time in its history, all China was truly under imperial rule.

The vast expense of these military exploits was matched by the colossal wealth of China at this time. During the reign of Ch'ien-lung, official corruption was, if not eradicated, greatly reduced, and between his accession and ten years before the reign was over, the imperial revenue had more than tripled. Agricultural productivity expanded as a result of official encouragement of peasant migration into the mountainous south and the introduction of such new hardy crops as maize and the sweet potato—in spite of which, it should be mentioned, a shortsighted land utilization policy ultimately resulted in soil erosion and famine. By the end of Ch'ien-lung's reign the population of China was more than 300 million, the largest of any country in the world.

Ch'ien-lung continued the imperial progresses through his lands that his grandfather had established—resulting, incidentally, in considerable local hardship. Whenever he and his retinue visited a particular village or town, food supplies were diverted, canal banks had to be reinforced to support the weight of the crowds that assembled to see the imperial barges and lavish entertainments were arranged in his honor. These preparations were said to have caused the ruin of many a local dignitary, and since any criticism of this wasteful program was frowned upon, it continued unabated for many years.

Apart from the deliberate forgery of historical annals, Ch'ien-lung was responsible for a widespread censorship of many literary works, especially during the period 1774–82. During this time, 2,300 works were totally suppressed, others partly so. The grounds for suppression were that they contained material which was in some way seditious or abusive, but these criteria were loosely applied. The motivation, in Ch'ien-lung's own words, was "in order to cleanse our speech and make straight the hearts of men." It was, in fact, so dangerous to make any sort of political pronouncement in print that for many years China was almost without statesmen of any ability, no one being prepared to risk the consequences of committing his beliefs to paper. Any anti-Ch'ing text, or any that offended a fellow frontier invader, such as Genghis Khan, however obliquely, was destroyed. The entire output of some authors was eliminated. A typical comment of an official censor was, "although there is nothing that shows evidence of treason in this work, still the words are in many cases lying nonsense, fishing for

Ch'ien-lung's red lacquer throne of carved wood. This gives an indication of the elegance of the imperial court during his reign.

praise. It should be burned." An extreme case was that of Wang Hsi-hou, whose dictionary criticized an earlier work, and dared to print in full the characters which represented certain taboo names, such as that of the philosopher Confucius. Wang and twenty-one members of his family were promptly arrested. He was executed, two sons and three grandsons were sent into slavery. Wang's property was confiscated and all his works were destroyed. Ch'ien-lung's remarkable comment on reading the offending passages had been, "My hair stood on end at this revelation of rebellion and lawlessness."

Although scholars find it hard to forgive Ch'ien-lung for his "literary inquisition," which destroyed many masterpieces, he partly vindicated himself by his great encouragement of officially approved literature. He was the nucleus around which gathered many of China's leading literary figures, and he personally wrote learned papers on and prefaces to many books. He was himself a competent poet —his collected poems were alleged to total over 40,000 (which, if true, would mean that he was China's most prolific poet!). His popular verse, *In Praise of Tea*, was for many years inscribed on teapots. It is related that soon after his succession, he took his chief ministers in boats on the lake at his summer palace and invited them to write poems, judging them and their fitness for high office on their productions. Early in his reign he had expanded the official dynastic histories, and continued to supervise the production of lavish "encyclopedias" of law and political affairs. His most outstanding literary achievement, however, was his *Imperial Manuscript Library* or *Complete Library of the Four Treasuries* which included a choice collection of

China's finest works under the headings of Classics, History, Philosophy and Belles-Lettres. It took 15,000 copyists twenty years to produce this vast work in 36,000 volumes. This prodigious undertaking, which the Emperor himself partly edited, contained transcriptions of some 3,462 texts. The catalog alone occupied ninety-two volumes. Seven manuscript copies were made, some of which were later destroyed, but others were preserved and later, printed in part, serve as a vital section of China's literary heritage and a monument to Ch'ien-lung's scholarship.

Ch'ien-lung was a great patron of the arts and a discerning collector of objets d'art. In fact, the very knowledge that a piece of porcelain, for example, was once in his collection, is enough to ensure its desirability among twentieth-century collectors. He was a fine calligrapher, though an indifferent and somewhat wooden artist who produced, in the words of a modern critic, "the sort of picture that Queen Victoria might have painted, had she been Chinese." His love of traditional Chinese art also gave what has been described as a "museum elegance" to the imperial court, but those treasures with which he surrounded himself were always of the finest quality and in the most excellent taste. He was capable of recognizing talent in others, and ever anxious to foster it. In consequence, his court was filled with the most notable painters of the Empire—and even a number from well beyond its boundaries. Several of the Jesuit missionaries who had been

residing at the imperial court for a number of years before his accession stayed on. Among them were fine artists, such as Joseph Castiglione, who produced portraits and scenes of court life, and reproductions of murals depicting Ch'ien-lung's great military campaigns. The latter were sent to Paris where they were engraved and served to promote interest in China. Ch'ien-lung personally encouraged the production of porcelain, especially the popular *famille rose* type made by T'ang-ying and his followers, *cloisonné* ware, and jade and ivory carvings. While he was in many ways narrow-minded about the potential of trade with the West in general, he was eclectic in his regard for European-made clocks and watches, even appointing European mechanics to build and repair them. Apart from Marco Polo, few European travelers had been accepted in China until the arrival in 1599 of the Jesuit Father Matteo Ricci, a noted clockmaker, later revered by the Chinese as "Li," tutelary deity of clockmakers. His presentation of timepieces to the Emperor, Wan-Li, and the immediate imperial enthusiasm for them, had created an atmosphere of mutual respect that endured for many years. The Chinese had, however, virtually no interest in any of the other novelties which the West had to offer at this time, and "trade" was almost a one-way traffic from China to Europe. The only other aspect of European culture for which Ch'ien-lung showed any appreciation was architecture. The result, when translated by Jesuit architects into actual

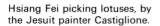
Hsiang Fei picking lotuses, by the Jesuit painter Castiglione.

buildings, was a very curious blend of traditional Chinese and European structures at the summer palace of Yüan-ming Yüan. The Jesuits, having been so long away from the mainstream of European architecture, were somewhat out of touch with changes in style, and so the buildings they designed were not only strange, but also antiquated, a generation or more behind the times. They were, nevertheless, magnificent, set in fine landscaped gardens with fountains, the innovation of the Jesuit hydraulic engineer, Michel Benoist. Sadly, this exotic merging of Eastern and Western architecture was destroyed by the British and French in 1860.

The Emperor was largely uninterested in anything else that contact with the West might bring to China. Inherent in his philosophy was the profound belief that China was the ultimate civilization, neither needful nor desirous of any of the technological advances or wealth that relations with Europe could provide. Accordingly, the colony of Jesuits was the only permanent contact with European ways that he permitted, constantly thwarting all foreign attempts at opening diplomatic relations. Although trading contacts with the Portuguese, Dutch and British based at Canton and Macao slowly grew—they were eventually joined by the United States—so many restrictions were placed on the traffic that all these countries tried over and over again to negotiate with Ch'ien-lung for concessions. A British embassy under Lord Macartney (1737–1806) was sent to the Emperor in 1793 to

present petitions, traveling under escort to Peking in carts with banners supplied by the Chinese that read, "Ambassador bearing tribute from the country of England." The British mission met Ch'ien-lung, finding him "firm and erect," though now aged eighty-two, exchanged gifts and left with many interesting impressions of imperial court life, and with a strange letter to King George III, the tone of which implied Ch'ien-lung's considerable superiority over the "barbarian" king. They did not, however, come to any firm trading agreements, and in fact the Emperor secretly urged the governor-general at Canton to guard against the development of trade with Britain.

Ch'ien-lung was also quite impervious to the missionary zeal of the Jesuit residents in Peking. As early as the first year of his reign he had issued a decree forbidding the Chinese to become Christians, but he tolerated the continued Jesuit presence in return for the practical work that they undertook on his behalf. Apart from their duties as clock-makers, court painters, engineers and architects, they had replaced the Moslem astrologers at court—largely because their instruments were superior and they were able to prove that the Moslems' astronomical predictions by which the dates of religious festivals were fixed, were in error. Under his predecessor, there had been an attempt to convert the Chinese to Christianity, but in a way that fitted in with the Chinese system of belief. The degradations of the Crucifixion were glossed over, and God referred to as "T'ien Chu"—"Lord of Heaven." The Office of Propaganda in the Vatican was appalled to learn of this modified and aristocratic version of Christianity, and dispatched an apostolic delegate to China. A publicly conducted quarrel with the Jesuits ensued, and as a result Christianity in China was largely discredited. The squabble also

A porcelain teapot decorated in colored enamels in "Ku-yueh" style. Ch'ien-lung encouraged the production of porcelain, and his poem *In Praise of Tea* was inscribed on many teapots.

Below A characteristic *famille rose* group of a European couple dancing.

Watering rice fields with a chain pump c. 1796, from Alexander Hamilton's book of watercolors. Chinese civilization, however, ignored many of the technological achievements of the West.

contributed to the later suppression of the Society of Jesus, after which the "exiled" priests remained in China with no official function, acting only as craftsmen and as interpreters of Western languages and culture to those Chinese at court who were sufficiently open-minded to listen.

Although the output of the Jesuits—the fountains of Benoist, engravings of Sickelbarth, paintings of Attiret, paintings and buildings of Castiglione, and the clocks and enamel products made at their workshops at Hait'ien—were Ch'ien-lung's closest dealings with Western culture, the traffic in the opposite direction was considerable. As a result of such trade as was permitted, and from correspondence and the writings and sketches of travelers, Europe became fascinated by Chinese culture. Chinese-inspired architecture, porcelain, furniture, enamel-ware, landscaping, lapdogs, China tea and tapestries—and even the eighteenth-century fashion for wearing pigtails—were China's chief contributions to the West under Ch'ien-lung. Louis XVI of

France copied a custom of Ch'ien-lung's and at New Year would plow a furrow to symbolize the closeness of the monarch to his land.

Had Ch'ien-lung died before 1780, he would have been remembered as China's most illustrious Emperor. By that time his territory and the wealth of his country were enormous. His major military conquests completed, the country was at peace with a rapidly growing population. Art in every field was flourishing, and the literary productions under his auspices were among the most spectacular in China's history. Unfortunately, however, as he grew old, like many rulers before and since, he became complacent and open to the flattery of the many courtiers who surrounded him. One of these rose to prominence and is particularly responsible for marring the good name of Ch'ien-lung in his last years. He was Ho-shen (1750–99), formerly an obscure soldier in the Manchu Red Banner Guard, who had attracted the Emperor's attention in 1775, when he was twenty-five and Ch'ien-lung

36

皇帝冬朝
服一
圖

Ch'ien-lung's design of a winter court robe for his own use. The collar and ornamented skirt are trimmed with undyed sable and the sleeves with perfumed sable. Other features are the dragon and cloud motifs. As the seasons of the year progressed different robes were worn.

sixty-five. Ho-shen had winning ways—a homosexual relationship between the two has even been hinted at—and he quickly entered the Emperor's confidence, becoming a grand councilor at the exceptionally early age of twenty-six and acquiring more and more high offices, a total of twenty at one time, including those of President of the Board of Revenue and Assistant Grand Secretary. Though corrupt and nepotistic—he secured marriage alliances between his own family and the imperial house and appointed his own relatives to important positions—he was able as an administrator, and had a photographic memory, but he angered many other officials by his rapid rise to power. By 1777 he was allowed to ride a horse in the Forbidden City of Peking, a privilege usually reserved for the most important senior ministers. Once in power, he rapidly eliminated all his opponents, gaining a vast fortune, mostly by confiscating property and by embezzlement, actually requisitioning government money to fight mythical wars.

While Ho-shen was draining the imperial coffers, weakening the army and reducing the prestige of important government institutions, Ch'ien-lung decided to abdicate. His main reason for doing so was that he was anxious not to reign for longer than the sixty years of his grandfather, and so in 1796 he stepped down in favor of his son Chia-ch'ing. In reality, the abdication was nominal, for Ch'ien-lung—and Ho-shen—continued to interfere in the politics of China until the Emperor's death on February 7, 1799. Ho-shen's unscrupulous "rule" marks the beginning of the decline of the Ch'ing dynasty, which had reached its peak during the middle of the reign of Ch'ien-lung. Thereafter, despite the suicide of Ho-shen after the Emperor's death, the dynasty began a downward spiral characterized by revolts that the now inefficient army was unable to suppress, and culminating in the total overthrow of the dynasty and of the imperial system in little over a century.

RUSSELL ASH

37

Colonial expansion provides new fuel

The failure of Chinese science

During the Middle Ages, science in China had been, in many respects, more advanced than in the West, but by the middle of the eighteenth century it was clear that the West had little to learn from China. The Chinese, however, were anxious to learn about Western science, although they showed little or no interest in its technology. The Jesuits were no less eager to teach than the Chinese were to learn. Historians have long sought to explain why Western science overtook that of China so rapidly. By 1700 China's lead had faded away, and the West had overtaken China not merely in economic growth and technological development but in most areas of pure science as well.

In many cases, however, the Jesuits were not trained scientists, and even the exceptions were often elderly men set in their ways. In 1710 a young Jesuit priest in China was refused permission by his superior to use up-to-date planetary tables on the grounds that this would "give the impression of a censure on what our predecessors have taken so much trouble to establish." The greater confidence of Western scientists in their information (or misinformation) was part of the reason for the abandonment of traditional Chinese scientific ideas and led to the development of the tradition of observation that contributed so much to scientific knowledge in the Middle Ages.

India

The Mogul dynasty of Delhi reached the height both of its power and its cultural distinction during the reign of Shah Jahan (1628–58), who built the Taj Mahal as a memorial to his wife. His successor, Aurangzeb (1658–1707), was a capable and strong ruler, but he abandoned the cultural and religious syncretism and eclecticism that had given the early Mogul rulers of Delhi their unique distinction.

Aurangzeb's successors were men of little ability. Bahadur (1707–12) and—after a period of anarchy—his grandson Mohammed (1719–48) ruled an empire that was rapidly decaying. The decline was due both to internal weakness and to external pressures. The govern-

Mohammed Shah, Mogul Emperor of India, with an attendant.

ment showed itself incapable of channeling discontent in any constructive way and there were almost continual outbreaks of rebellion. Meanwhile, from beyond the Empire's borders came two serious challenges. In 1739 the Persian leader Nadir Shah invaded India and captured Delhi. He made no attempt to hold the city—he was merely looking for treasure. He was not disappointed. He was able to take the magnificent Peacock Throne of the Mogul emperors—the symbol of their power—back to Isfahan with him. A more serious threat to the Mogul Empire came from the south. The Hindu Marathas, marauding horsemen who had established a group of independent states in central India, saw the troubles of the Mogul Empire as an opportunity to extend their territory.

The subsequent gradual disintegration of the Mogul Empire and its continuous warfare against the Marathas provided the conditions that made it possible for the British and French greatly to expand their territory in India during the course of the eighteenth century. While the Mogul Empire had remained strong the colonial empires of the West had shown little interest in Indian conquest, but they proved ready enough to pick its bones when its more glorious days were passed.

Colonial competition

During the century and a half from 1600 to 1750, the colonial possessions of the European states grew enormously. Although by 1600 European states laid claim

to large areas of the globe, their power in those areas was very often nominal. Settlements in South America, for example, were almost entirely along the coasts, except in Peru, where the search for mineral wealth had led to the foundation of towns inland. In Central and North America, Spanish settlements were few and far between. Africa was an almost entirely unknown continent, partly because fierce Negro tribes proved more effective at holding off the European invader than the Aztec and Inca empires in America had been. The vast mineral wealth of Africa was scarcely thought of until the twentieth century, and the continent was seen as little more than a source of slaves and an impediment to speedy sea communications with the East. On the mainland of Asia, too, the Europeans on the whole preferred to trade with the native rulers rather than to fight with them. Only among the Spice Islands and the Philippines was there any large-

scale settlement in Asia by 1600.

By the beginning of the Seven Years War in 1756, Europe was far more firmly entrenched overseas. The settlement of North America had proceeded rapidly throughout the seventeenth century, and the eighteenth century saw a continuation of this trend. The colonization of America's east coast was completed with the foundation of Georgia in 1733, and the land-hungry east-coast colonies were beginning to make extensive claims on the Indian land to their west. Beyond the Mississippi River lay the scarcely settled French colony of Louisiana. This was joined by a thin strip of French territory to Quebec, France's Canadian colony. On the other side of Quebec lay the British colony of Canada, which had few links with the other British possessions in North America, a source of concern to successive British governments.

Farther south, in Florida and the Caribbean, the competition

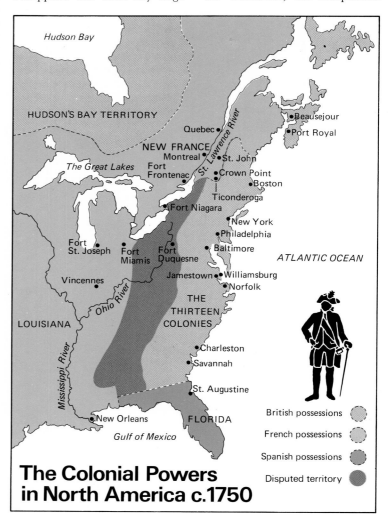

The Colonial Powers in North America c.1750

Hudson Bay

HUDSON'S BAY TERRITORY

NEW FRANCE

The Great Lakes

Quebec

Montreal • St. John

Fort Frontenac

Crown Point

Boston

Ticonderoga

Fort Niagara

Fort St. Joseph

Fort Miamis

Fort Duquesne

Vincennes

Ohio River

LOUISIANA

Mississippi River

New Orleans

Gulf of Mexico

Beausejour

Port Royal

New York

Philadelphia

Baltimore

ATLANTIC OCEAN

Jamestown • Williamsburg

Norfolk

THE THIRTEEN COLONIES

Charleston

Savannah

St. Augustine

FLORIDA

British possessions

French possessions

Spanish possessions

Disputed territory

for European rivalry

was between the British and the Spanish, although there were a few rather scattered French and Dutch possessions. Only in Mexico and South America did the old division between Spain and Portugal as the great colonial powers remain, and even there the French in Cayenne and the Dutch in Surinam intruded.

Africa still largely retained its independence, but there were scattered Portuguese, Spanish, French, English and Dutch settlements. The only substantial settlements were in the Portuguese colonies of Angola and Mozambique, and at the Cape of Good Hope, where the Dutch East India Company was established by Jan van Riebeeck (1618–77) in 1652. In order to prevent clashes with the nomadic tribes, van Riebeeck considered digging a canal to make the Cape Peninsula an island. To make up for the lack of any harbor near the Cape of Good Hope, the British drove the Dutch out of the South Atlantic island of St. Helena and the French took over the Indian Ocean island of Mauritius (Ile de France).

Russia's huge Siberian empire was far larger than the possessions in Asia of any other European power, but they were of little economic value and were scarcely populated. It was further south, in India, that the British and French were beginning to compete most seriously—even the North American struggles were dwarfed by the fight for control of the dying Mogul Empire. In the islands of southeast Asia, Portugal's role and possessions had been taken over by the Dutch.

England under Walpole

The British government's success in maintaining domestic tranquillity and restoring confidence after the bursting of the South Sea Bubble owed much to Sir Robert Walpole. As leader of the administration from 1721 to 1742, Walpole established the system by which England has since been governed, a system that made the cabinet collectively responsible for the government's policy and established the supremacy of the First Lord of the Treasury as Prime Minister in both the cabinet and the House of Commons. The cabinet, a group of ministers who were all members of Parliament, depended on the favor of Parliament and were collectively answerable to Parliament for their actions. This had not been envisaged in the Revolution settlement of 1689. Nor had the office of Prime Minister. But under Walpole both the cabinet and the office of Prime Minister evolved and developed in answer to the country's needs. There was no written constitution, nor apparently was there need for one.

Yet despite the general constitutional success of the British system of government and the high esteem in which it was held by foreign visitors, it had many serious defects. For one thing, religious

Sir Robert Walpole talking to the Speaker in the House of Commons.

toleration was severely limited; nonconformists could not enter Parliament, nor could they attend the universities of Oxford and Cambridge. Roman Catholics were even more seriously discriminated against, and until 1779 were not allowed to practice their religion in public. Furthermore, the government of England was still an aristocracy, and that aristocracy controlled Parliament. Many of the members held their seats through family influence or bribery, and under their rule social injustice flourished unchecked. Moreover, although it was often mitigated in practice, the penal code was ferocious. There was scarcely another country in Europe where so many crimes were punishable by death—and the number of capital offenses was being increased. Thirty-three new capital crimes were created in the reign of George II alone—roughly one for every year of that monarch's reign.

But except for the miseries of the unheeded and largely unseen poor, England was a stable, even a happy, country. The Industrial Revolution had not yet brought the problems of "dark Satanic mills" to the north nor the horrors of slum life to the cities, and agriculture flourished in most parts of the country. In the provinces, the power of the Tory squire to govern the life of his tenants and dependents went unquestioned. All in all, life in early Georgian England was stable, placid and self-satisfied. When a second large Jacobite rising attempted to overthrow the House of Hanover in 1745 it failed to arouse the English people, who refused to imperil the safe Protestant monarchy by rallying to the cause of a pretender, however romantic. Although the Young Pretender, "Bonnie Prince Charlie," the son of the Old Pretender, managed to persuade his army, which was largely made up of Highlanders, to march as far as Derby, causing the rich Whig merchants of London untold terror, he could go no further. His troops melted away in the hostile English countryside to return to the barren hills and valleys of their native Scotland. Not even the hope of plundering London could keep them loyal to the Stuart cause. At Culloden on April 16, 1746, Jacobite hopes were quelled forever by the army of William

Debtors in prison. Whig complacency ignored the social and economic evils of the time.

The Battle of Culloden at which Cumberland shattered the hopes of the Jacobites.

Augustus, Duke of Cumberland, the second son of George II. Cumberland came to be known as "the Butcher" because of his brutal treatment of the rebels, and by 1765 Horace Walpole, son of the former Prime Minister, could write that Jacobitism was extinct. That was not strictly true, but Jacobitism had ceased to be a political threat and had become no more than a romantic ideal.

Warfare in Europe and beyond

From the sixteenth century onward, wars in Europe had repercussions overseas; European colonies found it hard to avoid being dragged into disputes that were of little direct concern to them. In the eighteenth century, colonial fighting became an increasingly important factor in warfare. All the major European struggles of the eighteenth century were in a real sense wars of overseas aggrandizement. Often—as in the Anglo-Spanish War of Jenkins' Ear (1739–48)—the fighting took place largely outside Europe. The increasing complexity of international relations during the eighteenth century is largely due to the importance of trade and the effect of clashes in distant parts of the world. The most European of these wars, however, was that which arose from the rival claims to the Austrian inheritance.

39

The War of the Austrian Succession

The death of the Hapsburg Emperor Charles VI left his domain in the hands of his daughter, Maria Theresa. Fighting soon broke out to annex parts of her territory, with Prussia, Bavaria, Saxony, Spain and Sardinia making their various claims and England and France joining the shifting coalitions. Before the fighting died down, it had spread far from the confines of Europe and as far as India and North America.

The year 1740 offered an object lesson in the impermanence of princely rule. Within a few months of one another, the King of Prussia, the Empress of Russia and the Holy Roman Emperor all died. This coincidence was to have momentous consequences. In a sense, the death of the Hapsburg Emperor Charles VI had been anxiously awaited ever since his accession as Holy Roman Emperor in 1711, for when he ascended the imperial throne he had no children to succeed him. A son was born in 1716, but died within the year; two daughters followed, of whom the elder, Maria Theresa, was henceforth regarded as the Hapsburg heir. She could not, as a woman, become Holy Roman Emperor, but Charles wanted her to succeed to all his scattered dominions and hoped that her husband, Francis of Lorraine, would become Emperor.

The extinction of the Hapsburg line in Spain in 1700 and the cession of Naples and Sicily to the Spanish Bourbons in the 1730s had transformed the European position of the Hapsburgs, but had not necessarily weakened it. In 1740 the Hapsburg inheritance still embraced, besides Austria and Bohemia, the former Spanish Netherlands, Milan, Parma and Piacenza in northern Italy, and Hungary, where the Hapsburgs were still needed for defense against the Turks. By the mid-1720s, Charles VI had persuaded the ruling groups in all the Hapsburg territories to recognize Maria Theresa as his successor. Their agreement was embodied in the so-called Pragmatic Sanction. And, in return for suitable territorial or commercial concessions, this famous document had been ratified by every important European state except Bavaria by the time of Charles' death in 1740.

In October, 1740, no European ruler seemed likely to challenge the Pragmatic Sanction except Charles Albert of Bavaria (who wanted the imperial title himself) and he could not act alone. England and Spain were already at war with one another;

France, whose foreign policy was controlled by Cardinal Fleury, was bent on peace; Russia had a succession crisis of her own. That left the new King of Prussia.

The twenty-eight-year-old Frederick II (later to be called "the Great"), who had succeeded his father Frederick William I in May, 1740, seemed at first sight a cultivated young prince more devoted to literature and music than to politics and war. Voltaire predicted: "Under your auspices Berlin will be the Athens of Germany, perhaps of Europe." As it turned out, Rome seems to have been the more likely model. Within a month, Frederick was reporting to Voltaire not only the founding of the Academy of Science and Literature, but also that he had begun "by increasing the forces of the state by sixteen battalions, five squadrons of hussars and a squadron of lifeguards." These troops were not intended purely for ceremonial duties.

Frederick had determined to seize Silesia. He found a pretext in an antiquated dynastic claim long since abandoned by the rulers of Brandenburg-Prussia. His real reason was, of course, strategic. He could not foresee the economic importance of the mineral wealth of Silesia that a century later was to lay the industrial foundations of Bismarck's Germany, but he could see that the acquisition of Silesia would provide a solid central block amid Prussia's widely scattered provinces, besides increasing her population by half. His program is best stated in the bald words of his own memorandum: "We must occupy Silesia before the winter and then negotiate. When we are in possession we can negotiate with success." By the time his demands for the cession of Silesia had been presented in Vienna, his troops were already invading the disputed territory.

Frederick's contemporaries expected him to be defeated, not perhaps seeing just how vulnerable Maria Theresa's position was. She had not yet had

A gold and enamel snuffbox in its original case portraying an elderly Frederick the Great. Frederick's brilliant opportunism won Silesia from Austria and ensured Prussia's status as the new power in Germany.

Opposite The Empress Maria Theresa. Archduchess of Austria and Queen of Hungary and Bohemia, she was attacked by Prussia in a war that transformed the Hapsburg Empire and altered the European balance of power.

A contemporary engraving of Prussian troops on the march during the Silesian War.

time to receive the homage of the various provinces of her empire (in which no less than ten different languages were spoken) nor to take the measure of the ministers who had served her father. The death of Anna of Russia, who might have supported her, left the infant Ivan VI on the Russian throne. To add to her problems Maria Theresa was pregnant.

Frederick on the other hand had all the advantage of surprise and was backed by an economy and administration geared to the needs of war. Even so, in his first major encounter with the Austrians, at Mollwitz in April, 1741, Frederick's forces were all but routed. The cavalry gave way and Frederick fled with it; but the well-drilled and disciplined infantry stood their ground and saved the day. With a mere 22,000 men and three dozen field guns, Prussia had defeated a Hapsburg army, however narrowly. Well might historians describe Mollwitz as one of the decisive battles of the world.

Frederick's victory encouraged other European powers to demand a share of the Hapsburg inheritance. Charles Albert of Bavaria claimed not only the imperial title, but the Bohemian crown; Augustus of Saxony discovered a dynastic title to Moravia; Philip v of Spain, successor to the Spanish Hapsburgs, thought he had a right to all the Hapsburg lands; even Sardinia, under the House of Savoy, put in a bid for Milan.

This chorus of demands was in part orchestrated by the French. Cardinal Fleury had been in almost continuous control of French policy for seventeen years, and had done much to repair the economic ravages of Louis xiv's wars. He had, it is true, been forced into the War of the Polish Succession in 1733, but as recently as 1738 he had defeated the French war party and abandoned the attempt to put a French candidate on the Polish throne. Now, at one stroke, Frederick had wrecked Fleury's peacemaking, and at the age of eighty-six the Cardinal had not the energy to resist the belligerence of the Count of Belle-Isle. Belle-Isle made a tour of the European capitals, building up an anti-Austrian coalition from among the signatories of the Pragmatic Sanction and canvassing support for Charles Albert of Bavaria in the coming imperial election. Fleury died in 1743, his pacific policy abandoned.

In allying herself with Frederick and with Charles Albert, France was now reviving the traditional role she had played in the sixteenth century and during the Thirty Years War—that of weakening the Hapsburgs by dividing the Empire. In a matter of months Franco-Bavarian forces had secured for Charles Albert the Archduchy of Austria and the Bohemian crown. At the end of January, 1742, he was duly elected Holy Roman Emperor as Charles vii—the first non-Hapsburg for 300 years. Such rapid success did not please Frederick, who accordingly decided to betray his allies. By the secret Treaty of Kleinschnellendorf in October, 1741, Frederick had agreed to halt his offensive so that the Austrian armies could march against the French. This temporary truce was soon broken, but after another Prussian victory in May, 1742, at Chotusitz, peace negotiations were resumed. By the Treaty of Berlin in July of that year, Silesia was surrendered to Frederick.

That was the end of the First Silesian War. The second began in August, 1744, when Frederick, seeing that Austrian successes against Bavaria were placing his own gains at risk, marched first on Prague and then on Vienna. Prague fell. If the French had supported him more energetically, Vienna might have fallen too. As it was, Frederick was forced to retreat. Then, to complete his discomfiture, the new Emperor Charles vii died.

Bavaria bought itself out of the war by agreeing to back Maria Theresa's husband in the election to the vacant imperial throne. Frederick nevertheless managed in four quick victories to consolidate his position sufficiently to ensure that he retained Silesia under the terms of the Treaty of Dresden of Christmas Day, 1745.

Meanwhile the war continued in Italy, the Netherlands and the Baltic. In Italy a Neapolitan army, reinforced by the landing of Spanish troops, had advanced on Milan; but it had been checked when Charles Emmanuel of Savoy came to Austria's assistance—in return for the promise of some Milanese territory for himself. And in 1742, the Neapolitans had been persuaded to retreat south by a British threat to bombard Naples. British money, too, had underwritten the Treaty of Worms (August, 1743) by which Charles Emmanuel, having demanded even more compensation in Milan, agreed to combine with Austria to expel the Bourbons from the whole of Italy. The immediate result was a Franco-Spanish alliance which prolonged the Italian campaign by a further two years before it drifted into stalemate.

British involvement in the war was doubtless due partly to nostalgic memories of Marlborough's campaigns and partly to the Hanoverian connection. George II of England was also Elector of Hanover. He too had signed the Pragmatic Sanction, but England did not at first come to Maria Theresa's aid because neutrality seemed the best way of safeguarding Hanover—being landlocked it could hardly be defended by the navy, England's surest force. At the end of 1742, however, a British army of 16,000 was dispatched to the Netherlands, where it was to join Hanoverian, Hessian and Dutch contingents that would make up the "Pragmatic Army." The Dutch troops arrived late, and when

the army eventually began its advance, with George II at its head, it was lucky to escape being cut off by the French at Dettingen. Only a tactical blunder resulting from the impatience of one of the French commanders enabled the allies to evade the trap. Dettingen was celebrated as a victory in England, and Handel wrote a special *Te Deum* for the occasion. But never again would a British king lead his troops into battle.

It was in any case symbolic that George II had worn Hanoverian uniform when he rode at the head of his army. For the "victory" of Dettingen encouraged the British government to continue to embroil itself in the continental war—though from now on its contribution was mainly in money rather than men. In the closing years of the war, things went badly for the allies. The French, commanded by Maurice de Saxe, had invaded the Austrian Netherlands in 1744. By 1746 they had taken Antwerp, Brussels and the principal fortress towns. In 1747 the French entered Holland and defeated the allied army under the Duke of Cumberland near Maastricht. So desperate was the plight of the Dutch that they hired troops from Russia.

The Russians had not intervened sooner against France for two reasons. First, the disputed succession at home was not settled until December, 1741, when Ivan VI was ousted by Elizabeth Petrovna. Meanwhile, in August, 1741, France had persuaded Sweden to go to war with Russia. The Swedes rapidly regretted their mistake as the Russians overran Finland. But only after peace was signed in the summer of 1743 could the Empress Elizabeth divert her attention from the Baltic. So Russia never really took part in the central drama of the war. Before the Russians could respond to the Dutch appeal for help in 1747, Louis XV had called off Saxe's campaign in the Netherlands, and

The French Marshal Maurice de Saxe, by Quentin de la Tour. In order to weaken the Hapsburgs, France allied with Prussia, Bavaria and Spain, and clashed with the British in the Netherlands.

Cardinal André Hercule de Fleury, Louis XV's minister of state, whose pacific foreign policy was wrecked by the support lent to French activists by Frederick's aggressive moves.

43

Above The Battle of Fontenoy, 1745, in which de Saxe defeated the Pragmatic Army (British, Dutch, Hanoverians and Hessians), and began the conquest of the Austrian Netherlands.

Below The Battle of Dettingen, 1743, in which the Pragmatic Army under England's George II defeated the French forces.

peace negotiations had opened at Aix-la-Chapelle.

The terms of the peace treaty affected three continents. Macaulay wrote of Frederick II, in a famous phrase, that "in order that he might rob a neighbour whom he had promised to defend, black men fought on the coast of Coromandel, and red men scalped each other by the Great Lakes of North America." This is to credit Frederick with too much responsibility. The commercial struggle in India and North America, though linked with the Austrian Succession War, had separate causes

and an earlier starting point. When England and Spain went to war in 1739, what was really at stake was the future of the *asiento*—the exclusive right to supply South America with slaves—which England had been awarded at the Peace of Utrecht in 1713. The Spaniards thought, quite rightly, that the British monopoly of the slave trade to the Spanish West Indies was being used as a cover for illegal trading, beyond the one ship a year for general trade that the Treaty of Utrecht allowed.

The war in the West Indies did not prove very decisive. England had declared war on Spain in spite of the opposition of Sir Robert Walpole, still nominally the Prime Minister. He could hardly be expected to conduct the war with much enthusiasm. Admiral Vernon achieved a startling initial success when he captured Portobello on the Panama isthmus with a squadron of six ships and the loss of only seven men, but he failed to capture his other objectives and had to content himself with a policy of blockade. In this he was successful: only one treasure fleet got through to Spain.

But the real struggle for supremacy in the Americas was between England and France. British merchants, already worried about the growth of French trade in West Indian sugar, had been clamoring for war with France since 1740. As Sir Matthew Dekker wrote in that year: "Because the Incumbrances on our Trade at present have given the French so much the Start of us in time of Peace, that War seems absolutely necessary to obstruct their growing power." Frederick the Great could hardly be blamed for that.

The Anglo-French War in North America did not start until 1744. The French Canadians began

with a series of frontier raids on Nova Scotia and Massachusetts, while using Louisbourg (the port they had built at the mouth of the St. Lawrence) as a base for privateering in the New England fishing grounds and for general harrying of colonial shipping. In 1745, an expedition organized by the Governor of Massachusetts, and supported by a detachment from the West Indies squadron, blockaded Louisbourg and captured it. But the bulk of the British fleet was busy blockading the coast of Italy, and so the colonists could not exploit their advantage. Equally, the European war prevented France from assisting her settlers. A strong French squadron tried to recapture Louisbourg in 1746, but was beaten off and left to limp back to France, narrowly escaping interception and destruction. Thus the conflict in Europe ensured that the Anglo-French struggle for control of North America would be postponed for a decade.

It was not until the winter of 1744 that the news of Anglo-French hostilities reached India. Here the contestants were the two rival East India companies, the British, with its bases at Calcutta and Madras, the French at Chandernagore and Pondicherry. This was purely a commercial war, for the deeper political implications of the struggle were not fully understood at the time. The possibility of some sort of compromise between the two trading companies was forestalled by the arrival of Admiral Barnett's squadron in the Indian Ocean, where he cut the French trade routes and seized a number of merchantmen. Dupleix, Governor of the French East India Company, determined to defeat the British on land. He attacked and captured Madras— thanks to the timely death of Barnett and the no-less-timely arrival of La Bourdonnais' squadron from Mauritius with another twelve hundred men. Dupleix successfully defended Madras against a massive counterattack by the Nawab of Arcot, and

not even the arrival of Boscawen and a force of four thousand troops could secure a British victory before the war ended.

In the peace-making at Aix-la-Chapelle, the French agreed to give back Madras, while the British surrendered Louisbourg. In Europe the fruits of eight years of war seemed just as meager. Austria retrieved the Netherlands, but relinquished Silesia—and so Frederick at least was satisfied. Charles Emmanuel was rewarded for his support of Maria Theresa in Italy by gaining part of Milan. Spain gained Parma and Piacenza, but allowed England to retain the *asiento* until 1752. The Hapsburg Empire had emerged from the war maimed but very much alive.

Historians have marveled at Prussia's success in the two Silesian wars. In fact, it is more remarkable that the Hapsburg Empire did not fall apart. It is true that Maria Theresa had to abandon all hope of dominating the Italian peninsula, though the Austrian presence there would last into the second half of the nineteenth century. It is true, too, that Prussia's seizure of Silesia meant that there were now two major powers in Germany, and Austria's unsuccessful attempt to regain Silesia in the Seven Years War (1756–63) merely confirmed this fact. Meanwhile the loss of a million German subjects with the ceded territory meant that the Hapsburg Empire would in future contain proportionately fewer Germans and more Slavs and Magyars. To that extent, the war of 1740–48 foreshadowed the war of 1914–18.

Yet, like defeated nations in more modern times, Austria probably benefited more from defeat than she would have done from victory. The shock of Frederick's victory at Mollwitz provided a stimulus to military and administrative reform that could never have come about in peacetime. The provincial diets of Austria and Bohemia surrendered all their traditional administrative functions to ten new *gubernia* and, although Hungarian independence remained nominally intact, more and more business was gradually transferred from Budapest to Vienna. By various inducements—diplomatic posts, court dignities, generalships, titles, schools for their children—Maria Theresa enticed the Magyar nobles, the ruling class of Hungary, into the service of the Austrian Empire. The process of law reform was begun, even if it took half a century to complete, and the foundations of a new educational system were laid.

It is a strange paradox. Frederick the Great, flute-player, religious skeptic and patron of philosophers, sacrificed his educational program to the demands of war. Maria Theresa, Catholic, conventional and temperamentally conservative, was forced by the Austrian Succession War to introduce enlightened reforms which ensured that the Hapsburg Empire would be enabled to survive not only the wars of the eighteenth century, but also the impact of the French Revolution and the onslaught of Napoleon Bonaparte.

STUART ANDREWS

An allegorical engraving of the Treaty of Dresden, 1745, depicting Augustus III of Saxony, Maria Theresa and Frederick the Great. The terms of the treaty ratified Prussian possession of Silesia, recognized Maria Theresa's husband, Francis I, as Holy Roman Emperor, and stipulated that Saxony pay Prussia indemnity.

Rococo

The art of the eighteenth century developed from the sumptuous, often over-pretty, interiors in the Rococo style, by way of Neoclassicism, which was dominated by formal values, to the early manifestations of the Romantic style.

Rococo was predominantly a decorative style, which found its finest expression in Germany in the sculptures—mostly commissioned for churches—of Ignaz Günther (1725–75) and in France in the interiors of important domestic buildings, which were often hung lavishly with pictures of nymphs and shepherds in mincing dalliance. Rococo (from the French *rocaille*, rock-like), was an extreme development of the Baroque love of irregularity raised to a fundamental principle. By the use of light colors—white and gold predominate—and a lack of formal lines, Rococo decorators were able to produce a charming and airy informality. One of the major painters of the period, deeply in-

An allegory with Venus and Time, by Tiepolo.

fluenced by Rococo ideals, was the great Venetian decorative artist Giambattista Tiepolo (1696–1770). Many of the frescoes that he painted for churches and palaces in all parts of Europe show a freedom and strength of line and spirit considered to verge on the blasphemous. But, despite a mounting chorus of conservative criticism, Tiepolo was

recognized as the leading painter of his time, and art historians have not quarreled with the verdict of his contemporaries.

In France, too, the influence of Rococo was felt. François Boucher (1703–70) used the Rococo style to develop the traditions that he had learned from Watteau. The lightness, wit and wordly gaiety of much eighteenth-century French art is illustrated by the work of Jean Honoré Fragonard (1732–1806), Boucher's most talented pupil. Fragonard's early work was historical, but he was commissioned by a wealthy financier, the Baron de St. Julien, to paint *The Swing*: "I would like you to paint Madame [St. Julien's mistress] on a swing which is being pushed by a bishop. You should place me where I shall have a good view of the legs of this pretty little thing." Fragonard was happy to oblige, and pictures of this sort became his *métier*.

Hogarth, Reynolds and Gainsborough

English art, too, had its wit, though of a different kind. William Hogarth (1697–1764) produced series after series of moralities, usually six or eight meticulously detailed, savagely satirical pictures showing the triumph of good or the downfall of evil, such as "The Rake's Progress" and "The Harlot's Progress." These paintings, which were to enjoy an enormous and enduring success as prints, showed

a deep satirical relish in the portrayal of physical peculiarities and deformities. Although social caricatures had existed in art before Hogarth's time—the cartoons of Callot in the seventeenth century are an example—Hogarth was the first to see the individual as a representative of the whole society; and for him art was a medium of social criticism. He was the father of the cartoon in its modern sense—forerunner of the political cartoonists of the nineteenth and twentieth centuries.

But Hogarth was regarded as idiosyncratic by most contemporary English artists. The eighteenth century in English art was the great age of portraiture. Sir Joshua Reynolds (1723–92) played a major part in making portrait-painting the most important branch of art in eighteenth-century England. He combined historical painting with portraiture, as in *Dr. Beattie—The Triumph of Truth*, and his reputation was such that he portrayed almost all his famous contemporaries. The growing importance of portrait painting is seen too in the career of Thomas Gainsborough (1727–88), who began by painting landscapes. Although he continued to regard himself as a landscape artist—and certainly preferred painting landscapes to people—the bulk of his output is made up of commissioned portraits. After establishing himself in Bath, which was becoming a fashionable town, he moved in 1774

The Swing by Fragonard, leading French exponent of Rococo.

The Levée by Hogarth in the series of paintings "The Rake's Progress."

expression in its art

to London, where he became Reynolds' leading rival. He was technically superior to Reynolds—although his portraits often lack freshness and originality.

Neoclassicism

In the middle of the century the historical and critical ideas of Johann Joachim Winckelmann (1717–68) began to influence art, particularly German art. Winckelmann's *On the Imitation of Greek Works*, which was published in 1755, had the immediate effect of encouraging the return to the "simplicity and grandeur" of classical models, and gave birth to Neoclassicism, which was the most influential artistic style of the late eighteenth century. Painters such as Anton Raphael Mengs (1728–79) were much influenced by Winckelmann's ideas. Sculptors, of whom John Flaxman (1755–1826) and Antonio Canova (1757–1822) were the most distinguished, adopted the new style with great enthusiasm, and architects began to use it lavishly in about 1800. Even at the end of the century, when Romantic ideas were beginning to influence artists, Neoclassicism remained strong, and the pictures of Jacques Louis David (1748–1825), the greatest artist of the French revolutionary era, show the impact of both Neoclassicism and Romanticism.

Architecture

The eighteenth century was a period of fine domestic architecture. Although many great country houses were built, the most notable characteristic of the period was the development of urban architecture. The huge growth of population, particularly in towns and cities, from the middle of the eighteenth century onward made large-scale housing developments essential. The development of the English city of Bath, which became popular as a spa because of its hot springs, shows Georgian urban architecture at its finest. The terraces and crescents provided a graceful and, by the standards of the time, comfortable living environment at a relatively low cost. In capital cities a grander style of architecture was used by great nobles for their town houses and palaces, most notably in German

The Circus, Bath (1754–60), designed by John Wood.

princely cities. In many cities throughout Europe there was a growing realization that a degree of town planning was necessary, and the shape of many of Europe's cities today is largely an inheritance of the eighteenth century.

Music

During the first half of the eighteenth century music went through one of its greatest periods of creative advance—largely because of the genius of two men, Johann Sebastian Bach (1685–1750) and George Frederick Handel (1685–1759). Both were born in northern Germany and absorbed a musical tradition—largely a tradition of sacred music—that became increasingly important and influential during the second half of the seventeenth century.

The development of German music was largely due to Heinrich Schütz (1585–1672), who provided a link between the great sixteenth-century composers of unaccompanied choral music—men such as Giovanni Palestrina (*c.* 1525–94) and William Byrd (1542–1623)—and the great eighteenth-century composers of accompanied choral music and orchestral music, of whom Bach and Handel were the most distinguished. Schütz had absorbed much of the technique of Venetian music during a three-year stay in that city between 1609 and 1612.

A more immediate influence on Bach was the great organist and composer for the organ, Dietrich Buxtehude (1637–1707), a Dane who spent the latter part of his life at Lübeck. Bach was so impressed by Buxtehude's reputation that as a young man he walked several hundred miles in order to meet him and hear him play.

The birth of a strong local tradition in Germany did not at once end the musical dominance of Italy. Composers such as Arcangelo Corelli (1653–1713), who played a key role in popularizing the violin, and the youthful prodigy Giovanni Battista Pergolesi (1710–36), did much to keep the Italian musical tradition lively. Even more important were Alessandro Scarlatti (1659–1725) and his son Domenico (1683–1757) and Antonio Vivaldi (*c.* 1675–1741). The elder Scarlatti's operas were to be highly influential both in Italy and in Germany—his use of harmony was to have a great impact on Mozart and Haydn later in the eighteenth century. The younger Scarlatti, a close friend of Handel, was perhaps the outstanding keyboard performer of his generation and composed hundreds of sonatas. No less prolific was Vivaldi, whose *concerti* did much to create the mature form of the Baroque *concerto grosso*.

In France, too, the early eighteenth century was a period of great musical brilliance, encouraged by the patronage of Louis XIV. The three outstanding composers of the latter part of Louis' reign were Jean Baptiste Lully (1632–87), François Couperin (1668–1733) and Jean Philippe Rameau (1683–1764), all of whom were closely associated with the court for significant periods of their lives.

England produced only one great composer in the late seventeenth century, Henry Purcell (1659–95), and, owing partly to his very early death, his contribution was rapidly overshadowed by the influence of Handel. Among those who wrote under Handel's influence, the most important were Thomas Arne (1710–78) and William Boyce (1710–79), but they made little independent contribution to musical ideas or practice, and the great period of English musical innovation, which had begun with Byrd, ended with the death of Purcell.

But it was Bach and Handel who dominated the musical scene in the early eighteenth century. Bach had shown considerable talent as a violinist while he was still a child. Indeed for the rest of his life he was better known as a performer, particularly on the organ, than as a composer. His most productive years as a composer were spent at Weimar, where he held court posts from 1708 to 1717, and at Leipzig, where he was cantor of the Church of St. Thomas from 1722 until his death in 1750. He poured forth choral compositions for the feasts and fasts of the Church year, mostly in the form of cantatas, of which over three hundred survive. His greatest works, however, were more extended, his *Passions* and the heroic and passionately moving *Mass in B-Minor*. His production was not confined to liturgical music, but included *concerti grossi* (such as the *Brandenburg Concertos*), overtures (the suites), lighter choral works (such as the *Coffee Cantata*), exercises (such as the *Well-Tempered Clavier*) and a large body of organ preludes, toccatas and fugues. Bach's real importance lay less in his structural innovation and his use of new techniques or instruments than in the depth of his musical insight and imagination.

Like Bach, most German composers did not travel widely. Even composers who made considerable innovations, such as Philipp Telemann (1681–1767), were largely untraveled. But one of Telemann's pupils was Handel, who became an international figure. After training in Germany and Italy he settled eventually in Britain, where he was employed as court composer, and where his greatest work, the *Messiah*, received its first performance in 1742.

An etching of the English composer Thomas Arne at the organ.

First Performance of Handel's "Messiah"

After a brilliant career in Germany and Italy, George Frederick Handel moved to London. At first lionized, he suddenly found his popularity declining and his debts mounting. His response was feverish activity and in the incredible space of twenty-four days he completed an oratorio different from any that had gone before. Taking it to Ireland, he produced the Messiah *to great acclaim—and changed the course of music.*

The very familiarity of Handel's *Messiah* hides many of its qualities from us. The subtly melodic airs—such as "How beautiful are the feet"—and the majestic choruses—like "Lift up your heads"—survive even indifferent performances, often because the listener is willing to supply in his own mind what the performance lacks in actual quality. Familiarity with the *Messiah* leads not to contempt but to a too easy acceptance of its powers—although nowadays no choir would consider launching the "Hallelujah" chorus with only one tenor and one bass, as happened at St. Paul's Cathedral in the mid-nineteenth century. (The organist was nonplussed. He turned to his two singers and advised: "Do your best and I will do the rest with the organ.") The *Messiah* then, as now, was the acknowledged classic of English oratorio, its musical quality proof against all kinds of choral assault.

Looking back to the first performance of the *Messiah*, in the mid-eighteenth century, one is able to place the work in perspective, and realize its importance both in the history of music and in social history. For Handel himself the work marked a change of fortune. It was a triumph of spirit after discouraging setbacks. By his single-handed invention of English oratorio an entirely new tradition was founded, not just a transplant of the Italian genre. Musically, the *Messiah* contained much of Handel's most brilliant invention—a piece that is undramatic in form with its soloists as commentators rather than characters, but that is nonetheless exciting because of the dramatic power within the music. The oratorio is also a remarkable blend of two musical traditions. Handel, because of his background and training, combined the complex polyphonic techniques of northern Europe with the more melodic operatic styles of the south. So the *Messiah* contains ringing choruses with many intertwining voices and tuneful airs, an example of two traditions meeting that had often been mutually

exclusive in the past. His skills made Handel a greatly admired composer; witness the story of Haydn, who after hearing the "Hallelujah" chorus, rose to his feet and said of Handel, "He is the master of us all." Indeed, without the example of the *Messiah* before him, Haydn's own great oratorio *The Creation* might well have sounded very different. Anyone writing oratorio after the *Messiah* would find it impossible to ignore.

And the *Messiah* also had an interesting social as well as a musical impact. It rapidly became the mainstay of choirs and choral societies and thus both a stimulus and a burden to musical life in cities, towns and churches in Britain and North America (the first American performance was in New York in 1770). Its appeal was not just a musical one. Unlike many oratorios that have Old Testament subjects, the *Messiah* has a Christian subject, a fact that is easier to understand in the context of the eighteenth century than today. For the work provided the Protestants and the rapidly burgeoning Nonconformist movements of the time with something that they could regard as especially their own. And it was in English, readily understandable in Britain and America, unlike Latin and Italian. Moreover Handel had not written parts for *castrati*, those Italian imports who sounded all very well on the stages of London but whose voices and style could not very easily be reproduced by provincial choirs.

So the *Messiah* as well as providing marvelous music also satisfied other needs, a milestone indeed. How was this attained? Perhaps one should start with this report from *Faulkner's Dublin Journal* of April 17, 1742:

> On Tuesday last, Mr Handel's Sacred Grand Oratorio, the *Messiah*, was performed in the New Musick Hall in Fishamble-street; the best Judges allowed it to be the most finished piece of Musick. Words are wanting to express the exquisite Delight

The New Musick Hall in Fishamble Street, Dublin, in which the first performance of the *Messiah* took place.

Opposite George Frederick Handel, the German-born composer whose masterpiece, the *Messiah*, popularized oratorio as a musical form. From the National Portrait Gallery, London.

49

An excerpt from *Faulkner's Dublin Journal* of April 6–10, 1742, in which ladies were asked to attend the performance of *Messiah* without their hoops.

Right An engraving of Handel conducting. The success of his charity subscription concerts in Dublin prompted Handel to present his new work in Ireland.

it afforded to the admiring crowded Audience. The Sublime, the Grand, and the Tender, adapted to the most elevated, majestick and moving Words, conspired to transport and charm the ravished Heart and Ear. It is but Justice to Mr Handel that the World should know he generously gave the Money arising from this Grand Performance to be equally shared by the Society for relieving Prisoners, the Charitable Infirmary, and Mercer's Hospital, for which they will ever gratefully remember his Name: and that the Gentlemen of the two Choirs, Mr Dubourg, Mrs Avolio, and Mrs Cibber, who all performed their Parts to Admiration, acted also on the same disinterested Principle . . . .

The reviewer employed by *Faulkner's Dublin Journal* to cover the first public performance of Handel's *Messiah* on Tuesday, April 13, 1742, was skillful at his trade, dealing with time, manner, place and result with an admirable economy of style. The course of events, however, that led to this famous first performance is long and not always clear.

George Frederick Handel, born in 1685 at Halle in Saxony, had taken the British musical world by storm when he had arrived as a young man in early eighteenth-century London. He was fresh from four years in Italy where he had composed both operas and oratorios, mastering the fashionable Italian styles. But it was his operas that first became the rage among the English. His tunes from a work like *Rinaldo* were sung, whistled and hummed by all classes, and his operas dominated the London musical season for several years. Then came disenchantment, first gradual, then abrupt. For Italian opera, despite its initial reception, was not temperamentally suited to the English. Many of the plots and passions appeared contrived, and were unintelligible to most listeners anyway since they were expressed in Italian. Perhaps worse, the visiting Italian singers charged large fees—the elaborate stage machinery required to produce such expected effects as moving clouds, thunder-

storms, bolts from the blue and sudden godly interventions from the slopes of Olympus, was very expensive! In 1728 the appearance of John Gay's *The Beggar's Opera* with its English libretto, its down-to-earth plot, and its saucy piracy of some of Handel's best tunes as well as folk songs, hit hard at the popularity of Italian opera in London, which declined from then on. Handel, a businessman as well as a composer, recognized the trend, and while not abandoning opera composition entirely turned his hand more often to other forms, notably oratorio.

One obstacle to the presentation of such religious musical drama, however, was the attitude of the Bishop of London, Dr. Gibson. Handel decided to make the best of this opposition and present singers in their everyday clothes, in choral ranks, on a stage bare of scenery, and in 1732 his oratorio *Esther*, given under these conditions at the Haymarket Theater, was a huge success. Yet the London musical public once again proved fickle, and Handel was to find that within a few years his oratorios would be indifferently received—even such works as *Saul* and *Israel in Egypt*—and that he was falling into debt.

Handel's response to this situation was an amazing spell of hard work, during which he composed with such speed and inspiration that one cannot imagine even a Mozart outpacing him. He wrote the *Messiah* in a span of twenty-four days, from August 22 to September 14, 1741. Of course, popular legends have surrounded this feat. He is said to have been inspired by a vision, to have composed in a religious ecstasy; he is supposed to have quoted St. Paul, "Whether I was in my body or out of my body I knew not," and to have said in later years, "I did think I did see all Heaven before me and the great God himself." Certainly the original manuscript of the *Messiah*, now in the British Museum, shows the signs of haste, with its blots and hurried corrections. But it is wrong to imagine a divine efflatus suddenly surrounding Handel and compelling him to write.

The work did not just happen. The fifty-six preceding years of Handel's life were necessary for it to happen. The *Messiah* was the product of an accumulation of skills; Handel did not hesitate to use some of his earlier themes in the score.

One must also remember that the *Messiah* had another author. The libretto was not written by Handel himself but compiled from Scripture by Charles Jennens, a rich, eccentric Leicestershire squire who was conceited about his literary ability. Handel was fortunate in that the decision to choose texts from Scripture allowed a libretto to emerge that was neither absurd nor turgid. Even so, there are critics who cannot believe that Jennens was capable of such intelligent selection and who claim that the credit should go to an assistant of his called Pooley. Jennens, anyway, was not very impressed with Handel's treatment of the text: he wrote later that Handel "has made a fine Entertainment of it, tho' not near so good as he might and ought to have done."

When, in his London rooms, Handel had finished the *Messiah* on September 14, 1741, he did not appear to have any immediate plans for performance. It has been suggested that the oratorio was given in London that autumn, but no records of this exist, and Handel's other activities would have left little time for the intense rehearsals that would have been necessary. For he immediately set to work on *Samson* which he finished by the end of October, and then in early November he set out for Ireland.

The invitation to come to Ireland had been extended by the Duke of Devonshire, Lord Lieutenant of Ireland, some time during the previous months—indeed, Handel may even have written the *Messiah* with the visit in mind. Negotiations had also been going on with the representatives of three Dublin charities—the Charitable Infirmary, Mercer's Hospital and the Charitable Musical Society for the Relief of Imprisoned Debtors—who

hoped that Handel would be able to perform for their causes during his stay there. There were certainly great advantages for Handel in going to Dublin at this particular time. It was a chance for him to measure his musical success away from the London audiences that had grown increasingly critical; there was the attraction of a brand-new Musick Hall in Dublin's Fishamble Street; and he would have the opportunity to meet and work with an old friend, the virtuoso violinist Matthew Dubourg, who led the viceregal orchestra in Dublin. For a long time it was thought that the *Messiah* was the only major new work that Handel decided to take with him to Dublin, but evidence has recently come to light, in the form of advertisements in the *Dublin News-Letter*, that a performance of *Samson* may have been planned, but had to be canceled because of the difficulty of the parts.

Handel set out north from London at the beginning of November, 1741, but was obliged to interrupt his journey at Chester because of reports that the wind was unfavorable for the Irish Sea crossing. This short stay in Chester gave rise to a famous anecdote, reported by Charles Burney, author of the well-known *History of Music*, who was a schoolboy in Chester at the time. He recalls Handel staying at the Golden Falcon, smoking a pipe over a dish of coffee at the Exchange Coffee House, and one day going to the organist at Chester Cathedral and asking for the loan of some good sight-readers from the cathedral choir so that he could rehearse some of the choruses from *Messiah*. A group of singers assembled at the Golden Falcon, including a bass called Janson, a printer by trade. Poor Janson failed so completely to understand his part in "And With His Stripes We Are Healed" that Handel lost his temper, swore, and (to use Burney's transliteration) shouted at the printer, "You shcauntrel! tit not you dell me dat you could sing at soite?"—"Yes, sir, says the printer, and so I can; but not at *first sight*."

Detail from Hogarth's painting of *The Beggar's Opera* by John Gay. The success of Gay's musical satire led to a decline in the popularity of Italian opera in England and caused Handel to experiment with other musical forms.

The original manuscript of the *Messiah,* subsequently acquired by a Mr. Wass, whose name appears in the top right-hand corner.

During late February and March the rehearsals of *Messiah* got under way, with the performance planned for Monday, April 12. The custom of the time was to give a preliminary public rehearsal, and this was fixed for April 8, tickets for the rehearsal being presented free to people who had bought tickets for the actual first performance. It is interesting to note, as some Handel biographers do, that these tickets could be bought both at the Musick Hall and at "Mr. Neal's in Christ Church Yard," but not at Handel's own door in Abbey Street, as had been the case with the subscription concerts—an indication perhaps of the importance Handel attached to the performance of *Messiah* and his wish not to be bothered with financial detail during rehearsals.

The public rehearsal of April 8 was reported fully in both *Faulkner's Dublin Journal* and the *Dublin News-Letter* and was judged to have given "universal satisfaction to all present." The papers printed more details for the forthcoming official first performance which, because of a confusion over dates, was now to be put off until Tuesday, April 13. *Faulkner's Dublin Journal* requested ladies in the audience not to wear their whalebone hoops. In fact, by doing without the fashionable but bulky hoops of the women's dresses (and with some help from the gentlemen who left off their swords), the people of Dublin managed to crowd 700 rather than 600 of their number into the Musick Hall in Fishamble Street by midday on Tuesday, April 13, and showed great eagerness to attend the long concert, which included not only the first performance of the *Messiah* but also a number of organ concertos, played by the composer.

This performance of *Messiah* was different in many respects from what we are accustomed to today. There was a small choir and orchestra of possibly not more than forty altogether, the orchestra led by Matthew Dubourg, the choir composed solely of men and boys. What was lacking in numbers, however, was probably made up for in

Once in Dublin, where he arrived on November 18, Handel began to make his plans: a series of six subscription concerts was arranged to start on December 23, using the new concert hall in Fishamble Street which had only been opened a month or two earlier by the efforts of the Charitable Musical Society for the Relief of Imprisoned Debtors. The aim of this body was to raise money to repay the debts of men held in the notorious Marshalsea prison who would only be released once their debts were cleared. Handel's subscription concerts at the new Musick Hall were such a success —the program included such works as *Esther* and *Acis and Galatea*—that the Duke of Devonshire arranged for Handel to stay on in Ireland and present a second series, a fact that Handel notes in a letter to Charles Jennens dated December 29. An interesting implication of this letter, in view of the fact that no planned performance of the *Messiah* is mentioned, is Handel's uncertainty whether to give it in Ireland. Doubtless, if his second series of subscription concerts had failed, he could have taken the manuscript of *Messiah* back to England. But the concerts were successful, and Handel approached the deans and chapters of both Christ Church and St. Patrick's Cathedral in Dublin for the loan of some singers to present the new oratorio. He had a strange reaction from Dean Swift of St. Patrick's—the autocratic, unpredictable author Jonathan Swift who was then on the verge of insanity. Swift first gave permission and then withdrew it, writing angrily that he did not give "a licence to certain vicars to assist at a club of fiddlers in Fishamble Street." His attitude became favorable again when he learned that proceeds from the performance would go to charity.

Susannah Maria Cibber, actress and singer. Her notoriety enhanced the *Messiah*'s first performance.

precision—they had been well drilled by Handel in the previous weeks. The exact division of the solo parts is unclear. The newspaper report a few days later mentioned two of the female soloists, Mrs. Avolio and Mrs. Cibber. Of the former little is known other than her Italian origin and the brief period she spent as one of Handel's singers. Mrs. Cibber is a far more colorful character, an actress as well as a singer who had been promoting her acting career while she was in Dublin, appearing in productions of Richard Steele's *The Conscious Lovers* and Milton's masque *Comus*. She was the sister of Thomas Arne (a rival composer to Handel) and had been married to Theophilus Cibber, the squeaky-voiced, conceited and thoroughly objectionable son of the famous actor-playwright Colley Cibber. Not surprisingly she took a lover, named Sloper, which caused Theophilus to start court proceedings. It was judged, however, that he had connived at her intimacy, and the action did not succeed. All this surrounded Mrs. Cibber with an attractive cloud of notoriety to which she added a dramatic stage presence, despite her small voice and frame. *The Gentleman's Magazine* of March, 1742, had apostrophized her,

O wondrous girl! How small a space
Includes the gift of human race!

and her performance on April 13 of her arias in *Messiah* apparently led one clergyman, a certain Delaney, to forget all her marital misdemeanors and rise to his feet saying, "Woman, for this be all thy sins forgiven thee." As for the names of the male soloists, there remains no reliable record.

If the cast of the first *Messiah* is uncertain, however, the oratorio's reception definitely is not. The performance was one of the most successful that Handel ever experienced. Both the subject of *Messiah* and the charitable nature of the performance struck a chord of appreciation among the Dubliners. About £400 was made for the three charities from the one performance—a reward for their prolonged negotiations, first to get Handel, and then to get him singers. One appreciative citizen published a glowing poetical tribute in *Faulkner's Dublin Journal* that began:

What can we offer more in Handel's praise?
Since his *Messiah* gain'd him groves of bays . . .

The future of *Messiah* was set by that first performance, even though Handel subsequently altered many details in the work and though disappointments were to come. The first London performance of the work, for instance, at Covent Garden eleven months later, was mildly received and the work only gradually won the acceptance of the London public. The *Messiah*, which we automatically think so typical of Handel, is in fact a unique work in his canon, and it was to the credit of the people of Dublin that they immediately recognized its uniqueness and its power. Few descriptions can better that written by the reviewer in *Faulkner's Dublin Journal* as a summary of *Messiah*:

The Sublime, the Grand, and the Tender adapted to the most elevated, majestick, and moving Words, conspired to transport and charm the ravished Heart and Ear.

Handel's synthesis of polyphony and melody had produced a work that in itself was to become almost a definition of a musical form. To innumerable people, even today, *Messiah* is oratorio and oratorio *Messiah*.

IAN GILLHAM

The music room in Vauxhall Gardens. The changing tastes of the sophisticated London public had caused Handel to abandon opera for oratorio. Despite this bold move, recognition was slow to come from the metropolis.

Savoy supplants Venice as the leading

Music after Bach and Handel

Eighteenth-century music after Bach and Handel remained dominated by rigid forms. In many ways composers such as Bach's fifth son, Karl Philipp Emanuel Bach (1714–88), and Karl Stamitz (1745–1801) stood in the tradition of an earlier generation. There was, however, a noticeable move away from the choral tradition that had played such a large part in the music of the older masters. The orchestra, which at the beginning of the century had usually been a miscellaneous group of instruments brought together more by chance than by design, was becoming more defined in structure and was growing larger and stronger. Composers began to provide a rapidly increasing range of symphonic works for orchestral performance. In addition, individual instruments, particularly the piano—which developed rapidly in the middle of the century into a versatile and powerful instrument, almost completely replacing the harpsichord—were used in *concerti* in alternation with the rest of the orchestra. More intimate chamber works, too, such as the sonata for one instrument or a small group of instruments, were becoming popular.

The later decades of the eighteenth century were dominated by Haydn and Mozart, who were the key figures in the transition from Baroque to Classical music. Joseph Haydn lived from 1732 to 1809. Most of his creative years were

Mozart as an infant prodigy.

spent as musical director to the Hungarian noble family of Esterhazy. With a large musical establishment at his disposal, he was able to experiment freely, and was largely responsible for the creation of the classical symphony. But Haydn's talents, great as they were, were dwarfed by those of Wolfgang Amadeus Mozart (1756–91). Even the nineteenth-century German composer Wagner—who had little in common with Mozart—regarded him as "the greatest and most divine genius." A child prodigy, he performed in many of the great courts of Europe; his pitch and memory were so perfect that when he was in Rome he heard Palestrina's *Missa Papae Marcellae* in the Sistine Chapel and was able to reproduce most of it as a score. His later years were harder. Mozart's patron, the Archbishop of Salzburg, had none of the sympathy that Prince Esterhazy showed for Haydn. At the age of twenty-six, Mozart left Salzburg and his job, and for the next ten years, although living in considerable hardship, he poured forth a stream of brilliant works. He regarded his last work, a commissioned requiem mass, as his own requiem, and he died at the age of thirty-six, leaving six operas, over forty symphonies, and a large number of other works of exceptional beauty.

Italy in the eighteenth century

During the late fifteenth and sixteenth centuries, the kings of Spain had begun to build up a substantial empire in Italy. When the Hapsburg holdings were divided between the Spanish and Austrian branches of the family in 1556, Spain was the dominant power in Italy, and it seemed likely that the whole country, with the possible exception of the Papal States, would fall into Spanish hands. But by the late seventeenth century, the decline of the Spanish Hapsburgs was manifest.

The effect of the War of the Spanish Succession, however, was not to recreate the medieval Italian city-states; instead, the power of the now-defunct Spanish Hapsburgs was largely replaced by that of their Austrian cousins. The Kingdom of the Two Sicilies (Sicily and Naples), which had been the cornerstone of the Spanish empire in Italy, passed into Austrian hands,

as did the duchies of Milan and Mantua. However the Austrians were unable to hold the Two Sicilies against the attacks of the new Spanish royal family, the Bourbons, and they were lost in 1735. In the north, Austrian power continued to grow, and the southern loss was soon made good. The last of the Medici of Tuscany died in 1737, and it was agreed that his state should pass to Francis, Duke of Lorraine and husband of Maria Theresa of Austria. The Duchy of Parma, too, passed into Austrian hands. These Italian possessions were to prove valuable bargaining counters a few years later; by the terms of the Treaty of Aix-la-Chapelle in 1748, Parma was surrendered to Spain, and Sardinia gained a large strip of Milanese territory. Although—or perhaps because—the Austrians were unable to achieve the dominant position that Spain had previously held in Italy, they proved on the whole anxious to make administrative and ecclesiastical improvements and reforms. But, since the reforms were imposed from above by foreign officials and governors, the Austrians never succeeded in winning widespread popular support, a problem that was to aid Napoleon in his attack on Austria's Italian possessions at the end of the century. Austrian power had the important effect of continuing the enforced political fragmentation of Italy that was only to be overcome toward the end of the nineteenth century.

Among the independent states of Italy, the papacy continued to be so vexed by administrative problems that it was unable to see beyond the borders of the Papal States. Unable to rule effectively themselves, the popes cast jealous eyes on those who could, and were energetic in their condemnation of the ideas and practices of the Enlightenment such as the "enlightened despotism" of the Emperor Joseph II. Under enormous pressure from the major Roman Catholic states—Spain, France and, to a lesser extent, Austria—Clement XIV was forced in 1773 to dissolve the Jesuits, who had for so long been regarded as the right arm of the papacy (they were reestablished by Pius VII in 1814). But this humiliation was minor compared with what the papacy would have to suffer early in the nineteenth century under Napoleon—an experience that was

The mausoleum of Clement XIV.

to sour its relations with the rest of the world for most of the nineteenth century.

Venice, for so long the major independent state in Italy, continued its steady decline. Although military problems constituted less of a preoccupation for Venice in the eighteenth century than they had in the seventeenth, her inability to meet the changing economic needs and realities of the eighteenth century was more and more apparent. Venice's position as the major independent Italian state was gradually usurped by the growing status of Savoy. This was largely due to the ability of Victor Amadeus II, in whose long reign (1675–1732) Savoy became a European and not merely an Italian power. Although he lacked the military genius of his cousin Prince Eugene, Victor Amadeus made

Victor Amadeus II, Duke of Savoy.

independent state in Italy

up for this deficiency by his unequaled skill as a negotiator. The Treaty of Utrecht in 1713, which brought him Sicily, was a triumph only matched by Savoy's ineffectiveness in the war that preceded it. In 1720 Victor Amadeus exchanged Sicily for Sardinia, which had been held by the Austrians. This exchange made his possessions —now less far-flung—easier to govern, and reduced the danger of war with Spain, which was anxious to recover southern Italy. As the century grew older, Savoy's possessions in mainland Italy grew gradually larger. The dukes of Savoy, who came to be known after 1720 as the kings of Sardinia, saw their powerful neighbor France as their main enemy. As a result they opposed France during the revolutionary and Napoleonic wars. Although in the short run this proved a disastrous policy, it was to be richly rewarded later.

English literature in the eighteenth century

Both in art and in literature the eighteenth century in England was a period in which the smug self-satisfaction of both aristocracy and squirearchy provided an endless

Dean Swift by L. F. Roubillac.

source of material for satirists. Two writers in particular, the poet Alexander Pope (1688–1744) and the prose satirist Jonathan Swift (1667–1745), caught the public imagination. Pope developed the heroic couplet into a finely edged satirical weapon, which he used mercilessly on his enemies—and even, on occasion, on his friends.

An illustration from *Gulliver's Travels* by Swift, 1727.

His couplets, formal and concentrated, proved an excellent medium for the best of his work, *The Dunciad* (1728) and *The Rape of the Lock* (1712). Pope was conscious always that his role as a satirist was to protect and promote civilized society. Swift's satire was of a different kind. He was an Anglican clergyman who became Dean of St. Patrick's Cathedral, Dublin, and was also an ardent social reformer. He saw satire as a means of revealing the inequity and hypocrisy that existed in eighteenth-century society, and his works, such as *Gulliver's Travels* (1726), were usually strongly didactic.

Yet, just as Hogarth was untypical of English artists of the period, so were Pope and Swift eccentrics among English writers. More characteristic of the poets of the age were Thomas Gray (1716–71) and Oliver Goldsmith (1728–74), both of whom sought to achieve the ambitions of the new Augustan Age by imitating the qualities of the Latin poets of the reign of the Emperor Augustus at the beginning of the Christian era; they particularly admired the poetry of Virgil, Horace and Ovid. To some extent they succeeded in their aim; their works are usually cool, refined and clear, but often

lack any deep conviction. Nor did the Augustan enthusiasm pass without challenge; the praise of classical literature led to a lively war between the "ancients," who felt that classical standards could never be equaled, and the "moderns," who thought that they could be surpassed.

Yet even those who felt little sympathy for the supposedly superior qualities of classical literature could not entirely escape its spell. Despite the growing influence of the ideas of the Enlightenment, which suggested (in Pope's words) that "the proper study of mankind is man," many poets were finding a new interest in the contemplation of nature. James Thomson's (1700–48) *The Seasons* (1726–30) showed this new-found enthusiasm. Some, such as William Cowper (1731–1800) went further, expressing a profound horror of everything man-made. Cowper's *The Task* (1785) compared life in the man-made town adversely with that of the country, which was created by God.

But the growth of towns was producing a new breed of writers, of whom one, Samuel Johnson (1709–84), dominated the literary life of the century. Johnson emerged from the pages of his biography by James Boswell (1740–95) as the most urbane of men; his *Journey to the Western Islands of Scotland* (1775) presents the reader with the reactions of a cultivated mind thrust suddenly into an alien environment that it does not fully understand or like.

Although best known for his conversation, much of which was preserved by Boswell, Johnson wrote extensively. He was above

all a critic, but this did not prevent him from venturing into verse himself. Nor did it stop him from producing *A Dictionary of the English Language* (1755), the first critical work of lexicography in English and the basis of all later dictionaries. Despite the popularity of this venture—he subscribed over fifteen hundred to booksellers and friends before publication—it was so expensive to produce that it almost reduced him to bankruptcy.

Much of Johnson's critical work appeared in *The Rambler*, a journal which he founded in 1750. During its two-year life Johnson produced almost all of its material. After the demise of *The Rambler* he continued to write for the *Weekly Gazette*. His articles in these journals were written in conscious imitation of those in *The Spectator*, a magazine that had appeared at intervals from 1711 to 1714. During its life *The Spectator*—which was edited and published by Joseph Addison (1672–1719) and Sir Richard Steele (1672–1729)—had had a wide influence and sometimes sold as many as thirty thousand copies of a single issue.

The wide circulation of *The Spectator* shows how far literacy had spread in the early eighteenth century. The enormous expansion of the market for literature encouraged the growth of the novel. The English novel was largely the creation of Daniel Defoe (c. 1660–1731), whose books—particularly *Robinson Crusoe* (1719)—had a wide popularity. But it was Henry Fielding (1707–54), Laurence Sterne (1713–68) and Samuel Richardson (1689–1761) who formalized the structure of the early English novel.

The SPECTATOR.

Non fumum ex fulgore, sed ex fumo dare lucem Cogitat, ut speciosa dehinc miracula promat. Hor.

To be Continued every Day.

Thursday, March 1. 1711.

I Have observed, that a Reader seldom peruses a Book with Pleasure 'till he knows whether the Writer of it be a black or a fair Man, of . . . stinguished my self by a most profound Silence: For during the Space of eight Years, excepting in the publick Exercises of the College, I scarce ut-

First number of *The Spectator*, edited by Steele and Addison.

"Tom Jones" Revolutionizes Literature

1749

At the start of the eighteenth century few people could read and those who could found little on which to practice. Some plays and poems were produced, followed by journals and pamphlets. Then a noted pamphleteer became engrossed in the tale of a marooned sailor and wrote Robinson Crusoe. *Shortly thereafter a professional writer of letters for love-struck maidens wrote* Pamela. *Partly inspired and partly amused by these, Henry Fielding then wrote* Tom Jones *and with it the English novel truly began.*

Only over the last few hundred years has reading become a major form of entertainment and learning for most people. In Chaucer's time people listened to stories, usually told in verse; only a handful read them. By Shakespeare's time, printing had been invented, but still not many people read. They continued to listen to stories and now they went to plays. But by this time enough people could read for it to be worth a printer's while to publish plays and even a few prose narratives, the forerunners of the novel. By the eighteenth century a large number of people were literate. They still read plays and poems, and the new form of writing, journalism, but nobody in England wrote novels. Then, in 1749, Henry Fielding's *Tom Jones* was published and at last the public was presented with a new and important literary form.

Since the 1750s the novel has been the major literary form; almost every literate person has read a novel at some time in his life. For many people over the past two hundred years it has been the novel that formed their imagination and taught them what to expect of life. More than any other kind of writing, the novel shows what life is like, or what it might be like. At its worst it creates impossible fantasies in the reader's mind; at its best, it helps the reader to understand his own life and how it relates to all that goes on around him. In addition, the novel, if worth reading at all, is entertaining. Its multifaceted nature makes it one of the most important forms of art we have.

Curiously enough, the English novel came into being as a result of the mishaps of a young Scottish adventurer, Alexander Selkirk. The genre came of age with the first truly great novel in the English language, *Tom Jones*, in a period which saw the flowering of the two earliest English novelists, Daniel Defoe and Samuel Richardson.

At the end of the seventeenth century, the hot-tempered and adventurous Selkirk was charged with indecent conduct in church. Rather than face this charge, he ran away to sea and, several years later, found himself part of a privateering expedition against Spanish shipping. This was a disastrous trip for Selkirk for he quarreled so bitterly with his captain that he was, at his own request, put ashore on the uninhabited South Sea island of Juan Fernandez. As soon as his folly dawned on him, he begged to be taken back on board, but the captain would have none of him. Over four years later he was rescued by pure chance by another expedition, and both he and his story became famous in England. His adventures fired the imagination of a journalist who, on April 25, 1719, published a story based on them. This was the first English novel of any importance—*Robinson Crusoe* by Daniel Defoe.

Defoe (*c.* 1660–1731) was in his thirties before he began to earn a living by his pen. He had been for a time a successful merchant but had been ruined to the enormous extent of £17,000. Subsequently he took up a new career as a political journalist, but soon found himself in prison for antagonizing the government. Thereafter he enjoyed an amazing career of political opportunism, first supporting one party, then another, then pretending to work for the second party when really he supported the first. He was remarkably hard-working, writing an entire newspaper three times a week as well as producing numerous pamphlets and acting as secret agent for a government minister.

Defoe was almost sixty when, in the middle of his political activity, he produced *Robinson Crusoe*. He had already the reputation of not only having an "agreeableness of style" but also of being a master of the art of "forging a story and imposing it on the world for truth." So it was that in this and his later novels, all of which were narrated by the hero or heroine, he created strong and realistic adventure stories. Two new elements in these prototype novels were the attention paid to the thoughts,

The only known portrait of Henry Fielding, the author from whom the main tradition of the English novel derives. It is attributed to Hogarth.

Opposite Detail from *The Distressed Poet* by Hogarth. Babies and bills deflect the poet's attention from the muse. Hogarth was a close friend of Fielding, and his painting could well describe the straitened circumstances in which Fielding lived for a time.

57

The hypocrite unmasked. A Rowlandson etching showing Tom Jones, protagonist of Fielding's novel, discovering his tutor in Black Moll's bedchamber.

actions and feelings of individual people, and their contextual realism.

The literary world of the early eighteenth century was a complex one. A major aspect can be seen through Defoe's satirical journalism and pamphleteering; it was a time when satire was immensely popular.

The career of Samuel Richardson (1689–1761) illustrates another aspect. Richardson was a printer's apprentice who married his master's daughter. With her dowry he was able to set himself up in the profession, and he became very successful. However, his wife died ten years later, after bearing him six children, none of whom survived childhood. Richardson married another printer's daughter and continued to prosper.

It was not until he was in his fifties, however, that Richardson ventured to write anything for publication other than dedications or indexes. He had in fact been employed as a writer before he reached his teens. The ability to write was not common at that time, and not only was Richardson able to write, but he enjoyed doing so. As a result, he soon became the youthful letter-writer for all the lovesick girls of his neighborhood; what is more, he became their counselor and confidant. Thus, from early life, Richardson was a master of letter-writing and was versed in feminine psychology and moral counsel. This qualified him admirably to fulfil a commission now entrusted to him by two book-seller friends.

These friends, Charles Rivington and John Osborne, proposed that he should write, as they put it, "a little volume of letters, in a common style, on such subjects as might be of use to those country readers who were unable to indite for themselves." In other words, it was to be a pedestrian handbook of examples of different kinds of letters. Richardson wrote this volume, but, being the man he was, he gave it a moral purpose; it was, in his own words, "to instruct handsome girls, who were obliged to go out on service . . . how to avoid the snares that might be laid against their virtue!"

Some twenty-five years earlier Richardson had heard an anecdote which much appealed to him: a young girl of humble origins had been taken into the service of a family of some means and nobility; the young master of the house had pursued her amorously but she had resisted him so virtuously that in the end he married her. Now that Richardson was embarking on a writing career, this anecdote came to mind. So, as well as the volume of examples, he wrote a novel. This took him two months, and was called *Pamela; or, Virtue Rewarded*. It was published in 1740. Pamela is a country girl employed as a maid to a fine lady; the lady dies and the son of the house, Squire B., keeps trying to seduce her; her honor and virtue defeat him, so he marries her. Pamela herself tells the story through letters to her parents. To Richardson's real surprise, the novel was a tremendous success.

In fact, he need not have been surprised; there was no literature of real standing being written at the time, so his book had no rivals. Moreover, he had captured the fantasy of thousands of English women of his time and, in so doing, hit upon what

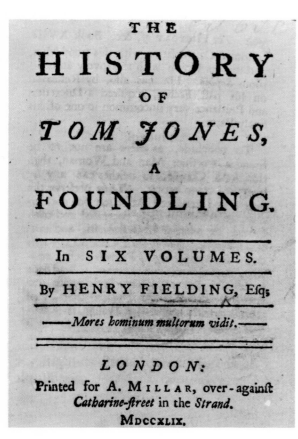

THE
HISTORY
OF
TOM JONES,
A
FOUNDLING.

In SIX VOLUMES.

By HENRY FIELDING, Esq;

—— *Mores hominum multorum vidit.* ——

LONDON:
Printed for A. MILLAR, over-against
Catharine-street in the *Strand.*
MDCCXLIX.

Left Title-page of the original edition of *Tom Jones* by Henry Fielding.

is still a predictable romantic suspense formula: will he get her? will she resist him? Like Defoe he too had written in a realistic manner about people who, though not ordinary in themselves, might be met with in real life.

Richardson's other two novels are less important, though his second work, *Clarissa*, constitutes the longest English novel. What mattered was what he had achieved in *Pamela* by adding the relationships of love and sex, in a non-romantic context, to the realism of Defoe. *Pamela* had one other direct effect on the English novel: it gave Fielding the starting point for his first important work.

Like Defoe and Richardson, Henry Fielding (1707–54) did not begin life as a novelist, but became one by chance. His career points to a third facet of the world of letters of the first half of the eighteenth century, for Fielding was a playwright in his twenties. He was born into a well-to-do family and educated at Eton. By the age of twenty-one, he was writing plays with varying success. He excelled in parody and satire, and became the major playwright of his time. But the English theater, which had thrived so gloriously under Shakespeare, and then been resurrected in the year of the Restoration for a brief flourish, was gradually declining. Unwittingly, it was Fielding himself who shaped the events that led to its eclipse.

Satire and political warfare were two of the main forces in writing at the time. Like Defoe, Fielding was adept at both. Unlike him, he kept out of jail; but, for the rest, his career has some strong similarities. He too went through grave financial difficulties but

eventually obtained some political reward, and he too was a journalist and a pamphleteer. As journalist, pamphleteer and playwright he attacked the political corruption of Sir Robert Walpole's Whig government. Fielding himself was a Whig, but there had been a division in the party and many distinguished men of the time opposed Walpole's administration. However, Fielding's satire on the government was so biting in two of his last plays that it provoked sufficient reaction for Walpole to be able to push the Licensing Act of 1737 through Parliament. This act made all plays subject in effect to the censorship of the Lord Chamberlain, and it put a stop to Fielding's career as a dramatist.

Thus, at the age of thirty, Fielding found himself with no career and with debts and a family to support. Some years earlier he had married Charlotte Cradock, to whom he was devoted throughout his life. The portraits of Sophia Western, the heroine in *Tom Jones*, and of Amelia, the heroine and title character of his last novel, show how much he loved her. Fielding was a man of great energy, able to make the best of any situation. He began to study law, supporting himself in the meantime by his journalism. He made sufficient headway in his legal work to be made a justice of the peace for Westminster, admittedly with the help of an old school-friend, Lord Lyttelton. Later his jurisdiction was extended over Middlesex. These justices of the peace were known as "trading justices" and had, as the name implies, a disgraceful reputation for corruption. But Fielding was a man of honor as well as a man of the world, and he brought dignity to the office. He was among the wisest and most

A scene from Fielding's *Joseph Andrews.*

59

humane legal men of his time. Even so, he is remembered and revered not as a jurist but as the greatest of the early English novelists.

Pamela set him on his way by provoking his skill in parody. Fielding's idea in writing *Joseph Andrews* was to mock Richardson's lofty morality by writing a novel about a man as virtuous as Pamela; accordingly, he invented a brother for her, Joseph Andrews. The novel begins with Joseph being dismissed from service for refusing not only Lady Booby's advances, but those of her attendant, Mrs. Slipslop. However, once Fielding had taken this richly funny opening from Richardson, he let his imagination and his knowledge of England and its people take over. Almost as soon as Joseph escapes from the clutches of the two ladies, he is set upon by thieves, stripped and robbed. It is while he is recovering from this misfortune that one of the great characters of English literature finds him. This is Parson Adams, as full and real a person as any novel can offer. He and Joseph travel together and, after many misadventures, wind up at Lady Booby's country mansion. At this point Fielding drew on his experience as a writer of stage farces to create a wild series of bedroom mishaps which eventually find Parson Adams innocently in bed with the delectable Fanny, Joseph's beloved.

In some ways this is Fielding's best novel, for he never wrote a funnier one; nor did he create a finer character than Adams. Both these qualities, strong character and comedy, were new to the novel, but the most important development here was the way in which Fielding succeeded in presenting so wide a picture of contemporary society.

In 1744 his wife died, and a bitter time for Fielding followed. He himself was in poor health because of gout and yet, over the remaining ten years of his life, he refused to admit defeat and continued as active as ever. The crowning triumph of this period was the writing of *The History of Tom Jones, a Foundling*, which was published in 1749. Two important qualities had been lacking in the novel up to this time—a really good plot and the creation of well-rounded characters. These qualities, as well as those noted in *Joseph Andrews*, are present in *Tom Jones*, which marks the climax of the early English novel.

In *Tom Jones* Fielding's knowledge and love of England and the English find fullest expression. The nature of the hero shows this: Tom is a fine, robust figure of a man, of a gay and carefree character. Women simply fall for him and, unlike Joseph Andrews whose chastity was phenomenal, he responds naturally to them. This leads him into various liaisons and mishaps—at one point he even appears to have slept with his mother. For all this, there is only one woman he truly loves, the beautiful Sophia Western; no matter how he may forget her

in the warmth of a moment, his heart remains always true to her. In this Tom contrasts with the evil Blifil, who is about the same age and who has been brought up with him. Blifil is grave, prudent and sober, but also lying and treacherous. To cap it all, he is Tom's rival for Sophia's hand. Significantly, Fielding was broadminded enough to accept Tom's worthiness as a lover in spite of his various escapades, and to give him his true reward, Sophia, in the novel's closing pages.

This is what makes *Tom Jones* the most important of these early English novels: in it Fielding showed the qualities of the human heart and made them more important than actions and appearances. Despite the fact that Tom appears to be a sinner and Blifil to be a saint, the reader knows the true value of their characters.

Defoe, Richardson and Fielding pioneered the novel form. Innumerable writers have followed in their footsteps, among them some of the major figures of both English and world literature. Jane Austen wrote in the early years of the nineteenth century; *Pride and Prejudice*, published in 1813, is one of the world's masterpieces. In the 1840s the Brontë sisters published *Jane Eyre* and *Wuthering Heights*, both remarkable love stories. Through the middle years of the century Dickens produced a series of comic and real characters, while George Eliot wrote *Silas Marner*, and created an entire

English society in *Middlemarch*. At the beginning of this century Joseph Conrad, a Polish seaman who settled in England, wrote *Nostromo*, one of the world's great novels, the story of a South American state dominated by a silver mine. A few years later saw publication of the work of yet another figure of world standing, D. H. Lawrence.

But this random list of English language authors serves only to indicate a continuing literary tradition to which millions today are heir. In an age of greatly increased literacy and heightened sensibility, both novelist and reader stand indebted to Henry Fielding's *Tom Jones*, which provided the first model for the English novel.   DAVID NORTON

Tom Jones, bloodied and bandaged, leaving his room in dead of night to surprise the ensign who had made light of his Sophia's name.

A true and exact representation of the Art of Casting and Preparing Letters for Printing. This view of the compositor's craft engraved for the *Universal Magazine* in 1750 reflects the growing interest in the printed word.

The decay of mercantilism

Attacks on the mercantilist idea were common even in the seventeenth century, and as the eighteenth century wore on they became ever more so, particularly in Britain. Sir William Petty (1623–87), for example, had written extensively on economics and taxation. He thought that many of Ireland's problems were due to discriminatory English legislation and business practice, and that the result of this discrimination was damaging not merely to Ireland but to Britain as a whole. Believing as he did that "Labour is the Father and active principle of wealth, as lands are the Mother," he held that British trade would triumph without the doubtful benefit that legal sanctions brought. He thought that the cause of France's prosperity lay in its rich soil and that of Holland in its large and hard-working population; since Britain had both rich soil and a large population, it was bound to grow faster than Holland or France.

But Petty and other critics of mercantilism were for a long time voices crying out in the wilderness of contemporary ideas. In France, too, there was growing publicity for the advantages of free trade; the term *laissez faire* began to be used early in the eighteenth century. The climate of the Enlightenment favored *laissez faire* doctrines, and both in France and Britain the large arsenal of laws protecting national trade fell increasingly into disuse. This change in practice was not, however, accompanied by any

An eighteenth-century market in London beneath the statue of Charles II.

Sir William Petty, Irish economist.

change in fundamental attitudes, as the refusal of the British government to give way to the demands of the American colonies in the 1770s was to show. The fundamental problem was that few writers—

Petty was almost unique in this respect—treated economic theories as a separate field of study; most regarded it as no more than a small part of politics, as the contemporary term, "political economy" suggests.

Adam Smith

The great intellectual contribution of Adam Smith (1723–90) was to establish economics as a separate discipline. After studying at Glasgow and Oxford, he returned to his native Edinburgh and formed part of a highly talented group that included the philosopher David Hume (1711–76). The problem of mercantilism had been brought home to Scotland by the failure of the Darien Scheme, when a Scottish trading company had been brought down largely because of the opposition of the English Parliament. It is no accident that the two most energetic critics of mercantilism—Petty in the seventeenth century and Smith in the eighteenth—were a Scot and an Irishman. In the 1750s, after his appointment as Professor of Philosophy at Glasgow University, Smith devoted himself to the study of economics and gradually became more and more convinced that mercantilism was an economic evil.

It was not, however, until 1776 that Smith published the fruits of his labors, *An Enquiry into the Nature and Causes of the Wealth of Nations*. Although Smith saw it as only one of a wide-ranging series of philosophical books in which he expounded his ideas on the need for freedom, it was seen from the

first in a narrower context, and Smith's other books were rapidly consigned to an ill-deserved oblivion. His book was the first large-scale treatment of wealth, a term that had previously been freely used but rarely defined. Smith defined wealth as labor.

Smith's basic importance as the "inventor" of economics was not, however, the reason for the book's enormous impact. He presented a view of an entirely different system of commerce from that which existed at the time. According to contemporary economic orthodoxy, in a fair exchange neither party gained, but it was essential for each party to ensure that the exchange was fair lest the other benefit. Rejecting this objective orthodoxy, Smith put forward a highly subjective alternative. He simply suggested that in a fair exchange both parties gained, since each received something that it wanted in exchange for something that it did not want. If this was so—and his view rapidly gained wide acceptance—there was no need for governments to regulate trade, since by its nature trade was beneficial. "The wealth of neighbouring nations," he wrote, "though dangerous in politics is certainly advantageous in trade. In a state of hostility it may enable our enemies to maintain fleets and armies superior to our own, but in a state of peace and commerce it must likewise enable them to exchange with us to a greater value and to afford a better market either for the immediate product of our own industry or for whatever is purchased with that product."

Part of the success of Smith's book, which at once became a bestseller, was due to the impact of the American Revolution, which was to necessitate a thorough re-examination of the whole understanding of trade. During the nineteenth century free-trade ideas were held throughout the developed world—although the very countries that so enthusiastically adopted them in Europe chose to ignore them in Africa and Asia.

Smith's ideas formed an important part of the intellectual substructure that helped the Industrial Revolution develop. The implication that an increase in wealth was to the benefit of all provided a spur to the search for industrial and economic growth that was to be so marked a feature of life from the late eighteenth

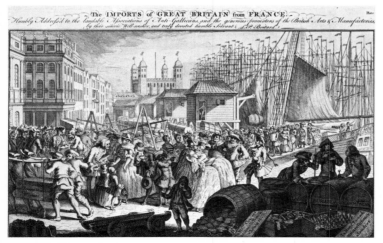

A satirical portrayal of the flooding of Britain with French imports.

theory leads to the decline of Mercantilism

century onward. It was only with the rise of environmental and ecological arguments that the fundamental assumptions that Smith built into Western thought have come to be questioned.

Other, no less serious, problems were also ignored. Smith admitted that in any exchange the gain that one party received might be greater (by its own subjective standards) than that of the other. If this happened frequently the country in question would eventually find its wealth and stability increased far beyond that of its trading partner. In other words, Smith was not interested in a situation that was to arise in the twentieth century, when the "gap" between the advanced, industrial world and the less advanced countries would rapidly widen.

Yet the growing criticisms of free trade in the twentieth century were only possible after two centuries of the most rapid growth in trade and industry that the world has ever known. Within the context of the eighteenth century, there can be no doubt of the beneficial effect of Smith's enlightened views.

The increase in literacy and of printing capacity led to the rapid growth of the publishing industry. The number of books that appeared each year rose steadily. Although interest in fiction grew as the century progressed, most books were in a broad sense educational. The interest in "useful knowledge" was almost insatiable, and books such as Smith's had an enormous success.

Voltaire and Montesquieu

Smith's work cannot be seen clearly except in relation to the Enlightenment as a whole. The English system of government aroused deep admiration among foreign observers of the time. Voltaire (1694–1778), who came to be recognized as the very embodiment of the eighteenth-century Enlightenment, arrived in England in 1726, and was profoundly impressed by what he saw. He was thirty-one at the time and had already achieved notoriety in France as a poet and dramatist—and as the satirist who had been banished from court and eventually imprisoned for lampooning the regent. He was forced to seek refuge in England after rashly challenging the Chevalier de Rohan-Chabot to a duel, and he arrived bitterly indignant at the tyranny and injustice that he had left behind him.

The French government that Voltaire railed against had failed to impose an equitable system of taxation, and in an effort to win the support of various sections of the community, exemptions had been granted to whole classes of the people. Not only the nobles and the clergy but a large proportion of the middle classes had been exempted from the *taille*, or property tax, and entire provinces had been given relief in other ways. Even worse, the French government appeared totally incapable of reforming the system.

Upon Louis XIV's death the *Parlement* of Paris was restored to its former authority, but its members (and those of the twelve provincial *parlements*) were blind to the need for reform and totally opposed to any proposal that might lead to it. A more representative legislative assembly, elected by the people and responsible to them, was so out of keeping with the French tradition that the idea was never even proposed with any sort of conviction. And even those writers who had found cause to criticize the autocracy during the later years of the King's reign suggested a return to ancient methods of government rather than a progression to new ones.

To Voltaire, the Englishman's freedom seemed so refreshing as to be an inspiration. In England the press was free, there was a measure of religious toleration inconceivable in France, and there was parliamentary government. Torture, arbitrary imprisonment and arbitrary taxation were evils of the past. The Frenchman's *Lettres sur les anglais*, a work that increased the disfavor in which Voltaire was held at the French court, provided his countrymen with a glimpse of a society

Montesquieu; full of praise for England's liberal political system.

that was much more fortunate than their own.

Charles de Secondat, Baron de la Brède et de Montesquieu (1689–1755), whose *Lettres persanes* was a biting satire on French society, arrived in England in 1729 to study its political and social institutions. His verdict was every bit as favorable as Voltaire's had been. "It is the freest country in the world," he decided. "I make exception of no republic and I call it free because the sovereign, whose authority is controlled and limited, is unable to inflict any imaginable harm on anyone."

By the middle of the eighteenth century, English optimism was shared by writers such as Voltaire and Montesquieu. For all their burning anti-clericalism and their lost faith in the doctrines of the Church, French intellectuals had not lost their faith in the dignity of man. Man was innately good, and good legislators could bring this to the fore. He could also be made better, and his environment improved, by increasing his knowledge—and it was with a view to increasing man's knowledge that Denis Diderot (1713–84) set about compiling his *Encyclopédie* in 1741, a project to which both Voltaire and Montesquieu contributed. "The aim of an encyclopedia," as he put it, "is to assemble the knowledge scattered over the face of the earth; to explain its general plan to the men with whom we live, and to transmit it to those who come after us, so that the labors of past centuries may not be useless to future times; so that our descendants, by becoming better informed, may in consequence be happier and more virtuous. . . ."

Adam Smith, the Scotsman whose advocacy of free trade was a spur to the Industrial Revolution.

An Encyclopedia for the Enlightenment

The task assigned to Denis Diderot in 1742 by a consortium of leading Parisian publishers was a relatively simple one: to translate Quaker Ephraim Chambers' single-volume Cyclopedia *into French. Diderot's immediate, ambitious revision of his employers' assignment led to the publication of a thirty-five volume* Encyclopédie *that both summarized and exemplified the Age of Enlightenment. The process took twenty-five years and was conducted semiclandestinely, without the approval of government censors. The series, which was suppressed by the State Council and expressly condemned by the Church, numbered among its contributors the greatest names of the Age of Reason: Rousseau and Voltaire, Quesnay and D'Alembert. The encyclopedia's influence on the courts, councils, and cognoscenti of Europe was profound. In France itself, Diderot's work was quoted at court to settle arguments—and was quoted elsewhere, by opponents of the King, to stir a revolution.*

Many of Diderot's friends wrote articles for his encyclopedia: Rousseau for example wrote on music.

Opposite Diderot, who developed the original idea of a translation of Chamber's *Cyclopedia* into French.

Soon after the publication of Diderot's *Encyclopédie*, a book of pirated selections was advertised as containing "the most interesting, the most pleasant, the most piquant, the most philosophical articles of the Great Dictionary," intended to attract all kinds of readers, "and in particular men of the world." The advertisement indicates something about the reading public of the *Encyclopédie*. Men of the world, including the crowned heads of many countries, did indeed have the volumes in their libraries. The Sultan in Constantinople instructed his engineers to make use of the illustrative plates to improve his gun foundry, and learned people all over Europe used the articles to better their knowledge and to write refutations. Army officers, lawyers, economists and clergymen are found on the various lists of subscribers. No other book has had such a dramatic impact on so widespread and influential an audience.

The great French *Encyclopédie* of Denis Diderot and Jean Le Rond d'Alembert is a landmark in the story of the human mind. It is a whole library, and its long list of contributors includes the most famous names of the age. The entire French literature of the eighteenth century is represented in these volumes—not only *belles lettres*, but also writings on philosophy, natural history, economics, politics and many other subjects. What is still more important, all the contributors were united in the task of creating a new and revolutionary way of thinking, in contrast to the still dominant traditions of the Church in politics and nearly all ways of life. New light was to be shed, and the term "Enlightenment" became the watchword for the whole epoch. The *Encyclopédie* was not the sole instrument of that great movement, but it was by far the most powerful and decisive vehicle.

The war on tradition had begun in the seventeenth century, when scientists and philosophers began attacking what for centuries had been the traditional patterns of European civilization: a divine monarchy; a privileged Church and hereditary aristocracy; a formally maintained, stratified social hierarchy; a legal system that favored the group rather than the individual; and decentralized state government that accounted for considerable local variety and regional autonomy. Both religion and the social order had been accepted on faith, unchallenged.

In addition, the seventeenth century saw new scientific discoveries—particularly Isaac Newton's investigations of motion—bring about startling changes in thought. Newton's investigations and the thinking of Descartes, Francis Bacon and John Locke helped develop a belief in natural law and a universal order. Most important, they developed the confidence that human reason, using the scientific method, could discover truth. Skepticism replaced blind faith, all the old orthodoxies were questioned, and the belief in change and progress replaced the commitment to stability. Nature, the new rationalists believed, was mechanical, ordered and subject to unvarying laws; man, through the use of reason, could discover these laws. Progress and perfection were possible on earth.

By the eighteenth century the Enlightenment—or the Age of Reason, as it has been called—was in full swing. The new ideas had by then become widely disseminated, popularized by the *philosophes*, who addressed themselves to the general public. Those *philosophes* were the men who contributed to the book that became the Bible of the Enlightenment, Diderot's *Encyclopédie*. That great work epitomized the rationalism and skepticism of the age, recording scientific achievements, the advance of industrial technology and the reorientation of thoughts. Its

Button making, a typical illustration from the *Encyclopédie* which dealt with practical matters as well as ideas. The first volume of plates was published a year after the first volume of the *Encyclopédie* itself.

The many faces of Voltaire; uncrowned king of the Encyclopedists.

point of view was that of the most enlightened, and it challenged sacred and hitherto impregnable institutions. Typical of its attacks was this veiled comment on the French monarchy: "A sovereign, absolute though he may be, has no right to touch the established law of a state, no more than its religion....He is, besides, always obliged to follow the laws of justice and reason."

D'Alembert, in his now famous introductory essay, the "*Discours Préliminaire*," gave full recognition to the debt the *philosophes*, or Encyclopedists, owed to their predecessors. He began with Francis Bacon, "born still in the deepest darkness" of the Middle Ages, the first who had broken the chains of scholasticism and metaphysical speculation and had placed empiricism firmly on the map. Empiricism was indeed the watchword of the Encyclopedists. It meant to explore not only the mind but all branches of knowledge and human activities: the arts, geography, zoology, botany, economics, agriculture, chemistry, architecture—even grammar and semantics. The *Encyclopédie* was truly universal, at least in its aims.

The beginnings had been very modest. Originally no more was intended than the French translation of the Quaker Ephraim Chambers' *Cyclopedia*, which had been published some decades before in London and had since been reprinted in several editions. A one-man work with modest aims and much useful information, it had shown that a public existed for this kind of dictionary. A small consortium of leading Paris publishers decided on a French edition and hired as editor Denis Diderot, who had already made himself known to the publishers as a translator of other English reference books and an author of books on mathematical problems, natural history and like subjects. Diderot at once changed the publishers' plan completely—substituting the very ambitious scheme that became the foundation of the *Encyclopédie*, and, in fact, the model for all future encyclopedias. A prospectus was printed, approved by the censor, and distributed. The response from the public was highly satisfactory, and the first virulent critics were shrugged off.

The main task for Diderot, as for any editor of an undertaking of that scope, was to find collaborators. D'Alembert, a leading mathematician who had been internationally honored with memberships in many academies, was willing to take over the section on mathematics besides contributing articles on other subjects. Other friends joined the venture: Jean Jacques Rousseau would be the author of articles on music; Baron Paul Henri Holbach would contribute articles on mining and geology; Voltaire promised his collaboration and delivered a few articles. Dr. François Quesnay, the court physician, wrote on economics, his private hobby. Quesnay proved to be one of the most valuable members of the team; his name now figures in all textbooks on the history of economics as the influential forerunner of Adam Smith.

But the *Encyclopédie* was by no means a mere repository. It was highly original in many places, and it paved the way for further development—not only in political and religious thinking but in such seemingly modest fields as veterinary science (then in its infancy and most important for a predominantly agricultural country). Almost no subject was overlooked. Articles in the form of "letters to the editor" came in as the work progressed, and they were gratefully accepted. An anonymous lady even provided highly professional information about frills and ribbons. Diderot, son of a master cutler and deeply interested in all arts and crafts, provided an article on stockings and the method of knitting them using improved machinery.

In 1751 a first volume appeared in Paris under the title *Encyclopédie, ou Dictionnaire Raisonné des Sciences, des Arts et des Métiers*. It was in folio format, printed in double columns and comprising nearly a thousand pages. The title-page mentioned Diderot as the general editor and d'Alembert as responsible for the mathematical entries. The volume carried on the title-page the official line of approval by the censor: "*Avec . . . Privilège du Roy.*" Another volume—well received by the public and fiercely criticized by powerful representatives of the Church and tradition—followed shortly. Then the first battle was lost; the censor intervened, permission was withdrawn

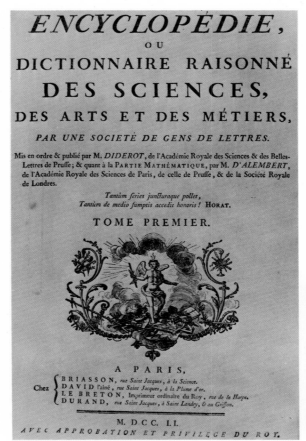

The title-page of the first edition of the *Encyclopédie*, published in 1751.

Above The French dramatist Beaumarchais.

Voltaire presiding at a philosophical dinner; others present include d'Alembert, Diderot and Condorcet. The Encyclopedists were regarded by their enemies as a group of dangerous conspirators.

and the entire work was banned under order of the King.

Half a year later, however, the great work was continued, although without official permission and on sufferance, because the chief censor and director of all publications, Chrétien de Malesherbes, sympathized in secret with the undertaking. And so the next five volumes came out. The number of subscribers reached four thousand, a colossal figure for the time, especially taking into account the very high price of subscription.

In 1757 the next battle was joined—and it ended in near catastrophe for the editors. The Attorney General denounced the work as dangerous and subversive from the point of view of religion as well as of politics and morals. The State Council gave the order for suppression. Worse still, some of the most important contributors deserted. D'Alembert resigned as joint editor. Jean Jacques Rousseau, who as a friend of Diderot had contributed numerous articles, attacked his former comrades-in-arms in public. The faithful band who had carried the great undertaking to such a spectacular success broke up and was scattered.

Diderot alone remained at his post and decided to continue. Many well-wishers advised him to transfer the *Encyclopédie* to some safer place, such as Berlin or

St. Petersburg, since both Frederick the Great of Prussia and Catherine the Great of Russia had taken considerable interest in the work and sympathized with its views. But Diderot stuck to Paris and his contract with the original publishers. Under his editorship, the final ten volumes of text were completed and printed in Paris. On the title-page, however, Diderot's name was replaced by an anonymous "Mr.——"; an obscure firm in the possession of the King of Prussia was listed as printer.

When the final set of volumes came out, Diderot discovered that the publisher, Le Breton, had secretly employed a censor of his own who had eliminated many lines and paragraphs that seemed too dangerous. Le Breton had also taken the precaution of destroying the manuscripts and the corrected proof sheets. Diderot could do nothing but rage and curse. Nonetheless, because he wanted to see his work finished, he began editing a further set of eleven volumes containing engraved illustrations of the industrial arts. Those finely engraved plates, covering the whole field of technical development known at the time, served not only to inform the reader but also to instruct and encourage owners of factories to introduce new methods.

In 1772, after twenty-five years of almost uninterrupted effort, the *Encyclopédie* was finished. Several volumes of supplements and plates followed, and in the end the whole work comprised thirty-five large folios and filled a fairly substantial bookcase. But Diderot refused to work on the supplements or on new editions. In fact he published no more books. The great dialogues and novels of his later years were published only after his death in 1784.

The fact that Diderot's *Encyclopédie* was published

in spite of solemn public condemnation by the Church and the highest legal authorities and an official ban by the State Council was puzzling to his contemporaries, especially to the enemies of the great undertaking. One explanation for the work's successful appearance is suggested by an anecdote: one day, it was said, a discussion about powder making was going on in the salon of the Marquise de Pompadour, the King's all-powerful favorite. Since nobody knew anything of the process, some well-wisher of the *Encyclopédie* produced the appropriate volume, which had a full and highly instructive article on the topic. The text was read out and generally applauded. There was general consensus that so useful a book should not be banned but should be in the hands of anybody interested in information. The King, the indolent Louis xv, agreed, although he did not see fit to lift the official order. According to another version, the article dealt not with the making of face powder, Madame de Pompadour's sphere of interest, but with the fabrication of gunpowder, which appealed to the King, a great hunter. The story, although apocryphal, is significant; the practical usefulness of the work was certainly directly related to its success—and to the limited tolerance accorded its distribution.

The Marquise de Pompadour's actual role in protecting the publication remains rather obscure. It may be best described as "benevolent neutrality." Yet even that attitude—when held by the de facto ruler of the country—was invaluable. In one of her portraits, painted by La Tour, the Marquise saw to it that among numerous objects displayed on a table to attest to her cultural interests and gifts was a volume of the *Encyclopédie*.

Another and far more powerful influence was the fact that the battle against the *Encyclopédie* took place at the same time as the great campaign against the Jesuit order. Waged by the main Roman Catholic countries—Portugal at first, then Spain and France—it culminated in the final suppression of the Society of Jesus by the Pope. After the ban on the first two volumes of the *Encyclopédie*, there had been elements at work to seize the papers and continue the work under the supervision of the order. The chief censor, Malesherbes, prevented this intrigue by taking the papers into his personal custody and returning them after some time to Diderot. Six years later, when the *Encyclopédie*'s continuation appeared almost hopeless, the Society of Jesus suffered an equally heavy blow; all activity of the order and its members was forbidden in France. The most active adversaries of the Encyclopedists were thereby eliminated from the scene.

Enemies remained, however: churchmen, satirists, defenders of the holy rights of absolute monarchy and the traditional moral standards (although the actual morals of the time, as everybody had to admit, did not exactly conform to the time-honored precepts that were being preached). The fight continued long after the publication of the original edition and finally merged with the ferment of the French Revolution. The *Encyclopédie* has often been described as

Experience Areostatique faite a Versailles le 19 Sept.bre 1783 en presence de leurs Majestes et de la famille Royale par Mr. de Montgolfier avec un Balon de 52 pieds d'hauteur sur 41 de Diametres. Cette Superbe machine a fond d'asur avec le Chiffre du Roi pesant 900 livres. Ce balon a eté enlevé avec toutes l'aplaudissement de tout les Spectateurs et a tombé dans le Bois de Vaucresson

one of the dominant intellectual influences paving the way to that great event.

The Encyclopedists were widely regarded as a faithful band of brothers, or suspected as a sect, or a church of their own, or a dangerous underground conspiracy. But they were by no means as united a movement as they appeared later. They had their personal squabbles, enmities and ambitions. Voltaire, as the uncrowned king of this movement, sent out exhortations and quasi-military instructions from his safe, strategically located stronghold on the border between France and Switzerland: "Form a square, gentlemen! Unity, O brethren!" However, he could not offer much more than praise for Diderot's work and diligence, although he did advise him to transfer the whole undertaking to a safer place, in Switzerland or perhaps Berlin, when the position in Paris seemed hopeless.

Yet history's view of the Encyclopedists as a movement of the greatest consequence is justified. The work came at the right time and it found the right people as collaborators. The names of the antagonists are rightly forgotten and can be found only in very detailed historical surveys of contemporary pamphlets, skits or dramatic productions of the most ephemeral kind. The Church was very poorly served; the monarchy and all traditional powers fared even worse. Half a century later, writers of caliber and standing—members of the generations that had gone through the school of the Encyclopedists—appeared in defense of traditional values. The half-century that preceded them belonged to the *Encyclopédie* and its friends.

RICHARD FRIEDENTHAL

Montgolfier's balloon; the publication of the *Encyclopédie* coincided with scientific advances in aviation and electronics.

Malesherbes, the writer and lawyer who, as chief censor, confiscated Diderot's papers.

The upbringing of Frederick the Great

The French *philosophes*—as the Enlightenment writers were called—revered no monarch in Europe as highly as Frederick II, King of Prussia. Jean Le Rond d'Alembert (*c.* 1717–83), the philosopher and mathematician who contributed numerous articles to Diderot's *Encyclopédie* and edited part of it, wrote that Frederick was "a prince greater even than his fame, a hero at once *philosophe* and modest, a king worthy of friendship, in fact a true sage on the throne."

The young Frederick as a Grenadier.

Frederick, whose rule ran from 1740 to 1786, was the first son of Frederick William I (1688–1740); he was born in January, 1712. The child's father was a harsh, narrow, boorish man whose eccentricities verged on insanity and whose tastes for order, regularity and the military life were reflected not only in the government of his country but in the architecture of his capital. Determined that his son should be a hardy, practical soldier, Frederick William devised a system of education for him that excluded from its curriculum all studies that he considered peripheral to that goal. And when his son displayed a keen interest in learning those very subjects that had been specifically denied him, the King looked upon the boy as an idle wastrel whose character must be molded by stronger and stronger discipline.

Frederick William's disappointment in his son soon turned to dislike—and then to positive hatred. The King did not trouble to hide his enmity, which he frequently voiced in public. He customarily referred to his offspring with contemptuous disdain—and before the boy was twenty he had decided to run away and to seek protection at the English court. The plan was discovered, and a young friend who had been implicated in it was condemned to death. The execution took place outside Frederick's window, and Frederick William—who conceived that the experience might awaken his son's sense of responsibility—forced young Frederick to watch.

"The whole town shall be his prison," the King wrote after the execution, upon learning that his son had promised not to disobey his commands in the future. "I will give him employment from morning till night in the departments of war and agriculture and of the government. He shall work at financial matters, receive accounts, read minutes and make extracts. . . . But if he kicks or rears again, he shall forfeit the succession to the crown, and even, according to circumstances, life itself."

His future thus threatened, Frederick devoted himself to his duties with so much conscientious application and such marked talent that his father's attitude toward him began to change. The young prince's interest in poetry and philosophy and his correspondence with Voltaire were not likely to arouse Frederick William I's unqualified approval, but the practical mind that Frederick brought to the business of government assured the King that he did indeed have an heir of whom he need not feel ashamed.

Frederick proved to be more concerned with the substance of power than with its shadow. When he saw an anonymous broadsheet criticizing his government stuck high on a wall, he moved it so that it would be easier to read from the sidewalk. But in reality he would allow no opposition that could reduce his freedom of action.

Frederick comes of age

For his part, Frederick recognized that his father—whom many dismissed as a violent martinet—was in fact a dutiful, economical sovereign who had done much good for his country. Indeed Frederick William had provided Prussia with an adequate treasury, sound schools, a strictly organized system of taxation and a large and well disciplined army.

"Prussia's entire government was militarized," Frederick wrote. "The capital became the stronghold of Mars. All the industries which served the needs of armies prospered. In Berlin were established powder mills and cannon foundries, rifle factories, etc. . . . The military character of the government affected both customs and fashions. Society took a military turn." After he succeeded to the throne of Prussia in 1740, Frederick had good cause to thank his father for the strong army and sound finances that Frederick William had bequeathed him.

In truth, Frederick William I was not solely responsible for that legacy. Prussia had begun its climb to power in Europe in the seventeenth century under Frederick William (1640–88), the Great Elector of Brandenburg and Duke of Prussia, whose efficiency in the government of his possessions was celebrated all over Europe. The Elector's son, Frederick I (1657–1713), obtained the Emperor's permission to adopt the title of King of Prussia, and he placed the Prussian crown on his own head in the cathedral at Königsberg in January, 1701. At that time the territories governed by the royal House of Hohenzollern were all but separate entities: Brandenburg, where Frederick's forebears had been established since 1417, lay at the center and had its capital at Berlin; to the east was Prussia, which had been won by Brandenburg in 1660; to the west, beyond the Elbe, were the isolated duchies of Cleves, Mark and Ravensburg.

It was young King Frederick II's determination to unite and extend those hereditary possessions, and thereby to make Prussia a mighty

An allegorical engraving showing Frederick the Great dispensing justice.

emerges as Germany's giant

Frederick in the field at Leuthen, where in December, 1757, he gained a sweeping victory over the Austrians.

force in European affairs. His first opportunity came with the outbreak of the War of the Austrian Succession in 1740. By the Treaty of Aix-la-Chapelle (Aachen), signed in 1748, Frederick gained Silesia, although he also won the undying hostility of Maria Theresa as a result of his greed and his treacherous behavior. Some of Austria's Italian possessions—Parma, Piacenza and Guastalla—were lost to the Bourbons of Spain. But Maria Theresa retained the rest of her patrimony, and on the death of Charles VII her husband became Holy Roman Emperor. Both France and England were satisfied with comparatively modest colonial gains.

After his early successes, Frederick, still in his early thirties, set about the task of building Prussia into a powerful and respected state, economically stable and militarily strong. His formidable talents in many fields earned him envy as well as admiration, while his caustic wit, which was frequently directed at the leading women of Europe—the Empress Elizabeth of Russia, Madame de Pompadour and Maria Theresa—earned him their undying detestation. "The King of Prussia," the Hanoverian King of England declared, voicing a popular opinion, "is a mischievous rascal, a bad friend, a bad ally, a bad relation and a bad neighbour, in fact the most dangerous and ill-disposed prince in Europe."

The Seven Years War

Because so many European rulers agreed with the English King, Maria Theresa experienced little difficulty in organizing a coalition of states to crush the Prussian upstart; a coalition that Russia, France and Saxony all willingly joined. Learning (through the treachery of a clerk in the Saxon foreign office) of the clandestine measures that were being taken to destroy him, Frederick attempted to forestall his enemies by advancing to the attack himself. In the summer of 1756 he marched into Saxony at the head of his army, provoking the outbreak of the Seven Years War. In that war, Prussia found herself surrounded by enemies: France (in unnatural alliance with Austria), Saxony and Sweden.

Even Elizabeth of Russia, for years torn between suspicion of Maria Theresa and distrust of Frederick, joined the alliance against him. Like Maria Theresa in the War of the Austrian Succession, Frederick was almost friendless. But like Maria Theresa sixteen years earlier, Frederick found one useful ally in England, where William Pitt—recognizing the importance of Prussia in England's challenge to France—subsidized Frederick's army and supported his one powerful ally on the Continent, the Duke of Brunswick.

The fortunes of war

The war in Europe remained Frederick's responsibility nonetheless, and the loneliness and weight of that responsibility all but overwhelmed him. There were times when it seemed that nothing could save him from crushing defeat. After victories in Saxony and Bohemia, he was driven from the field by the Austrians at Kolin, and as his enemies moved in to what seemed the certain kill, he contemplated suicide. But within weeks he and his forces had rallied, and at Rossbach, in November, 1757, he surprised and overwhelmed a French army led by the Prince de Soubise. A month later Frederick's army—weak in numbers and tired out by its long campaigning—was to achieve an equally stunning victory over the Austrians at Leuthen.

Leaving Ferdinand of Brunswick to keep the French occupied in the west, Frederick then turned upon the Russians, whom he defeated at Zorndorf. He was less fortunate against the Austrians at Hochkirch, and he fared so badly against the combined armies of the Russians and Austrians at Kunersdorf in August, 1759, that he became as gloomy and disheartened as he had been two years before. "All is lost," he reported to Berlin. "The consequences of this battle will be worse than the battle itself. I shall not survive the ruin of the Fatherland. Adieu for ever."

The crestfallen monarch soon recovered his spirits, however, and at Liegnitz and then at Torgau he reversed the tide of his fortunes. Nonetheless, by the end of 1761 it once more seemed that Frederick's cause was doomed. His countryside had been ravaged by Russian troops, towns had been occupied and all but destroyed, his army had suffered terrible losses, and he himself was worn out by the long and tragic war. His enemies watched eagerly for his final collapse—only to see him saved by the death of the Russian Empress Elizabeth. Elizabeth was succeeded by Peter III, who was one of Frederick's most zealous admirers, and the Russians withdrew. With the loss of Russia's support, with the Turks threatening her borders in the southeast, and with Frederick's final victory over her army at Freiburg, Maria Theresa was forced to agree to the Treaty of Hubertusburg in February, 1763. The Treaty of Paris had been signed a few days before; the war was over.

The year before that war began, a disastrous event had occurred in Europe—an event that seemed even more terrible than war itself, and one that brought an age of optimism suddenly to an end. That age, reflected so complacently in Alexander Pope's 1733 *Essay on Man* and based so contentedly on what Voltaire called the *tout est bien* philosophy, ended in November, 1755, when a shattering earthquake destroyed one of the oldest and richest cities in Europe.

The Battle of Prague, May, 1757, in which Frederick defeated the Austrian army and went on to invest the city.

Disaster Strikes Lisbon

November 1, 1775, was All Saints' Day in Lisbon, Portugal's bustling capital city and principal port. Thousands of Lisbon's faithful jammed the city's numerous churches to celebrate the Holy Day—and thousands of them died in their pews shortly before ten in the morning as a series of earth tremors sundered the city. Cathedral vaults collapsed, church walls cracked and buckled inward, and fires—many lit by holy candles—swept the city. As few as 10,000—or as many as 40,000—persons died in the holocaust that followed, and as Lisbon's dazed citizens began the task of rebuilding their devastated city, scientists and seers alike attempted to explain the disaster. The former could offer no answer; the latter were certain that the quake was Divine Retribution for Portugal's collective sins. Both groups recognized that the earthquake had irrevocably shattered an age of optimism.

The Marquess of Pombal who, after the earthquake had wrecked the city, took command of the situation and headed the commission that rebuilt Lisbon.

Opposite The Church of Carmo, which was damaged in the earthquake and remains today as it appeared in 1755.

After the event there was talk of signs and omens, of crossed swords appearing in the sky and prophesies, but on that momentous November 1, 1755—a religious holiday—the weather was perfect and an unusual stillness in the air and a certain nervousness among the animals passed almost unnoticed. No one was worried about such things on that glorious morning of All Saints' Day, a day filled with the sounds of ringing church bells, the hurrying of the faithful to the churches and the lively bustle of the town and port of Lisbon.

King Joseph and the court had gone to Belém to attend Mass at the monastery of the Jeronimos, and certain wealthy middle-class families had their own chaplain say Mass for them in their private chapels. The majority, however, preferred to go to the Carmo or the San Roque, where they sang the long Masses. All the churches were packed to overflowing.

Suddenly, just a few minutes before ten o'clock, while the Service of the Holy Ghost was being celebrated, there were three violent shocks, one after another, accompanied by a terrifying uproar. All over the city the ground was splitting apart, walls were cracking and vaults were collapsing. A blinding curtain of dust clouded the sky and tongues of fire began to curl upward from the first fires; wax candles overturned on the altars and set fire to the hangings and the gilded woodwork, and stoves vomited forth their burning embers. A strong wind arose, blowing the smoke in all directions and fanning the flames.

Those who had not been buried under the ruins or swallowed up by the crevices in the ground rushed toward the Tagus River, hoping to escape from the scene of the disaster in one of the many boats moored in the estuary. To their horror, they saw that the waters of the Tagus were rapidly receding and that the boats were breaking up, their hulls crashing into one another and becoming stuck in the oozing mud. Then, just as abruptly, the waters began to rise again and came rolling onto the banks in a rushing tidal wave that carried corpses and debris alike as far as the center of the Lower Town.

Thus, within the space of a few minutes, the four elements had joined together: the earth splitting open like an overripe fruit, the wind swirling violently through the air, fire springing up in a thousand places at the same time and the waters angrily barring the way on all sides.

It was a merciless disaster, and terror reigned supreme. No one ever established the exact number of victims, although a total of 100,000 was first suggested. The figure was later reduced to 40,000, and that too was probably an overestimation. But even if one accepts the lowest estimate, of around 10,000 victims, the Lisbon disaster was still a great tragedy.

The 1755 earthquake affected all of Europe. Its tremors had shaken the whole of the Iberian Peninsula and had reached as far as Scandinavia, affecting the springs there. More important, however, was the fact that it had destroyed a city that served as a center for European trade. It seemed that Lisbon had been especially chosen—or cursed—by God, who had used the quake to reveal His wrath toward the whole of Christianity. Such a belief was enough to provoke the less fearful into a serious examination of conscience, while the more credulous were plunged into a state of total religious hysteria. Everyone was afraid, confessed his sins and did penitence. King Louis XV of France went so far as to promise his confessor that he would break off relations with the Marquise de Pompadour; she, in turn, vowed she would give up the wearing of rouge as an atonement.

King Joseph, his family and his court—as well as the monastery and tower of Belém—had escaped the catastrophe. The pathetic King, who was concerned only for his own personal safety and the salvation of his immortal soul, abandoned the task "of burying the dead and taking care of the living" to the man who already wielded the real power behind the throne—his minister, Sebastião José de Carvalho, who was to become famous in the annals of history as the Marquess of Pombal.

In 1755, Lisbon was the prosperous capital of a poverty-stricken country. Travelers who came there

were dazzled at the sight of so many palaces and by the treasures they contained: the rarest of goldware, silks and porcelain, paintings by Rubens and Titian and precious books. (Seventy thousand volumes and many priceless documents were destroyed when the royal palace was burned.)

The churches of the city were even more ostentatious, with their giant organs, their gilt woodwork, their panels of *azulejos* (glazed tiles) and their ciboriums and tabernacles of massive silver encrusted with precious stones.

By 1755 the huge Portuguese Empire had begun to disintegrate. Joseph's predecessor, John v, the last great King of Portugal, had squandered all the gold that he obtained from Brazil by building churches, clothing his prelates in purple and decking out religious ceremonies with pagan ostentation.

Lisbon suffocated under the weight of this inert wealth. The whole country was paralyzed by the King's narrow, pious attitude and by his total indifference to his subjects' interests. Thus paralyzed, Portugal fell without a struggle into the hands of its powerful ally, Great Britain, and was devoured alive. Indeed, the turn-of-the-century Treaty of Methuen, which laid down the terms for trading between the two countries (roughly speaking, Portuguese wines in return for British wool), was such that every Englishman who came to Portugal enjoyed a king's privileges.

A sudden shock, a violent emotion, can sometimes cure a paralyzed person. Pombal had a presentiment that the earthquake might serve as such a shock, reviving the energies of the Portuguese people and rousing the country from its state of hopeless apathy.

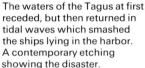
The waters of the Tagus at first receded, but then returned in tidal waves which smashed the ships lying in the harbor. A contemporary etching showing the disaster.

In attempting to restore order in Lisbon, Pombal was faced with many urgent and acute problems, all of which had to be dealt with immediately. One section of the city had been completely destroyed. The remainder was tottering on the verge of collapse, endangered by the earth tremors that followed one after another for many months, unpredictable in their timing and their volume. In spite of the rain, the discomfort and the bands of looters, the inhabitants of Lisbon who had not already fled into the country preferred to camp outside, to sleep in the open air under the stars or under any temporary form of shelter that came their way, rather than stay in the city.

With remarkable coolness and clarity of vision, Pombal immediately took the necessary steps to deal with the emergency. The dead were buried or unceremoniously thrown into the river, panic was allayed, famine averted and looters were severely and publicly punished. The complaints of the English merchants, who had lost their stocks as well as money owed to them, were coldly received. They were told that nothing prevented them from returning home to England; none of them did so, however. The situation soon improved, for Pombal had a very clear idea of both the difficulties and the resources of Portugal.

He decided to rebuild the city on exactly the same site that it had occupied ever since its foundation (which, according to legend, dated back to Ulysses). Two months after the catastrophe, the plans for this new city of Lisbon had already been drafted, revealing a boldness of conception, a practical genius and a clear vision of the future.

Pombal made no attempt to reconstitute Lisbon

LISABONA

in its former medieval style, with one section of the city clustered around the port and the rest scattered between the convents and the properties of the nobles. On the contrary, he commissioned a plan for a modern city with wide, well-drained streets laid out at right angles to each other. The façades of the buildings were uniform but dignified in style. They were constructed out of prefabricated sections for the first time in the history of town planning, and they were enhanced by beautiful wrought-iron lanterns and balconies and by the harmonious lines of their mansards and roofs.

Pombal's new Lisbon was dedicated to trade—of vital importance in his plans for the future prosperity of the country—as well as to industry, the growth of which he tried to stimulate. Such a policy soon met with the strong disapproval of the nobility—who considered Pombal an upstart—and of the Church. How could Pombal concern himself with such mundane preoccupations at a time when Divine Wrath had struck down Lisbon as a warning to others? The only thing that mattered was to obtain God's mercy by repentance and resignation. Pombal's detractors wanted more public confessions, processions of penitents, mortifications of the flesh and hymns of praise to ward off even greater evils. They were all agreed that they had deserved to be punished, but at the same time they were quick to point out the guilt in others. Thus the priests were accused of simony, the nobles of corruption, the middle classes of religious apathy and avarice, and the masses of lubricity. Fanatics, acting as Jeremiahs, predicted new catastrophes and cast curses on Lisbon, which they believed should remain a city in ruins like Sodom and Gomorrah.

Pombal had the utmost difficulty in persuading people that the disaster had been caused by a natural phenomenon. His difficulties were aggravated by the fact that science—which for some years had been accepted throughout Europe as the source of all truth—found it almost impossible to provide an explanation for this phenomenon. Famous scientists suggested that the quake might have been caused by the influence of the moon, or by fire and water that had become overheated in the center of the earth or by the little known force called electricity. None of the explanations was satisfactory. People preferred to listen to the oracles and to sermons.

In defiance of Pombal's orders, the Jesuit Malagrida wrote and distributed his *Judgment on the True Causes of the Earthquake*. According to Malagrida, Lisbon—the sixteenth-century center of operations for the Jesuits—had been punished for having sought to deprive the Jesuits of the Maranhão, an area of land claimed by both Brazil and Paraguay. Malagrida was a religious visionary who had great powers of fascination. He was considered a prophet, and he might have reduced Lisbon to a state of superstitious terror had he not been banished to the port city of Setubal. He was soon surrounded by a nucleus of loyal supporters, including some of the most illustrious families of the kingdom, who hatched a plot to kill King Joseph and thereby rid themselves

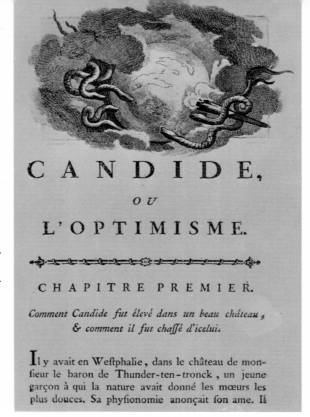

An early edition of Voltaire's allegory *Candide*. Writing twenty-three years after the earthquake, Voltaire still felt the event important enough to describe in great detail.

The city of Lisbon was almost totally destroyed. This picture shows how even the strongest buildings had crashed to the ground after the series of tremors.

of his first minister. The plot was discovered, however, and Pombal took advantage of the opportunity to bring all his enemies, aristocrats and Jesuits alike, to trial at the same time. The prisons were filled with them for the next twenty years; the Inquisition condemned Malagrida to be garrotted and burned at the stake and many of the most illustrious heads in Portugal rolled beneath the executioner's blade.

Pombal's hands were red with the blood of his enemies, but at last he was free to do what he wanted—set up a government of technocrats. He founded the *Compagnie Royale* in order to wrest control of the vineyards that produced Port wine from the English. Moreover, he sent to France, Italy and Germany for specialist craftsmen to start up or revive such local industries as ceramics, silk, cutlery and smelting

The royal palace at Lisbon.

The statue of King Joseph, a timid and ineffectual ruler.

works. He was a great believer in technical progress, in individual effort and in hard work, and he overcame all obstacles impeding his plans. The Society of Jesus had become progressively weaker and lacking in authority and finally was driven out of the country altogether. An ambitious, active and dedicated middle class did its best to carry out the great aims of Pombal. Before he fell into disgrace, Pombal saw Lisbon rise once again out of the ruins and saw the statue of his master erected in one of the most beautiful squares in the world, a plaza dedicated to commerce. But Pombal was to die a slandered, ruined man, and with his death all the fragile structure of his work collapsed. For the next 150 years, Portugal sank into oblivion, disorder and decadence.

The deadly earth tremors that had destroyed Lisbon had shaken the world. It was not only buildings that had collapsed, but also beliefs; the cracks carved out abysses not only in the ground, but also in the minds of the most well-balanced men.

It was true that this misfortune, befalling a country that could count on few friends at the time, was viewed very severely by many people. The Protestants saw in the earthquake a just retribution for popish idolatry; the Jansenists were overjoyed that the "cradle of the Jesuits" was destroyed; others believed that the crimes committed by the Inquisition had been expiated in this way.

Even compassion tended to be condescending. Emergency aid was generous to begin with, but soon people grew irritated with Pombal's claim that his country was capable of recovering by its own efforts and would soon take its place again alongside the other European nations. The scientists felt resentful toward Portugal because they had been asked to find an explanation for a phenomenon that was beyond their comprehension.

The philosophers, too, were troubled. The Lisbon disaster was a deadly denial of the complacent optimism that had reigned during a century when science served merely as a diversion for the government, and when religion was a pleasant way of making sure of a place in the next world. After all, the finest minds of the time had established, mathematically, that everything was "for the best in the best of all possible worlds." God had been proven infallible as well as just and good.

Why then had God struck down so pitilessly the innocent at the same time as the guilty? Where was His justice, His goodness? If, on the other hand, He had not wanted such a catastrophe to happen—if the phenomenon had been fortuitous—how could He be the Almighty, the wisest of all? What about the perfection of His creation?

People were reluctant to accept the doctrine of collective responsibility that so carelessly sacrificed innocence in its cause. Their belief in God was shaken. They began seriously to question Divine Providence. Man became bitterly aware of his own insignificance, of the precariousness of his existence. Prayer no longer sufficed to reassure him.

Just after the event Voltaire wrote a passionate poem that is one long cry of despair, pity and revolt. Rousseau, although he did not go quite so far, declared that man, and man alone, was responsible for his own misfortunes. If he had lived as a "noble savage" in the midst of nature, instead of crowding together in the cities for sordid motives of profit, there would never have been so many lives sacrificed. Goethe, then a child, was terrified at the thought of the blind wrath of Almighty God that struck indiscriminately at both the good and the wicked. If God were not just, if there were no mercy in Heaven, if, as Voltaire had cried so passionately, "evil is in this world," then there was no longer any joy in living.

Thus, a complete way of life, of thought, of hoping had disappeared, to be replaced by a new approach to existence. Menaced by the hostility of a cruel world, man had to accept the responsibility for his own actions. Pombal had shown him how he could conquer his fear, and tackle with courage the task of rebuilding a city to make it more beautiful and prosperous than the one that had been so cruelly reduced to ashes.

A Portuguese poet advised people to "stay at home in their villages and tend their sheep"—in other words, to concentrate on making the most of their own resources without depending on others or interfering in their affairs. This philosophy still prevails in Portugal today. Man must fend for himself without expecting God's help; the existence of Heaven is doubtful.

While all these ideas were merging and blending one with another, the old established order was gradually falling apart. Like the decrepit, worm-eaten palaces and gilded churches of Lisbon, the old world was crumbling down to its very foundations. New currents of thought emerged as a result of the traumatic shock that had swept across the whole of Europe: Choiseul expelled the Jesuits from France, the Pope dissolved the Society of Jesus, and the education of young noblemen—which up to that time had been in the hands of the Jesuits—henceforth changed direction. Daring new ideas, no longer contradicted or forbidden, began to circulate.

The Lisbon disaster, by causing men to doubt the wisdom of Divine Providence, marked the end of an era, an era dominated by faith and respect for the established authorities: the head of a family, the king and God. The senseless cruelty of the disaster had not only aroused compassion, Christian solidarity and simple human love, it had also led to objective, nonmaterialistic speculation and to a disdain for individual life which, although still precious and unique, was subordinate to larger goals. This concept was to lead directly to the conclusion that "the end justifies the means." Without a Divine Justice to separate good from evil, man was responsible for his own actions and had a perfect right to sacrifice the liberty or dignity of others in order to achieve his aims.

The reactions and shock provoked by the Lisbon earthquake in the eighteenth century can perhaps be compared to everything that man experiences in face of the horrifying reality of modern warfare: his confusion in face of the annihilation of the individual, the iciness weighing down his spirit, the despair that finds no relief in understanding. Today, as then, this anguish is perfectly expressed in Voltaire's lines:

What am I, where am I, where am I going to and from
where did I come,
A thinking atom, an atom whose eyes,
Guided by thought, have scanned the heavens?

SUZANNE CHANTAL

The Inquisition in session. For twenty years after a plot to murder Pombal was discovered the Inquisition executed the most able men in Portugal, and thus helped establish Pombal's position.

A picture painted at the time of the earthquake showing the dead and wounded inhabitants of Lisbon lying in the streets while fires rage throughout the city.

As Mogul power declines, India falls

British politics under Pitt

The resignation of Walpole did not reduce the power of the Whigs in British politics, but no individual of comparable talent could at first be found to replace him. The government was able to maintain itself in office, although the ministers changed rapidly. The dominant figures in the cabinet were aristocrats of little merit or ability, men whom Walpole had brought into the government partly because they would not present any serious challenge to his leadership and partly to repay political favors. They were men such as the Earl of Wilmington (Prime Minister 1742–43), Lord Henry Pelham (First Lord of the Treasury and effectively Prime Minister 1743–54) and his brother the Duke of Newcastle. Of the three only Newcastle (1693–1768) had much talent. He showed himself to be a brilliant dispenser of patronage and manager of parliamentary business, and was largely responsible for the continuance of the Whig majority in Parliament after the fall of Walpole—although he was assisted by the support given by many Tories to the Jacobite rising of 1745, which led to widespread suspicion of Toryism.

In 1746, however, a man of ability equal to that of Walpole was brought into the cabinet. This was William Pitt the Elder (1708–78), created Earl of Chatham in 1766, who became Paymaster General of the Armed Forces. Although egotistical—he once claimed, "I know that I can save the country and that no one else can"—and difficult to work with, he was a man of vision, and—no less important—able to inspire others with his vision. Unlike Walpole, Pitt believed in following an aggressive line in foreign affairs, particularly against France. He regarded France as an unacceptable danger to British foreign and colonial policy, and thought that his life's work should be to humble France. But he was not at first able to pursue his plans.

When Pelham died in 1754, Newcastle succeeded him as Prime Minister, but he quickly showed himself to be no less opposed to an all-out trade war with France than his brother or Walpole had been, and in 1755 Pitt was dismissed from the cabinet. In the following year, largely because of the need to fight the Seven Years War energetically, Pitt became in effect, though not in name, Prime Minister. His popularity was immense in 1758, and when the British captured Fort Duquesne it was renamed

Pittsburgh in his honor. Britain's success in the Seven Years War was largely due to Pitt's subordination of all other matters to military and above all to naval strength. But by 1761, the cabinet, Parliament and the public was tired of war, which, however successful, was a drain on the British economy. The new King, George III (1738–1820), influenced by his favorite, Lord Bute, wanted peace too, and Pitt resigned, deploring the peace terms of the Treaty of Paris. He became Prime Minister again in 1766, but illness reduced his effectiveness, and although he favored a conciliatory policy toward the American colonies, his advice was ignored.

In the years after Pitt's death, British politics lacked any real driving force. The King's efforts to expand the royal prerogative found little support among politicians. Pitt's vision of a powerful empire built on mutual trade was not fully understood by his successors, who saw the colonies primarily as valuable sources of raw materials for British industry and as valuable markets for British manufactured goods. The mercantilist ideal continued to dominate British political thinking, despite the growing chorus of criticism by economists. It was only as the result of the success of

the American Revolution and of rapidly increasing industrial output in the years after about 1760 that British politicians began to abandon the mercantilist ideals they had held so readily.

India

In India, the dissolution of the Mogul Empire had provided opportunities for both France and England to extend their influence and power. The trade of the English East India Company, which had bases at Surat, Calcutta and Madras, eventually grew to be considerably greater in bulk than that of the French (whose bases at Chandernagore and Pondicherry were less advantageously placed), but in the earlier rounds

Robert Clive, who became governor of Bengal and commander-in-chief of the East India Company's army.

of the struggle it was the French who were more successful. The talents of the French sailor Mahé de La Bourdonnais (1699–1753) and those of the brilliant governor of the French East India Company, Joseph François Dupleix (1697–1763), contrasted sharply with the meager talents of Nicholas Morse, the English governor of Madras. Morse surrendered Madras to the French in 1746 after a few days' half-hearted resistance. In the summer of 1748, the British attempted to recoup their losses by launching an abortive siege operation at Pondicherry, only to be obliged to withdraw.

By the Treaty of Aix-la-Chapelle, Madras was given back to the British in exchange for Cape Breton—but French prestige was much enhanced by her conduct of the

Publish'd according to Act of Parliament 1781. by Will.ᵐ Hinnell at y.ᵉ White Horse under y.ᵉ Piaʐʐa Royal Exchange London.

William Pitt the Elder is made Prime Minister by George III.

prey to rival European conquerors

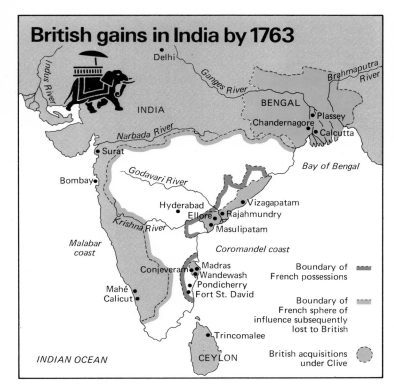

British gains in India by 1763

Delhi

Indus River

Ganges River

Brahmaputra River

INDIA

Narbada River

BENGAL

Chandernagore • • Plassey

• Calcutta

Surat •

Bay of Bengal

Godavari River

Bombay •

Hyderabad • • Vizagapatam

Ellore • • Rajahmundry

Krishna River

• Masulipatam

Malabar coast

Coromandel coast

Conjeveram • • Madras

Mahé • • Wandewash

Calicut • • Pondicherry

• Fort St. David

Boundary of French possessions

Boundary of French sphere of influence subsequently lost to British

• Trincomalee

INDIAN OCEAN

CEYLON

British acquisitions under Clive

---

war and French garrisons were greatly strengthened against the time of its continuance. After 1748, however, the French grip on India began to loosen. Dupleix extended French influence in southern India by manipulating numerous Indian alliances, and he set up puppet governments in the Carnatic, in the Deccan and in Hyderabad. But in 1754 he had overreached himself and had all but exhausted his finances. Dupleix was recalled to France—and as he departed, another figure of remarkable talents appeared on the Indian scene. This man was Robert Clive.

Clive had emigrated to Madras at the age of eighteen to become a clerk in the East India Company, and he was there—homesick and miserable—when the town was captured by La Bourdonnais in 1746. He entered the army a short time later and greatly distinguished himself during the siege of Arcot (where rival claimants, supported respectively by France and Britain, were contesting for the position of Nawab). By 1756 Clive had become governor of Fort St. David and a lieutenant-colonel in the British army. He took up his post as governor on the day that the young Nawab of Bengal, Siraj-ud-Daulah, captured Calcutta.

Like his predecessors, Siraj-ud-Daulah had originally been on friendly terms with the British

East India Company. But when the British government refused to remand a rich fugitive who had fled to Calcutta to escape what he regarded as the extortionate demands of the new Nawab, Siraj-ud-Daulah had advanced on Calcutta with an army of forty thousand men.

The town's defenses had been much neglected during the peaceful years that had preceded this outbreak of violence, and the garrison numbered only 250 men. At the approach of the Nawab's army both the governor and the military commander fled to the safety of British ships harbored in the river, and the garrison was left to its fate.

Siraj-ud-Daulah, Nawab of Bengal.

It surrendered on June 20, and that night—a night of stifling heat —146 prisoners were locked up in the small punishment cell of the fortress, the Black Hole of Calcutta. All but twenty-three of them died before dawn.

Clive at Calcutta

Although war with France was considered imminent, it was decided that the British forces in the area must concentrate on the recapture of Calcutta. Supported by Rear-Admiral Charles Watson and five men-of-war, Clive set out from Madras with nine hundred European troops and fifteen hundred native soldiers. On February 4, 1757, he overwhelmed the massed ranks of the Nawab's immense army. A treaty was soon concluded and Siraj-ud-Daulah was forced to return all the territory that he had taken from the British.

The long-anticipated conflict with France finally erupted, and Clive was urged to return to Madras. He refused the summons, however, believing that it was more important to capture Chandernagore, the base of the French East India Company in Bengal. He succeeded in achieving his objective only after the gallant defenders of the French fort had been driven into submission by Admiral Watson's determined onslaught from the river.

Siraj-ud-Daulah, who was known to be supporting the French, had actively sought to renew his attack on the English while their attention was occupied at Chandernagore. Therefore, a conspiracy was arranged to replace the Nawab by Mir Jafar, a noble who was more acceptable both to the English and to his own people. While the conspirators were plotting his dethronement, Siraj-ud-Daulah took to the field with over fifty thousand men and fifty pieces of heavy ordnance served by French artillery men. Clive moved out of Chandernagore to meet the renegade with just over a thousand Europeans, two thousand native troops and nine field pieces. The two armies met amid the mango groves of Plassey, a few miles outside Murshidabad. Clive hesitated to move against so large an army with his tiny force—but, after initially refusing to attack, he soon changed his mind, remembering his earlier victory. On

June 23, 1757, he defeated the Nawab in one of the most fateful battles of modern history. Siraj-ud-Daulah fled from the field on a camel, Mir Jafar was installed as a puppet ruler in his place, and the British were masters of Bengal.

The Dutch, no less appalled than the French by the sudden triumph of their rivals, responded by dispatching several armed ships to the Ganges. When these Dutch warships seized some English merchantmen, Clive's response was immediate and determined; seven Dutch ships were captured and the Dutch army was defeated by one of Clive's best officers, Francis Forde. The Dutch were allowed to retain their settlements in Bengal, but the terms on which they were able to do so removed the threat of Dutch competition in the subcontinent.

The British were equally successful in southern India, where the French general, the Count de

Count de Lally on the ramparts of Pondicherry.

Lally, son of an Irish Jacobite, vainly endeavored to prosecute an aggressive war against the British settlements. But he was inadequately supplied and had insufficient money. In December, 1758, Lally advanced against Madras, which was ably defended by Major-General Stringer Lawrence and the city governor, Lord Pigot. Lally and his unpaid, ill-supplied and mutinous troops were quickly forced to withdraw. The following year was to add still further to the already triumphant record of British arms.

CONQUESTS in the Glorious 1759, from the London Gazettes Extraordinary.

Basseterre the Capital of Guadalupe taken by Gen. Hopson & Gen. Barrington.

Goree
taken by Commodore Keppel.
(Vide L. G. E. Jan.ry 29th 1759)

The Courier riding thro' Cleves,
gives an account of Contades defeat
(L. G. E. Aug.t 8th)

THE TOULON FLEET
of Mons.r De la Clue, destroyed
by Admiral Boscawen.
(L. G. E. Sept.r 7th)

Niagara
Surrendered to S.r Will.m Johnson Bart.
(L. G. E. Sept.r 10th)

Admiral Pocock
defeats Mons.r Zally, in the East Indies.
(L. G. E. 12 Octr.)

Fire Ships and Rafts
sent down the River S.t Laurence
by the French with design to
destroy his Majestys Ships, under
Admirals Saunders Holmes, &c.
(L. G. E. Nov. 16)

QUEBEC.
taken by Wolfe, Townsend Saunders, &c.
(L. G. E. Octr. 17th)

Brest Fleet
under Conflans, destroyed by Adm.l Hawke
(L. G. E. Nov.r 30th)

The thundering Guns proclaim,
Great George's glorious name.

The gloomy throngs look terrible from far,
Disclosing slow the horrid face of war;
The thick Battalions move in dreadful form,
As low'ring Clouds advance before a storm.

The Cannons roar bid distant regions scare,
Shake all the shores and torture all the air.

On either side the Foe outrageous grew,
And Deaths unseen in dreadful tempests flew;
Destruction they exchange, by turns they give,
Exploded Ruin and by turns receive.

James Cooper
Whitsuntide 1760

Published according to Act of Parliament, April 30, 1760, & Sold by S. Hawkins Printer in Snow Lane, Temple Bar London.

The Year of Victories

By the mid-eighteenth century, Britain and France were vying for power and influence every-where in the world. Then came the year 1759. With victories in West Africa, the West Indies, the Mediterranean, the North Atlantic, the battlefields of Europe and India and the Plains of Abraham outside Quebec in French Canada, the British consistently turned back the French and established the Empire on which the sun never set.

When Lord Carteret, the minister dealing with foreign affairs, persuaded his colleagues in the British government to send 16,000 troops to support the cause of Maria Theresa in the dispute over the Austrian succession, no one had any idea that the campaign of 1742 was in fact the beginning of a struggle with the French for an empire extending all over the world. The year 1759 was the climax of that struggle, and never before in the course of Britain's history had there been such a year of triumph.

In the last days of December, 1758, a small British force attacked the island of Gorée, just off Cape Verde in Senegal. The French garrison there surrendered after a brief bombardment, yielding over 300 prisoners and 100 guns. The significance of this action was that the new year began with the acquisition by Britain of the French settlements in West Africa.

On January 3, another expedition, consisting of six battalions led by the elderly Major-General Peregrine Hopson, arrived at Barbados, the base for all British operations in the West Indies. An attack was launched against the island of Martinique. "Never was such a country," wrote the General, "the Highlands of Scotland for woods, mountains and continued ravines are nothing to it." His men went ashore at Negro Point at the northern side of the harbor of Fort de France, but, unable to move his artillery over such terrain, Hopson reembarked his force and made for Guadeloupe, wealthiest of the Antilles and the nest of French privateers operating in the Caribbean Sea. The town of Basseterre was taken and the French commander withdrew his troops into an impregnable position some six miles away. By the end of January, a quarter of Hopson's force was on the sick list. He himself died on February 27. With great skill and determination Hopson's successor devised and pursued a plan of campaign that resulted in the defeat of the French garrison, and on May 1, the island of

Guadeloupe, with a harbor large enough to provide shelter from hurricanes for the whole British navy, passed into British hands.

Since trading interests had no voice in the councils of the French King Louis xv, these losses in Africa and the West Indies were regarded only as minor military incidents, of little importance in relation to the war in Europe or events in India and Canada. France would take her revenge in the coming invasion of England. For some time there had been a great stir and bustle along the French coast, centered on Le Havre, and flat-bottomed boats to convey cavalry, infantry and artillery across the English Channel were being collected in many harbors and inlets. In England, the militia—the local defense force—was called out, and 24,000 French prisoners-of-war were placed under stronger guard and marched inland, away from the southern counties where they might have assisted an invasion force. In an attempt to meet and disperse the storm before it could break, Admiral Rodney bombarded Le Havre, setting fire to the town.

In the Mediterranean, Admiral Boscawen attacked the outer harbor at Toulon. He withdrew after this show of strength and the commander of the Toulon fleet, Admiral de La Clue, seized what appeared to be an opportunity to slip through the Strait of Gibraltar and join the fleet from Brest commanded by Marshal de Conflans. Boscawen's watchful frigates saw him go, and on August 18, the British battle fleet fell upon the French off Cape Lagos on the coast of Portugal. Admiral de La Clue, fighting with great gallantry, was mortally wounded. His ship and three other first-rate ships of the line surrendered to Boscawen and a fifth was driven ashore and burned. Though this defeat added to the problems of the invasion of England, which had depended to some extent on the junction of the Toulon and Brest fleets to protect the passage of the land forces, the French did not abandon the plan.

A coin commemorating the capture of Quebec in 1759.

Opposite A special edition of the *London Gazette* commemorating the conquests of 1759. In this year Britain's victories in different parts of the globe secured the future of her burgeoning Empire.

The Battle of Minden in Westphalia where on August 1, 1759, the allied army commanded by Ferdinand of Brunswick defeated the French under Marshal de Contades, thus ending the French threat to Hanover and Prussia.

In November, winter storms forced Admiral Sir Edward Hawke's fleet to break off its blockade of Conflans in Brest. Hawke returned on November 20 to learn that Conflans, who was now responsible for convoying the military transports across the Channel, had escaped. He also learned that the French fleet, sheltering from a storm then raging, had anchored in nearby Quiberon Bay. Ignoring the storm and the dangers of a lee shore notorious for its uncharted reefs and shoals, Hawke led his ships into an action deemed by Conflans to be impossible. Lying among rocks and sandbanks, the French felt safe from any attack, until the British men-of-war came at them through narrow and dangerous passages. Commodore Howe drove in so close to the great French ship *Formidable* that her bow struck the waist of his warship and smashed in the lower tier of guns. Of the French fleet of twenty-one ships, two—one of them Conflans' flagship— were grounded on rocks and were burned, two more were sunk, one was taken, and another struck her colors but managed to get away when British sailors were unable to board her in the storm. Seven others escaped up a small inlet, from which the last one was not able to work itself free for two years. The re-

mainder of the French fleet took refuge in Rochefort.

Admiral Hawke had twenty-three ships, but in the howling wind and the gloom of that short November day, less than half were able to take up station with him. Not more than ten came into action. Two of these were wrecked but the crews were saved. This decisive victory, for a time, put an end to French hopes, and English fears, of invasion. For the rest of the war the little fishing port of Quiberon was a British naval base where the sailors tilled French soil and grew vegetables to supplement their rations.

In the land operations in Europe, the French had invaded Germany with the main object of taking vengeance upon Prussia for King Frederick the Great's "insulting" treatment of Louis xv's mistress, Madame de Pompadour. Frederick insisted on referring to her always as Mademoiselle Poisson, which was in fact her proper name. It is significant that whereas Louis sent hundreds of thousands of French soldiers into Germany on this ridiculous mission, he left the French colonies to take their chances. His colonial governors were forced to carry on the war as best they could with little hope of any effective aid from France. William Pitt the

Elder (later Earl of Chatham), who had become Secretary of State in 1757, appreciated that the more employment found for French armies in Europe, the fewer were the men who could be spared for operations in India and Canada. Bearing in mind his own global commitments, he gave all possible support to Frederick.

Defeated at Krefeld in 1758, the French recrossed the Rhine in April, 1759, moved up the valley of the Main and occupied Bergen. Here, on April 13, they were attacked by Ferdinand, Duke of Brunswick, Frederick's commander of the western forces, who had beaten them at Krefeld. This time Ferdinand was defeated. Forced to withdraw north to hold the line of the Weser River which was his main supply route from Germany and England, he resolved to hold Minden.

His force of 45,000 men included six regiments of British infantry and a detachment of fifteen squadrons of British cavalry. Lord George Sackville was in charge of this body of Horse.

The French army, 60,000 strong, commanded by the Marshal Duke Louis de Contades, followed up Ferdinand's withdrawal, making for Hanover. During the night of July 31, Contades sent his army across the Weser to battle positions on the plain of Minden, and early in the morning of August 1, it drew up in the unusual formation of a center of cavalry with wings of infantry.

Ferdinand's army was formed into eight columns: of these, the first or right-hand column consisted of twenty-four cavalry squadrons under Sackville, the second of German artillery and the third, commanded by Major-General von Spörcke, was British infantry. Seeing the French moving into position, Ferdinand ordered his troops to occupy prearranged locations with the cavalry on the flanks and infantry in the center. Seven out of the eight columns marched away at once. In Sackville's column all was confusion; some of the units were ready to move, some were not. Sackville himself could not be found.

While the British were deploying from column into line, Ferdinand sent a message saying that when the time came for the advance, it should be made with drums beating. But there was some misunderstanding, and the ranks of scarlet, joined now by Hardenberg's Hanoverian battalion and two battalions of Hanoverian guards, began to move forward immediately. With drums rolling, in perfect order and steadiness, the Line Regiments,

A detail of the Battle of Quiberon Bay, November 20, 1759. Admiral Hawke's decisive victory over the French fleet under de Conflans put an end to French plans for invading Britain.

83

unsupported by the rest of the battle line, marched forward into the crossfire of more than sixty enemy cannon to attack the French Horse, drawn up in three lines. During their advance of some two hundred yards great gaps were torn in the British ranks by the French guns, but nothing could stop their measured approach to the huge mass of enemy cavalry. Suddenly this wall of men and horses came to life; eleven squadrons detached themselves and charged the oncoming infantry. The battalions halted to receive them, standing motionless until the horsemen were only ten yards away. Then one volley strewed the ground with dead and wounded men and animals, breaking and hurling back the charge, and the advance continued.

The enemy cavalry rallied. Contades sent forward four brigades of infantry and thirty-two guns to engage the British. The second line of Horse, eager to make good the first repulse, thundered down upon the nine isolated battalions. Under this triple attack the British and Hanoverian infantry seemed for a moment to waver, but they were merely closing their ranks before meeting the squadrons with a storm of musketry which swept them from the field. Turning then upon the French infantry, they beat them back with appalling loss and Ferdinand realized that he had an opportunity to annihilate the French army. He sent an order to Sackville, telling him to charge with the whole of his column. But Sackville, who already had a reputation for reluctance either to obey orders or to expose himself to enemy shot or saber, did not move. Four messengers were sent. Finally a fifth was dispatched direct to the Marquess of Granby, commanding the squadrons of Sackville's second line. He was just moving off when Sackville came

up and forbade him to advance. The moment passed. Contades, who had lost 7,000 men and forty-three guns, was able to withdraw in good order.

Sackville was subsequently court-martialed and found unfit ever again to hold the King's Commission, but his cashiering had little effect on his career. Changing his name to Lord George Germaine he later became Minister for War in George III's government and played a conspicuous part in losing the colonies in the American Revolution.

The Battle of Minden ended the French threat to Hanover—and Prussia—at a cost to the allies of 3,000 men, half of them British.

In India the success of British arms was unbroken. On January 28, Colonel Forde of the 39th Foot followed up the achievements of Captain Knox who, in the last days of 1758, had taken Rajahmundry, key to the district of Vizagapatam, with all its French artillery, ammunition and stores. Moving forward from Rajahmundry, Forde occupied Ellore, forty-eight miles north of Masulipatam, the most important town and the center of French influence in the Carnatic, held by the Marquis de Conflans (not to be confused with the Marshal-Admiral). Forde and Knox between them took the outpost forts at Narsipore and Concal, and on March 6, came in sight of the fortifications of Masulipatam. These had been considerably strengthened by the French during their years of occupation since 1751. The siege lasted for a month and was complicated by the southern monsoon which broke on April 5 with floods of rain and turned the ground around the fort into a morass. At length, after a daring three-fold attack on April 8, 500 Frenchmen and 2,000 of their sepoys laid down their arms; the whole district came under British control

Right The conquest of Guadeloupe by the English; the wealthiest of the Antilles islands and former operational base of the French privateers, it afforded the Royal Navy a large natural harbor.

Below A cartoon of Wolfe's predicament before the capture of Quebec, by George Townshend.

An allegorical engraving of the triumph of Britannia. Sea nymphs carry shields bearing images of the victorious commanders.

and the court of Hyderabad ceased to support the French.

Meanwhile the French commander Count de Lally de Tollendal, further south along the Coromandel coast, determined to capture the British trading center and port of Madras. He laid formal siege to it and remained under the walls for just over two months. His plans were ruined by the sudden arrival in Madras harbor of two frigates of Admiral Pococke's battle squadron and six East India Company ships carrying six hundred British troops fresh from England. Lally withdrew as silently as he could during the night of March 17, his unpaid troops by now in a state bordering on mutiny, and concentrated his force at Conjeveram. On April 6, Major Lawrence set out after him with 6,000 men— 1,156 of them being Europeans—and ten field pieces. For three weeks the French and English troops lay encamped within sight of each other, and then Lawrence moved south to Wandewash, entered the town and began to besiege the fort. Lally hurried to defend the place, whereupon Lawrence evaded him, slipped back and took the far more valuable fort of Conjeveram.

On May 28, both commanders put their troops in cantonments for the hot weather. Madras had been saved and, in addition, French influence along

the Coromandel coast had been destroyed for ever.

On August 20, Admiral Pococke, who had defeated the French Admiral d'Aché in an engagement off Madras in April of the previous year, sailed for Trincomalee in Ceylon where he was surprised to find his old adversary with eleven ships of the line and four frigates. Although Pococke had only nine men-of-war, one frigate, two East India Company ships and a fireship—an advantage to the French of 174 guns—he at once offered battle, but wind and currents prevented any real engagement for several days. On September 10, after a fight lasting two hours, d'Aché withdrew and found safety in Pondicherry. The French in India had reached the stage where they could no longer compete with the combination of British sea power and frequently reinforced ground troops.

In Canada, Pitt's plan of campaign for 1759, worked out from inaccurate maps thousands of miles from the area of operations, was far too ambitious for complete success. The great measure of success it did achieve was due very largely to the brilliance of a young officer of his own choice, James Wolfe, and to Wolfe's three brigadiers, the Hon. Robert Monckton, the Hon. George Townshend and James Murray.

Wolfe, who had held a commission since the age

85

The death of General Wolfe, by Benjamin West. Wolfe's surprise tactics forced the French to give battle on the Plains of Abraham southwest of Quebec town.

of fourteen, was then thirty-two. Recently promoted on Pitt's instructions to major-general, he was an admirable soldier: literally at his happiest when under fire, competent, enthusiastic, devoted to his men and trusted by them, a fine, aggressive but wisely cautious commander. To him was entrusted the task of seizing Quebec, capital of the French provinces, in a coordinated design involving two other expeditions. General Lord Geoffrey Amherst was to occupy Crown Point, reduce Fort Ticonderoga, cross Lake Champlain and then go down the St. Lawrence River to join Wolfe. At the same time, General Prideaux, with a force containing a considerable number of unpredictable Indians, was to take Niagara, embark on Lake Ontario, capture Montreal and afterward link up with Wolfe and Amherst for the final assault on Quebec.

Amherst succeeded in taking Crown Point and Ticonderoga. Prideaux's force captured Niagara, though he himself was killed by the premature explosion of a shell from one of his own guns. Sir William Johnson took his place, secured the whole region of the Upper Ohio and cut off from Canada all the French posts in the American west. Amherst was brought to a standstill on Lake Champlain, for the French had four gunboats on the lake, capable of blowing his flotilla out of the water. By the time he had constructed similar craft for his own pro-

tection, the season was too far advanced into winter for further operations.

The mastheads of British ships were first seen by the garrison of Quebec on June 21. The Marquis of Montcalm, the French commander, had been confident that no foreign ship would attempt the intricate navigation of the St. Lawrence River, particularly after the removal of all buoys and marks which made the river usable. But there was a junior officer in the British fleet, of the same age as Wolfe, who was to become one of the world's greatest explorers. His name was James Cook, and his early career as a navigator very nearly came to an abrupt end one night while he was taking soundings close to the river bank. A scalping party of Indians jumped into the stern of his boat while he leaped from the bows. It was he who made a chart of the St. Lawrence River so accurate that it was not superseded for more than a century, and as a result of his work, ships of the line passed where the French had not dared to take a coasting schooner. By June 26, the whole fleet and all the transports were safely at anchor off the Isle of Orleans, a few miles below Quebec. Two days later the French sent fireships down the river, but the British sailors rowed out, grappled the blazing craft and towed them ashore where they could do no damage.

No longer able to count on the support of Amherst

and Prideaux, Wolfe was faced with an apparently insoluble problem, for if he was to take Quebec he had to force Montcalm to give battle against his will. The only possible battlefield was the open ground known as the Plains of Abraham on a plateau to the southwest of the town, at the top of apparently unscalable cliffs two hundred feet high. Wolfe learned of a path up to the heights.

At two o'clock on the morning of September 13, two signal lanterns were hoisted to the maintop shrouds of H.M.S. *Sutherland* and the night was filled with quiet movement. Wolfe handed to Captain John Jervis of H.M.S. *Porcupine* the portrait of the girl to whom he was betrothed, asking Jervis to return it to her if he were killed. He and his officers then stepped into their boat and, with the rest of the force, floated silently down the river on the ebb tide. At sunrise, 4,500 men had climbed the cliff and were drawn up on the Plains of Abraham.

Montcalm seems to have lost his head. Though there was plenty of time for him to assemble all his troops and artillery, he hurried into battle with the 5,000 men of the town garrison and did not wait to be joined by seven more battalions that had been deployed to defend the river banks. Shortly before ten o'clock, with loud shouts and in somewhat ragged order, his line advanced to the attack. While still two hundred yards from the British force his men opened fire—the effective range of a musket was little more than fifty yards. Wolfe was hit in the wrist. He bandaged the wound, calling on his men to stand steady and hold their fire. When the opposing armies were only thirty-five yards apart the British fired their first volley, described by

Fortescue, historian of the British Army, as "the most perfect ever fired on any battlefield, which burst forth as if from a single monstrous weapon, from end to end of the British line." It shattered the French. One more volley was fired and Wolfe gave the order to charge with bayonets and swords. He led, at the head of the 28th Foot. A bullet struck him in the groin but he did not even pause. Moments later another passed through his lungs.

"Support me, support me," he gasped to an officer beside him, "lest my gallant fellows should see me fall." Two or three men carried him, dying, to the rear, just as Montcalm, shot through the body but supported in the saddle by an aide-de-camp, rode back through the gates of the town. Montcalm died in the house of a surgeon as his broken force fled in wild confusion. Wolfe refused to see a surgeon.

"There is no need," he said. "It is all over with me." His eyes closed.

"How they run!" called out one of the men near him, watching the fleeing French.

"Go one of you to General Burton," said Wolfe, making a great effort, "and tell him to march Webb's regiment down to Charles River to cut off the retreat from the bridge." He paused, turned painfully over on his side, whispered, "Now, God be praised, I will die in peace," and died.

The year of victories drew to a close. Britain had won her empire—in the West Indies and West Africa, in India and Canada. Her arms were triumphant in Europe and her navy supreme on all the oceans of the world.

In soothing the pique of a king's mistress, France had lost everything.   JOCK HASWELL

A view of the taking of Quebec, showing British troops from the fleet on the St. Lawrence River scaling the escarpment of the Plains of Abraham. The opposing armies are engaged in formal battle on the plateau.

The Aufklärung

Although they were an important part of the movement known as the Enlightenment, the French Encyclopedists had no monopoly on advanced thought in their generation. The fathers of the Enlightenment were men as varied in nationality, discipline and culture as England's Sir Isaac Newton (1642–1727) and Germany's Gottfried Leibnitz (1646–1716) in natural philosophy and mathematics, and France's Pierre Bayle (1647–1706) in theology, and their heritage was not confined to France.

In Germany, the philosophers of the *Aufklärung* (Enlightenment) had a major impact on contemporary thought. Like the *philosophes*, they attacked ideas that were based on supernatural religion and they tended toward idealism and a vague deism. The dramatist and poet Gotthold Lessing (1729–81) was a key figure in the attack on religious orthodoxy. He made important contributions to biblical scholarship—including the discovery that the synoptic Gospels were based on a common Aramaic source—but was interested chiefly in inculcating belief in religion as a humanitarian morality. It was, however, Immanuel Kant (1724–1804) who in a famous essay *What*

Immanuel Kant, the leading German philosopher of the eighteenth century.

is Enlightenment (1784) most perfectly expressed the aim of the Enlightenment as man's emergence from a state of dependence in which he was unable to use his intellect. Only by the determination to think for himself can man escape from this crippling dependence.

Frederick the Great visiting Voltaire in his study.

Man must dare to know (*sapere aude*).

But as Rousseau showed, the individualism of the Enlightenment was tempered by a high regard for the authority of the state. Man's relationship to society became a matter of great importance. Kant's studies of logic and metaphysics are his main contribution to the history of philosophy, but to contemporaries he seemed no less interested in "establishing the rights of humanity." It was in Germany that the philosophical ideals of the Enlightenment had most impact on politics: both Frederick the Great of Prussia and the Empress Maria Theresa were keenly interested in the writings of Enlightenment philosophers.

Josephism

It was the Emperor Joseph II (1741–90), however, who most perfectly exemplified the phenomenon of "enlightened absolutism." He regarded property ownership as a major problem and from 1781 he passed a series of laws attempting to improve the lot of the peasantry and to reduce their dependence on their landlords. He carried out a major land survey and in 1789 introduced a uniform tax rate, from whose payment the aristocracy were not exempted. He also introduced a comprehensive system of social welfare, including hospitals and orphanages. It is uncertain whether this concentration on improving the lot of the poor was based simply on an ideological acceptance of the values of the Enlightenment or whether it was also part of an economic policy designed to increase Austrian trade and industrial output. Joseph some-

times justified his policy on the grounds that the working population was "the most useful class of the nation," and that "nothing is more necessary for commerce and industry than liberty."

Joseph's religious policy, however, suggests that ideology did play a key part in his policy making. Even during Maria Theresa's lifetime he had put forward a far-reaching plan, based on Enlightenment ideas, for the reform of the Church. This was not accepted by his mother, but after her death he passed legislation granting Protestants and other religious nonconformists—including the Jews—full right to worship in their own way. He also withdrew all civil disabilities from religious minorities. But Joseph's reforms, whether political or religious, were designed only to increase liberty in society. Joseph did nothing to reduce the power of the state itself; indeed in ecclesiastical matters he actually increased it. He reduced the Church's property rights—an example that was to be followed in France during the early years of the French Revolution—banned direct communication between the Church hierarchy and the papacy and suppressed 876 monasteries and convents.

In its political dimension, however, the Enlightenment had only a shortlived effect. Even during his lifetime many of Joseph's reforms had to be abandoned, and those of Catherine of Russia and Frederick the Great lasted little longer. Enlightened absolutism

Joseph II, "enlightened despot."

raised serious problems as to the nature of political authority—by what right did Joseph impose his reforms on society? A substantial measure of democracy was implicit in most Enlightenment ideology, but Joseph, Catherine and Frederick remained absolute rulers, whose power was based on family, military and religious considerations rather than on any recognizable and meaningful social contract. Ironically, it was in England, where none of the Hanoverian kings could by any stretch of the imagination be described as enlightened despots—despite George III's unsuccessful efforts—that Enlightenment ideas had by far their widest circulation.

The Enlightenment in England

In England the relationship between reason and belief was much closer than in France or Germany, and the problems of belief in God were gradually whittled away;

David Hume; his empiricism led to a lessening of interest in metaphysics.

reason came to replace God as an explanation of the world. Both orthodox believers and deists—those who believed in a vaguely defined divinity rather than a specifically Christian God—used similar arguments, and as the century wore on their conclusions grew closer and closer together.

British philosophy was dominated by empirical—observational—methods, and the chief object of its interest was man. Both the Anglican Bishop George Berkeley (1685–1753) and the skeptical Scot David Hume (1711–76), the most notable British philosopher of the eighteenth century, sought to answer the questions: "How does man acquire knowledge and what is the knowledge that he acquires?" This

to institute reform

epistemological interest is apparent in Berkeley's phrase: "To be is to be perceived" (*esse est percipi*). To Berkeley the perception of an object gave it being; that perception could, however, be God's rather than man's. Hume's empiricism went still further. Reason itself was a product of experience and could prove nothing that has not been observed. As man does not see God, no argument about God's existence could have any logical value. Historical evidence as to the existence of God is valueless, too, since "it is contrary to experience that a miracle should be true, but not contrary to experience that testimony should be false." (Hume's skepticism was carried still further, as he publicly proclaimed that he did not believe in the existence of atheists.)

Hume's arguments did not, of course, disprove God's existence, and Kant and others could argue on non-rational grounds that God must exist. Such skepticism did, however, lead to a lessening of interest in metaphysics.

India

After the successes of the year of victories, the British were able to continue their Indian campaigns with little difficulty. A well-equipped army, led by Colonel Sir Eyre Coote, defeated Lally at Wandewash in January, 1760, and Coote went on systematically to attack the French forts in the Carnatic. By September Lally had been forced back to Pondicherry, the capital of French India. The arrival of a British fleet finally ended his beleaguered forces' already slight hope of resupply and in January, 1761, he was obliged to surrender. His surrender marked the end of French dominion in India. Although the Treaty of Paris in 1763 was followed by the return of most of the French territory, the French were forced to agree that they would not fortify any of their towns.

Clive, who had left India the year before at the age of thirty-five, had established the base of British power there. In the process he had become an extremely rich man. He was not home for long enough to enjoy the pleasures that his fortune could buy, however; in May, 1765, he returned to India as governor of Bengal and commander-in-chief of the army.

Corruption in the Company

In Clive's absence, Bengal had been notoriously misgoverned by a succession of administrators. (Clive's own behavior had unfortunately set the precedent for such venal conduct.) Mir Jafar had been deposed in favor of his son-in-law, Mir Kasim, from whom the Bengal Council accepted £200,000-worth of gratuities. Indeed, the whole of the English East India Company had been corrupted by the bribes, commissions and gifts that its servants had come to expect as a matter of course. It was to be Clive's duty to carry out extensive reforms and he did so with a dispatch that was widely resented by those who felt it was Clive himself who had been largely, though not entirely, responsible for the tradition that money should be extracted from the natives through fear of the power of Britain.

Clive raised the Company's salaries so that its employees had less reason to accept bribes; he forbade the acceptance of gifts and the participation of company employees in private trade; and he

An Indian portrayal of a European civilian. Corruption was rife in the British East India Company.

carried out a thorough reform of the army. Above all, he secured from the Emperor of Delhi—whose forces had recently been defeated by Major Hector Munro at Buxar—a document that granted the company the provinces of Bengal, Bihar and Orissa. Clive thus became the virtual ruler of thirty million people, and through his hands passed more than £4 million each year.

Clive left India for the last time in 1767, and on November 22, 1774, he killed himself in one of the fits of depression to which he had always been subject. Clive's work was continued by Warren Hastings, who became governor of Bengal in 1772 and Governor-General of India in the following year. Hastings reformed the government of Bengal, supported the Nawab of Oudh against the Rohillas, who had led plundering raids against his northern frontiers, and saved British India when a renewal of the French war in 1778 led to its being threatened by a coalition of Indian princes who could rely on French support. By the time that Hastings arrived back in England in 1785 (to face charges of impeachment for his

Warren Hastings, Governor-General of British India.

supposedly ruthless conduct as Governor-General), he had succeeded in extending the East India Company's influence over even larger areas of India.

In 1784 Parliament passed William Pitt's India Act, which transferred the control of much of the Company's power to the British government. Responsibility for Indian affairs was given to a board of six privy councilors appointed by the king.

India was but part of a huge and growing British Empire. Lally's 1761 surrender at Pondicherry was soon followed by other French territorial losses. The French and Indian War (1756–63) had not gone well for France. In 1745 and again in the following year the brilliant generalship of Maurice de Saxe had resulted in French victories (at Fontenoy and Lauffeld), and in the French and Indian War she had enjoyed several initial successes. But the great British successes of the year of victories—1759—included a successful attack on France's Mediterranean fleet at Lagos in Portugal. Nor was the loss of Quebec one that France could afford. It reduced the benefit that France could derive from her remaining American colony, Louisiana, the reason that was eventually to prompt the sale of that huge colony to the United States for a purely nominal sum.

By the Treaty of Paris France was forced to acknowledge the loss of these territories and to recognize England's right to much of her former territory. But, while England benefited enormously from these gains, this did not prevent her from having further imperial designs. In 1768 an expedition set sail for the South Pacific that was to add a whole new continent to Britain's burgeoning empire.

"Terra Incognita"

Captain James Cook was only one of dozens of eighteenth-century Englishmen who firmly believed that an undiscovered continent lay somewhere in the South Pacific. Cook was convinced that the "Great South Land" had to exist—to balance the known land masses in the northern hemisphere and thereby preserve the earth's orbital stability. Dutch and Portuguese navigators had purportedly touched the shores of Terra Australis Incognita *in the preceding century, but the continent remained virtually unexplored when Cook sailed south from Tahiti in 1769. On April 19, 1770, a crewman aboard Cook's ship, the* Endeavour, *sighted a low promontory on Australia's southeast coast—and before returning to England, Cook investigated and mapped most of the new continent's eastern and northern coastlines. The captain's journals aroused considerable interest at home and led, less than half a century later, to England's annexation of the entire continent.*

It was originally a matter of stargazing that led James Cook to the shores of Australia. A rare occurrence called the "transit of Venus" was to take place in 1769. (During a transit, Venus passes directly between the earth and the sun and appears projected on the sun's disk as a small black dot. Important deductions—such as the scale of the solar system and the distance of the earth from the sun—can be made from its passage.) Astronomers' charts recorded only two previous transits, the first of which had occurred in 1639. The next had taken place in 1761, but observation of the 1761 phenomenon had been unsuccessful and it was therefore of particular importance that the 1769 event be properly charted.

The Royal Society, which was devoted to the cause of natural enlightenment, took a lively interest in the coming transit and petitioned King George III not to neglect the chance of furthering the fame of British astronomy, "a science," the members pointed out, "on which navigation so much depends." Several European nations, among them Russia, wanted to establish points of observation, and England, the Society argued, should certainly do the same. The Royal Society was considered the world's most distinguished scientific body, and its petition carried weight with the King, who was particularly interested in science and exploration.

Because it was essential that the observers follow the transit from a point south of the equinoctial line, the recently discovered island of Tahiti was suggested as a suitable place. The idea of sending an expedition to the Pacific appealed to the King. He promptly gave the project his approval, and the Royal Society approached the Admiralty for a ship and a competent man to sail it. James Cook, a forty-year-old British naval officer who had already surveyed the coasts of Newfoundland and Labrador, was chosen to command the H.M.S. *Endeavour*.

In 1768 the expedition set out. Sailing with Cook were Joseph Banks, a young naturalist of twenty-five with an independent fortune who was later knighted

by the King; Charles Green, an astronomer; Doctor Daniel Charles Solander, a Swede who had been Linnaeus' favorite pupil; and two artists, twenty-five-year-old Sydney Parkinson and Herman Dierich Spöring, another Swede who joined the ship at Cape Town and seems to have acted as Banks' secretary. In his journal Cook always referred to Banks and members of his party simply as "the gentlemen."

The transit of Venus was successfully observed from Tahiti, but it proved to be a task of secondary importance to the expedition, for Cook had been given secret instructions by the Admiralty. After exploring Tahiti and the neighboring islands, he was to search for the Great South Land that was supposed to exist in the South Pacific. Known as the *Terra Australis Incognita*, it was a shadowy area sketched in around the South Pole on many old charts.

Geographers had been struck by the fact that, unlike the northern hemisphere, the southern Pacific had no large land masses. Having accepted the spherical nature of the earth, they came to the conclusion that in order for the earth to keep its stability, the amount of solid land in the two hemispheres must balance. Hence there must be a great unknown continent in the southern part of the Pacific. Dutch mariner Abel Tasman was supposed to have touched it when he sailed along the western shores of New Zealand, and many believed that Portuguese navigator Pedro Fernandes de Queiros had seen yet another part of it when he landed on Espiritu Santo in the New Hebrides in 1606—but no one was quite certain. Beyond these tentative probes, nothing definite was known about the mysterious continent.

Cook and Banks between them had an extensive geographical library on board, and among the books was Charles de Brosses' useful *Histoire des Navigations aux Terres Australes*, published in Paris in 1756. In his work de Brosses explained, "I call Austral lands all that is beyond the three southern points of our known world in Africa, Asia and America." Accompanying

An engraving of a kangaroo from Banks' *New System of Geography*. Kangaroos were first sighted on the coast of Australia on Cook's first expedition.

Opposite A Wedgwood cameo portrait of Captain Cook made in 1784.

The *Endeavour*, after narrowly escaping shipwreck, is laid up on the banks of the Endeavour River in New South Wales.

the text were maps by the celebrated French cartographer Robert de Vaugondy.

In one of his maps, Vaugondy marked out Tasman's discoveries—the southern part of Van Diemen's Land (now Tasmania) and the western coast of New Zealand's North Island. The imaginary eastern coast of New Holland (the early name for Australia) was shown by vague hatchings and was joined to the discoveries of de Queiros, which were displaced westward. Van Diemen's Land was also shown connected to the mainland.

These, then, were the geographical uncertainties that faced the crew of the *Endeavour* as the ship left Tahiti. Cook sailed from the Society Islands in August, and by the end of March of the following year, 1770, he had already charted New Zealand and had circumnavigated its two islands, thus disproving any continental connection. By April 1 he had turned northwest toward Tasmania, but strong southerly gales drove the *Endeavour* north, so that the English arrived at the southeast corner of Australia itself. Had the weather been fair, Cook would almost certainly have discovered Bass Strait, which separates Australia from Tasmania.

On Wednesday, April 18, certain birds were spotted—a sure sign, Cook noted, of the nearness of land. The following day Lieutenant Hicks sighted a low hill and Cook named the point after him. (Few modern maps bear Hicks' name; the British ship's landfall is known today as Cape Everard.) Sailing northward, the *Endeavour* hugged the shore, looking for a safe anchorage. The calm, noble landscape that they saw had a certain haggard beauty of its own— green and wooded, but with a shore of white sand. Dark figures could be distinguished against the glare. Smoke curled up through the dusty green hanging foliage of the eucalyptus, only to be lost against a pale sky. At night fires pricked the flat shoreland.

Cook, Banks, Solander and Tupaia, a Tahitian chief whom Banks had persuaded to join the expedition, tried to land in a yawl but were prevented from doing so by the heavy surf. Banks noted the parklike aspect of the land, the trees separate from each other "without the least underwood." Passing within a quarter of a mile of the shore, he was surprised at the total lack of interest that their presence had aroused in the natives; they did not seem to notice the passing of the yawl, although an old woman who was gathering sticks and was followed by three children "often looked at the ship but expressed neither surprise nor concern." On Sunday, April 29, the *Endeavour* stood into Botany Bay and anchored off the south shore. Midshipman Isaac Smith, Mrs. Cook's cousin (and later an Admiral of the British fleet), was the first to land. Young Isaac, eighteen at the time, later recalled how Cook, on the point of stepping ashore, said, "Isaac, you shall land first." Cook was forced to fire a musket loaded with small shot between two natives when a party of them threatened the explorers with spears.

Cook originally called their anchorage Sting Ray Harbor, "occasioned by the great quantity of these sort of fish found in this place." Banks' and Solander's prodigious haul of new plants later provoked him to change the name to Botany Bay. The plants were kept fresh in tin chests, wrapped in wet cloths, while Parkinson and Spöring drew them. (Parkinson worked with such alacrity that he averaged seven meticulous drawings a day.) Banks, who preserved his specimens by spreading them out on sails to dry in the sun, wrote that the aborigines "seemed never to be able to muster above fourteen or fifteen fighting men." He seemed undecided about their actual color—"they were so completely covered with dirt, that seemed to have stuck to their bodies from the day of their birth"—and on one occasion he spat on his fingers and tried to rub it off. His actions altered the color very little, and he judged their skin to be chocolate-colored.

The *Endeavour* remained at Botany Bay just over a week. On May 7 Cook resumed his voyage. A few miles north he passed present-day Sydney Harbor, which he named Port Jackson in honor of one of the secretaries of the Admiralty. Cook slowly worked his way north, charting the coast. He frequently landed, and he never sailed very far without sending boats ahead to cast shoreward and seaward and take bearings.

As they neared the northern end of the island continent, the voyage nearly came to an abrupt end when the ship grounded on a coral reef twenty miles from land. Cook's seamanship was, however, equal to the occasion: the *Endeavour* was freed and, much damaged and leaking severely, was guided up the estuary of a small nearby river, where she was banked and careened. There the men saw their first kangaroo, which Cook described as "an animal something less than a greyhound, of a mouse color, very slender made and swift of foot." During Cook's stay, natives came to the camp, but they always left their women on the opposite bank of the river. Banks, busy with his glasses, commented on their nudity, noting that they "did not copy our Mother Eve even in the fig-leaf."

Although repairs on the ship finally were finished, a strong wind further delayed Cook's departure. Eventually he managed to creep out and slowly thread his way through the tortuous mazes of the Great Barrier Reef. Inch by inch the group advanced to the northern point of Australia, which Cook named Cape York in honor of the King's late brother. Sailing west, they rediscovered Torres Strait, and before departing for Batavia and England they landed on a small island off the coast of Cape York. Cook made no claim regarding the strait, but he did claim the land. Accompanied by Banks and Solander, he made for the island and climbed the highest hill—from which he saw nothing but islands to the northwest.

Cook admitted that to the west he could make no new discoveries: "The honor of which belongs to the Dutch navigators; but the east coast I am confident was never seen or visited by any Europeans before us." He had already claimed several places along the coast; now he "once more hoisted the English colors and in the name of His Majesty King George III took possession of the whole eastern coast," christening it New South Wales. Three volleys of small arms were fired, and they were answered by a like number from the ship. Why, one asks, did Cook pick on so improbable a name? It has been suggested that since there already was a New England and a Nova Scotia, and since Cook wanted to associate the recent discoveries with his own country, he decided on New South Wales.

The most immediately striking aspect of early maps of Australia is the marked Dutch flavor of their nomenclature. The earliest explorers—before Cook's time—had been Dutch captains serving the East India Company, and rather naturally they perpetuated their sightings by their own names or those of their employers or ships. Some fifteen different landings took place during the first half of the seventeenth century. The first was made in 1606 by the *Duyfken* under the command of Willem Janz, who sighted the present Cape York Peninsula and advanced down the west shore as far as Cabo Keer-Weer, or Cape Turn-Again. Ten years later Dirck Hartog, sailing from Amsterdam in the *Eendracht*, entered present-day Shark Bay, which he named after his ship. Hartog left a pewter plate nailed to a post to commemorate the event; the plate, crudely carved with the men's names and the date, still exists.

Other landfalls followed in quick succession. In 1619 Jacob Dedel came in sight of the mainland in the vicinity of Perth, and in 1622 the *Leeuwin* discovered Australia's westernmost point. Later came Tasman's two voyages. His second, in 1644, proved the most rewarding; he sailed along the whole north coast from Cape York to the North West Cape, some three thousand miles—a greater distance even than Cook's northward passage up the eastern side.

By the middle of the seventeenth century three-quarters of Australia's actual coast had been mapped, and one wonders why it took another century and a quarter before Cook completed its outline. The answer is simple; the Dutch regarded this enormous island, about the size of the United States, as completely valueless. No place had been found where they could revictual their ships, and more often than not the crews, in their searchings for water, had been obliged to dig in the sand, unearthing only an evil brackish fluid. From the reports of the time one pictures a low, desolate shoreline dotted with burning fires but otherwise apparently uninhabited. On the rare occasions that the aborigines did make their appearance, they were judged to be "a race of savages more miserable than any creatures in the world." Further discoveries would cost money, and the expeditions had brought in no returns. It was obvious that to establish colonies in a land of this size would be a prodigious undertaking, more than the East India Company or even the Republic of Holland could manage. It was thought best to drop the whole matter.

William Dampier, the first Englishman to visit Australia, agreed with the Dutch about the inhospitable nature of New Holland's shores. A merchant-sailor as well as a privateer, Dampier had visited Australia twice—once in the *Cygnet* in 1688, and

Navigational instruments used by Cook on his voyages.

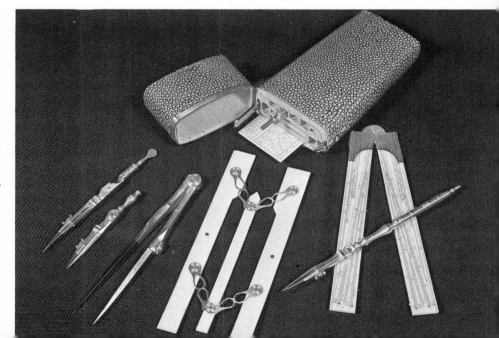

again in the *Roebuck* ten years later. Both times he had touched the country's arid northwest shore, and his two celebrated books, *A New Voyage Around the World* (1697) and *A Voyage to New Holland* (1703), did nothing to excite the British government's curiosity. No one in London thought much about Australia until Captain Cook's expedition discovered the well-watered, attractive eastern coastline seventy years later. His report was far more favorable and it led to the British taking possession of the continent.

The first suggestion for establishing a Pacific colony in Australia was made by Joseph Banks before a committee of the House of Commons in 1779. In 1776 the United States had declared its

independence, and the loss of her American colonies meant that England could no longer send her convicts across the Atlantic. Nevertheless, English judges continued sentencing convicted persons to transportation, and jails were overcrowded; a new outlet for offenders had to be found.

It was at this point that Banks enthusiastically recommended Botany Bay for that purpose. "The proportion of rich soil was small in comparison to the barren," he noted, "but sufficient to support a very large number of people .... The country was well supplied with water. There were no beasts of prey," and the natives were peaceful when compared with those in New Zealand. Banks did make the proviso that any body of settlers going to the country must take a full year's allowance of such things as victuals, raiment, tools, seeds and stock. Cook, in his journals, had stated similar views. "We are to consider that we see this country in the pure state of nature, the industry of man has had nothing to do with any part of it and yet we find such things as nature hath bestow'd upon it in a flourishing state. In this extensive country it can never be doubted but what most sorts of grain, fruit, roots etc. of every kind would flourish were they once brought hither."

By 1786 Lord Sydney, the Secretary of State, had appointed forty-nine-year-old Captain Arthur Phillip, a man with a fine naval record, to lead a fleet to Botany Bay. His fleet consisted of six transports, three storeships and two ships of war, carrying a total of 1,138 people, of whom 820 were convicts.

When Captain Phillip sailed into the bay, he realized that it had an exposed situation with an indifferent supply of water, and that settling there could lead only to disaster. Instead, exploring a few miles to the north, he entered Port Jackson, the future Sydney, an infinitely more satisfactory loca-

tion—"the finest natural harbor in the world," according to Phillip, "in which a thousand sail of the line may ride in the most perfect security."

At this point Great Britain, still under the belief that New South Wales might be separated from what the Dutch called New Holland, did not lay claim to the whole of Australia, but just to the eastern coast and all the islands adjacent in the Pacific. But by 1815 Australia's entire perimeter had been examined—and by 1820 Britain had formally annexed the entire country.

Thus the ultimate result of Cook's exploration of the Australian coast was to give Great Britain a whole new continent. But this was not his only achievement in the southern hemisphere. The 1768 expedition had proved that New Zealand was an island group and had closed off Australia's missing coastline—but it also disproved the existence of one enormous southern continent to counter-balance Europe and Asia.

Cook's second voyage, begun in 1772, settled that question once and for all; in the three years Cook was absent, he sailed between 60,000 and 70,000 miles and made vast sweeps in hitherto unexplored parts of the Pacific. He traveled in a giant, irregular zig-zag, penetrating as far south as 70° 10' latitude, a record not bettered until 1823. During that voyage he made numerous major geographical discoveries, one of them being New Caledonia, the largest island in the South Pacific after New Zealand. Ironically, it was what Cook did *not* discover that was to count as his most important contribution on that voyage; his conclusive proof that there was no great southern continent put our knowledge of the South Pacific on a sound basis. Indeed, maps of that part of the world remain essentially as Cook left them.

RODERICK CAMERON

Opposite Top A picture of many of the natives discovered by Cook during his expeditions.

Opposite Bottom The death of Captain Cook. Cook was killed by natives on the island of Hawaii on February 14, 1779.

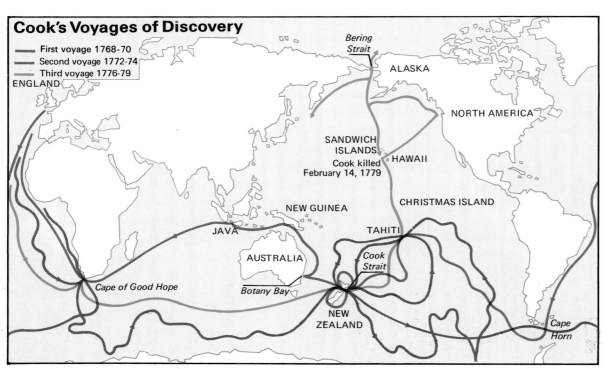

Cook's Voyages of Discovery

— First voyage 1768-70
— Second voyage 1772-74
— Third voyage 1776-79

ENGLAND
Bering Strait
ALASKA
NORTH AMERICA
SANDWICH ISLANDS
Cook killed February 14, 1779
HAWAII
CHRISTMAS ISLAND
NEW GUINEA
JAVA
TAHITI
AUSTRALIA
Cook Strait
Cape of Good Hope
Botany Bay
NEW ZEALAND
Cape Horn

Methodism and Latitudinarianism

Eighteenth-century religious controversy, in general, lacked the fire and fervor it had in the seventeenth century. Largely as a result of the Enlightenment, there was a strong feeling against religious enthusiasm and a broad acceptance of differing religious beliefs, an attitude characterized by the word "Latitudinarianism." The best known of the Latitudinarian clergy was Benjamin Hoadly (1676–1761), Bishop of Winchester, an opponent of those who believed that a particular form of Church government was taught in the Gospels. Many Latitudinarian theologians attempted to prove the truth of Christianity on purely rational grounds, and to define belief as no more than intellectual acceptance. As a result an almost purely mechanistic view of the universe became popular; the most famous argument was advanced in the *View of the Evidences of Christianity* by Archdeacon William Paley

Archdeacon William Paley fishing.

(1743–1805), in which the universe was compared to a watch, which was capable of running perfectly efficiently for most of the time without interference and needed no more than to be wound up occasionally. In England the close relationship between science and religion in the seventeenth century meant that theologians accepted the need for rational argument without difficulty; scientists such as Newton and Robert Boyle (1627–91) were little less interested in theology than in science, and this close relationship persisted into the eighteenth century.

However, intellectualized views such as Paley's had little appeal for the common man and still less for religious enthusiasts. There were a number of reactions against Latitudinarianism and Rationalism, the most successful of which was Methodism. After a religious conversion in 1738, John Wesley (1703–91) made it his sole ambition "to promote as far as I am able vital, practical religion and by the grace of God to beget, preserve and increase the life of God in the souls of men." He spent the rest of his life preaching. At first he was able to use churches, but as his enthusiastic evangelism became unpopular with most of the clergy he started preaching in the open air, which brought him into contact with the people outside the bounds of any organized religious body. His preaching, together with that of his friend George Whitefield (1714–70), proved immensely effective, and although Wesley remained an Anglican all his life, he had in practice created a new Church, which after his death formally became an independent body. Methodism appealed to the new middle class of prosperous men created by the Industrial Revolution and to poorer people, but it never had much appeal for the rich and powerful.

Methodism flourished in America. Although the Church of England had a privileged position in most of the thirteen colonies—even Maryland, which had been set up by Roman Catholics to provide a home for religious minorities—it had almost entirely failed

to use its advantage. Only among the rich and powerful was Anglicanism to be found. The Congregationalists of New England, the Roman Catholics of Maryland, the Quakers of Pennsylvania, and even the small religious minorities from the European mainland (particularly Holland and Germany), were all more or less active evangelists. Only the Anglicans, despite the efforts of the Society for the Promotion of Christian Knowledge, founded in 1698, failed entirely to promote their religion. There was not even an Anglican bishop in America; hence the clergy were either English expatriates or else had had to go to England to be ordained by the Bishop of London, whose diocese was considered to include all the English colonies. The close relationship between Anglicanism and loyalty to the British crown did not improve the situation. It was not until 1784—when the United States had already gained its independence—that Samuel Seabury (1729–96), a former loyalist, was consecrated as Bishop for America. Even then, the English bishops had refused to perform the ceremony, and he was consecrated by the Scottish bishops, whose Church, being disestablished, was less dependent on the government.

It was in this climate that Methodism found a firm root in America and rapidly became the largest of the Protestant denominations in the United States. Wesley himself encouraged this growth by ordaining a minister to work in America, although he had always refused to do the same in England.

John Wesley, founder of Methodism, preaching to American Indians. Methodism flourished in America where it rapidly became the largest of the Protestant denominations.

Expansive Russia

While England continued to expand her empire overseas, Russia was concentrating on expanding her frontiers in Europe. Aided by Austria, Russian troops invaded Prussia during the French and Indian War (1756–63) inflicting an overwhelming defeat on Frederick the Great at Kunersdorf. The Russians captured Colmar, advanced as far as Frankfurt and Berlin, and occupied Prussian Pomerania. Frederick's tenacity, despite the reduction of his army by the end of 1761 to a meager thirty thousand men—combined with Russia's inability to coordinate plans effectively with the Austrians—spelled doom for the Russian campaign. At the death of the Empress Elizabeth and the accession of her half-German nephew as Peter III in 1761, Russian troops withdrew from Prussia.

Catherine the Great

The new Tsar, a weak and incompetent ruler, was poisoned within a few months of his accession by the supporters of his dynamic German wife Catherine, who succeeded him on the throne and is known to history as "the Great." Catherine's determination to Westernize and modernize Russia was clearly influenced by the ideals of the French *philosophes*. Indeed the Empress claimed that Voltaire was her master and Diderot's *Encyclopédie* her Bible. However, the vast size of her empire, the political power of her nobles and her own determination to extend Russia's frontiers blocked any real attempt to implement the ideas of the Enlightenment. When Diderot (whose library she bought) pressed Catherine to institute more reforms, she retorted, "You only work on paper, while I, poor empress, work on human skin, which is much more ticklish."

Catherine did succeed in abolishing most of the state monopolies and in reforming the provincial administration of Russia. She increased the number and efficiency of the *gubernii*—local authorities administered by a governor and elected councils—and subordinated the Orthodox Church to the state by secularizing ecclesiastical lands

despot—makes Russia a force in Europe

Workmen moving the granite base of Peter the Great's memorial by Falconet.

Detail of map showing the Crimea, annexed by Russia in 1783.

and granting religious freedom to non-Church members. When Pope Clement XIV's bull *Dominus ac Redemptor* dissolved the Society of Jesus in 1773 she refused to expel the Jesuits from Russia.

Compared with her over-ambitious and liberal *Instructions to the Commissioners for Composing a New Code of Laws*—most of which she plagiarized from Montesquieu's *Spirit of Laws* and Beccaria's *Crimes and Punishments*—the legal reforms that Catherine actually instituted were minor: the establishment of a new system of courts and the separation of civil from criminal cases. The Empress had more success in reforming the educational system. She established free public primary schools in towns, extended the scope of Peter the Great's Academy and set up a college of medicine.

Peasant discontent

Despite the benefits that certain sections of Russian society gained from her rule, Catherine did relatively little to improve the lot of the serfs. By giving estates to her discarded lovers and introducing serfdom to newly conquered territories she actually increased their numbers. The extent of peasant discontent was dramatically revealed in 1773. An illiterate Cossack named Pugachev, pretending to be the murdered Peter III, announced that he was marching to St. Petersburg to punish his wife and place his son Paul on the throne. Pugachev gained so much support from the salt miners, Cossacks and peasants of the Lower Volga that he was able to capture and pillage several towns, and to hang hundreds

of priests, officers and government officials before his defeat in 1775, when he was taken in an iron cage to Moscow, and executed for the crime of *lèse majesté*.

The discontent that had generated Pugachev's revolt was to last throughout Catherine's reign, and was further exacerbated by her aggressive and extremely expensive foreign policy. Determined to expand Russia both to the west and to the south, she used the Duke of Courland's refusal to allow Russian troops returning from the French and Indian War to pass through his territory as a pretext for invading his duchy. She replaced the Duke, a son of Augustus III of Poland, with her own nominee. The death of Augustus himself in 1763 gave Catherine the opportunity to interfere directly in Polish politics. She nominated her former lover Stanislas Poniatowski as Augustus' successor—and by spending a fortune in bribes and threatening

Flogging in eighteenth-century Russia.

military action Stanislas obtained his unanimous election as King of Poland in September, 1764.

The French government, disturbed by Russia's territorial ambitions and alarmed by the friendship between Frederick of Prussia and Catherine, encouraged Turkey to attack Russia. The Turkish army was overwhelmed on the Dnieper in 1768, and the Russians were able to occupy Bucharest; the Turkish navy was defeated off Chios, and the Russians moved into the Crimea, Moldavia and Wallachia. By the terms of the 1774 Treaty of Kuchuk Kainardji Turkey ceded Azov and Kertsch to Russia, thereby extending Russia's frontiers to the Black Sea and the Lower Danube. Victory in a second Turkish war confirmed Russia's annexation of the Crimea, and secured her hold on the Black Sea.

Catherine's success in Turkey was made possible by her role in the War of the Bavarian Succession.

Upon the death of the Elector Maximilian Joseph in 1775, the Emperor Joseph II claimed Lower Bavaria for Austria, offering to compensate the Elector Palatine, Karl Theodore, the legal heir to the throne, with money and titles for his illegitimate children. But Frederick the Great, having persuaded Karl Theodore's nephew and legitimate heir, the Duke of Zweibrucken, to reject the Emperor's arrangements, invaded Bohemia. The Treaty of Teschen, which ended the war, guaranteed the rights of the Elector Palatine and the Duke of Zweibrucken in Bavaria and gave Austria only a small slice of Bavarian territory. Russia, having acted as mediator in the dispute, was in a good position to influence Austrian affairs. She obtained the support of Joseph II in her designs on Turkey. Thwarted in his attempt to add Bavaria to his empire, Joseph decided that an alliance with Russia might win him parts of Turkey's European possessions; Russia's gains were considerable, but Joseph's disorganized and disease-ridden army was defeated.

The partition of Poland

Meanwhile Catherine's protégé in Poland, Stanislas Poniatowski, was hampered in his attempts to rule as an enlightened monarch by a constitution that inhibited his initiative. The constitution was guaranteed by both Catherine and Frederick the Great, neither of whom felt any enthusiasm for the resurgence of Poland as a healthy and powerful state. Both saw that their interests might be served better by the partition of Poland.

The First Partition of Poland

By a combination of duplicity and craft, Prussia's Frederick the Great and Russia's Catherine the Great, joined by Austria's Maria Theresa, conspired to dismember their vast neighbor, Poland, dividing Polish territory among themselves. The partition took place in three stages, throughout which the voracious monarchs led the rest of Europe to believe that it was all in the best interests of the Poles. Poland would not again emerge as an independent nation until the twentieth century.

The partitioning of Poland, effected in three stages, 1772, 1793 and 1795, was without precedent in modern European history. Although victorious powers habitually stripped their defeated rivals of territorial possessions and were not averse to dividing the spoils of India, America or Africa among themselves, there is no other instance when they deliberately annihilated one of Europe's historic nations and one of its largest states. Poland was the victim of political vivisection.

The wags of the Enlightenment sharpened their wits on Poland's misfortunes. Frederick II of Prussia, a Protestant prince and one of the principal conspirators, boasted that he had "partook eucharistically of Poland's body." Voltaire uttered his famous witticism: "One Pole, a charmer; two Poles, a brawl; three Poles, ah, that's the Polish Question." Their audiences tittered elegantly, believing that Poland had somehow deserved her fate. As Vorontsov, the Russian Chancellor, declared in 1763, "Poland is constantly plunged in disorder; as long as she keeps her present constitution, she does not deserve to be considered among the European powers."

Poland's label as "the Republic of Anarchy" did not lack foundation, however. For over sixty years, since the death of John Sobieski in 1696, she had fallen prey to foreign intrigue. The state was a dual commonwealth or *Rzeczpospolita*, in which the conflicting interests of the two parts, the Kingdom of Poland and the Grand Duchy of Lithuania, obstructed all attempts at reform. The monarchy was elective, not hereditary, and in the hands of the Saxon House of Wettin, had become a plaything of international diplomacy. The Diet, or *Sejm*, was crippled by competing factions and by the extraordinary practice of *liberum veto*—the absolute right of any member to terminate its proceedings by a simple expression of dissent. The constitution permitted the formation of armed leagues or confederations, whose purpose was to safeguard the rights of the nobility against the pretensions of state or king. Despite a population of eleven million and a territory of 282,000 square miles, which made the *Rzeczpospolita* larger than either France or Spain, there was no central treasury, and a royal army of only 12,000 men. The "Golden Liberty," which her noble citizens saw as the glory of their republic, was meaningless in a land where all was customarily arranged by the promise of French gold or the threat of Russian intervention. Every incident spelled trouble, not least the death of the last Saxon King, Augustus III, on October 5, 1763.

Yet it must be understood that Poland's troubles were largely the deliberate creation of her more powerful neighbors, particularly Russia. Russia had been interfering in the internal affairs of the *Rzeczpospolita* for over a century, since 1654 when Tsar Alexis offered protection to the rebellious Cossacks of the Polish Ukraine. In 1686, in the "eternal treaty" by which the Dnieper lands were lost to Poland for ever, Peter I had proclaimed himself the patron of the *Rzeczpospolita's* Orthodox minority. In 1697, he had successfully schemed to put the puppet House of Wettin on the Polish throne. And in 1718, it was the presence of Russian troops in Warsaw that forced a silent *Sejm* to pass the limitations on finance, army and reform that blighted public life thereafter. Not only Russia, but Sweden, Prussia, France and Austria used Poland as a battleground on which to settle their quarrels inexpensively—the Great Northern War, the Wars of the Polish and Austrian Successions, and most recently, since 1756, the Seven Years War.

Poland's "anarchy" suited her neighbors most conveniently. Moreover, whenever the Poles took steps to put their house in order, both Russia and Prussia took counter-steps to see that nothing

A Prussian hussar from the army of Frederick the Great. Where military might failed, however, Frederick pursued a policy of diplomatic intrigue.

Opposite Detail from the *Election of Stanislas Augustus*, by Bernardo Bellotto. The last king of independent Poland, Stanislas was well-meaning but weak. He abdicated at the third partition in 1795.

Poland partitioned by
Catherine of Russia and
Frederick of Prussia. The
despots' obsession with
raison d'état—the need to
protect or strengthen their
countries—led to the dis-
memberment of Poland.

Europe, and Poland in particular, came in two
variations. On the one hand, the military party
was openly in favor of direct annexation. Its members believed that Russia's interests could best be
protected by seizing her neighbors' territory on
every possible occasion. Chernyshev, the Vice-
President of the War College, expressed this view
when, at the new Empress Catherine's council,
called to discuss the death of the King of Poland,
he proposed an invasion of the Polish province of
Livonia and the counties of Polock, Witebsk and
Mścisław. He commanded the support of those who,
the previous year, with the Russian Army in Berlin,
had urged the late Empress Elizabeth to dismantle
the upstart Kingdom of Prussia. The politicians,
on the other hand, were more cautious. Panin,
Catherine's principal adviser on foreign affairs,
held to the older and deeper Russian game whereby
rivals were disarmed by promises of protection, and
where the victim was not gobbled suddenly but
chewed at leisure. Panin had hopes of a "northern
system," where alliances with Prussia, Sweden and
England could be used to confound the "southern
system" of Louis xv's minister, Choiseul. In Panin's
scheme, the *Rzeczpospolita* was to continue as
Russia's advance post in Europe, a vassal state
whose dependence could be perpetuated by endless
manipulation and at minimal expense. Catherine
undoubtedly shared his intentions, and one vital
strand in the partitions' history can be traced in
her progressive abandonment of leisurely rumination
for the policy of instant consumption.

Prussia's outlook was somewhat different. In
comparison to Russia, it was a tiny state, whose
marvelous efficiency could not always preserve it
from the consequences of insatiable ambition.
Prussia's seizure of Silesia in 1742 had provoked
two decades of war that all but overwhelmed their
instigator. In 1762, the treasury empty and Berlin
occupied, Prussia had only been saved by the timely
death of the Empress Elizabeth and the accession of
Peter III, Frederick's most fervent admirer. Prussia
was an international parasite. In one century it
had grown from a Polish ducal fief into a recognized
kingdom. On two occasions, in 1656 and 1720, it
had been party to abortive plans for dismembering
the *Rzeczpospolita*. In 1752, Frederick's *Political
Testament* had likened his Polish neighbor to "an
artichoke, ready to be consumed leaf by leaf." For
Prussia did not possess a consolidated territorial
base. The possessions of the Hohenzollerns were
scattered across northern Europe in unconnected
clutches. The two largest elements, Brandenburg
and Ducal (east) Prussia, were still separated by
the broad Polish province of Royal (west) Prussia,
which Frederick saw as the first leaf of the artichoke.
After the crisis of 1762, Prussia's policy was no more
repentant than before, but more circumspect.

The *Rzeczpospolita's* other neighbor, Austria,
lacked both Prussia's dynamism and Russia's
resources. Exhausted by the Seven Years War
which had failed to recover Silesia, the Austrians
still possessed more than enough territory to keep

changed. In 1764, for example, when the *Sejm*
appointed a commission of finance to create a
general customs system in line with other modern
states, Frederick of Prussia set up a fort on his side
of the Vistula River to bombard and terrorize
Polish shipping until the new proposals were
dropped. In the same year, the Russians dispatched
the latest of their military expeditions to see that
the coming royal election was held as planned. If
the Poles are judged to have contributed to the
catastrophe themselves, it was more by their
desperate efforts to escape from the anarchy than
from their supposed desire to wallow in it. It should
have been clear to all that the despots of St. Petersburg and Berlin, who denied their own subjects
most civilized liberties, could never be the genuine
champions of "Golden Liberty" in Poland.

The same sort of hypocrisy was current in matters
of religion. Poland was a predominantly Roman
Catholic state which, despite a long tradition of
toleration and freedom of worship, did not allow
her religious minorities, Orthodox and Protestant,
full political rights. Russia took this as an excuse to
pose as the defender of oppressed minorities. But
Prussia was in advance of its time, with Catholic
and Calvinist refugees equally welcome in Lutheran
Berlin. Yet Frederick himself had no illusions. He
knew his collaborators well, but did not flinch in
joining them in their pious demands for religious
rights in Poland. If Poland had been strong, and
her favors sought, there is no doubt that the
diplomatists would have praised her tradition of
religious enlightenment instead of cultivating the
grievances of the "dissidents."

Russia's expansionist policy toward Eastern

their creaking administration busy. They had no plans for expansion. Their mountain frontier in the Carpathians, dividing them from Poland and northern Europe, was complete except for one minor gap at Spisz (Zips). Besides, like the Poles, they were Catholics and still remembered the legendary occasion in 1683 when Sobieski broke the siege of Vienna and saved Christendom from the Turks. They hated the Prussians and feared Russia. It was inconceivable that they might make common cause with Poland's assailants. But they did.

Ruling personalities played a part. Frederick of Prussia, brilliant, cynical and unscrupulous, knew exactly where he was going. He was dealing with a couple of empresses whose weaknesses he exploited with consummate skill, flattering the one, teasing the other. Catherine II, recently elevated to the throne of All-the-Russias after the death of her husband, was equally unscrupulous, but impatient, and as harsh with her allies as with her innumerable lovers. Maria Theresa, Queen of Hungary and Empress of Austria, "the widow of Silesia," was devout and anxious. Finally, there was Stanislas Augustus Poniatowski, the polished, pliable, cosmopolitan nephew of the Czartoryski family, the most powerful, and Russian-backed, faction in Poland. As minister of the *Rzeczpospolita* in St. Petersburg in 1755–58, he had been Catherine's most passionate lover. Unlike her, he was enlightened but not despotic. He was the obvious choice to displace the somnolent Saxons from the throne of Poland.

The prospect of a royal election in Poland accelerated existing intrigues. Both Frederick and Catherine had anticipated the event, the one in 1762 by coordinating his plans with the ill-fated Peter III, the other in January, 1763, by imposing her candidate by armed force on the Duchy of Courland, a fief of the *Rzeczpospolita*. Now they conspired together. On April 11, 1764, a treaty was signed in which Frederick persuaded Catherine to accept the points he had agreed upon with Peter: both would support a *Piast* candidate (a native-born Pole) for the Polish throne and act together in defense of the "Golden Liberty" and the rights of religious dissidents. Frederick was to unseat the Saxons, his neighbors in Germany, from their Polish base and to create room for maneuver. Catherine was to smooth the way for Poniatowski. At this juncture, she was sufficiently ingenuous to issue a declaration to all the courts of Europe, denying the rumor that a partition was being prepared.

However, Poniatowski's road was smooth enough. The electoral field at Wola near Warsaw was lined with Russian soldiers and retainers of the Czartoryski. On September 6, 1764, those nobles of the *Rzeczpospolita* who had not left in disgust, acclaimed their new King with a unanimous shout.

Stanislas Augustus' position was far from comfortable, however. In the first four years of his reign his independence of mind only succeeded in offending all those who had regarded him as the servant of their interest. He soon fell out with his Czartoryski relations, who resented his plans for constitutional reform. He had a difficult relationship with Catherine's agent, Repin, whose threats and violence made a mockery of his prerogatives. He angered Frederick by the customs proposals, and disappointed the "dissidents" who had been led to regard him as their patron. He particularly incensed the established Church by failing to make his position clear on the religious issue. The first *Sejm* of his reign, in 1766, turned into a fiasco. The King's proposals for ending the *liberum veto* were rejected, while the efforts of the Bishop of Cracow, Kajetan Sołtyk, to obtain a declaration on "the Security of the Faith" led to repeated uproar. By the end of the year, the country was dividing into several armed camps.

The year 1767 marked the nadir of Polish "anarchy," in which the Russians' hostile provocations were plainly revealed. Ready were two armed confederations of "dissidents," one at Toruń for the Protestants, the other at Słupsk for the Orthodox. The extent of genuine religious motivation in these developments may be judged from events at Toruń, where the confederation was organized by a Russian officer who, having affirmed the protection of the Empress, proceeded to arrest everyone, including the city corporation, who protested against "the will of the people." At Radom had emerged a more serious confederation, which gradually spread into a countrywide or "general confederation." Some confederates, like the Radziwiłłs in Lithuania, were aiming to dethrone the King. Some were merely trying to block his program of reform. Others thought they were saving the Church. All were being manipulated. On this occasion Repin not only managed to patronize both the opposition and the King; he actually persuaded the King to join the confederates. In October, he showed his hand. Having arranged an extraordinary meeting of the *Sejm*, he promptly arrested four leading oppositionists—Sołtyk, Bishop of Cracow; Załuski, Bishop of Kiev; Rzewuski, Governor of Cracow; and Rzewuski's son—and sent them in chains to Kaluga. His adherents suspended the *Sejm* in favor of a special commission which then proceeded to pass the so-called "cardinal laws," perpetuating the reign of anarchy. The nobility

An eighteenth-century engraving of Warsaw.

Frederick the Great under whom Prussia developed into Germany's leading state.

Europe about 1740

- Hapsburg dominions
- Bourbon dominions
- Prussian dependencies
- House of Savoy
- - - - Boundary of the Holy Roman Empire

were confirmed in their monopoly of political rights. The *liberum veto* was retained. Royal elections were to be "free." In short, the "Golden Liberty" was exposed for the sham it was, and the only person empowered to change it was the Empress of Russia.

At this point Catherine was well pleased. Poland lay prostrate before her in an agony of self-induced paralysis. She had no further demands. But she was cornered. Her moment of satisfaction soon passed; for the Empress had not taken into account the Poles, the Turks or Frederick of Prussia, and was soon obliged to rethink her policy.

In 1768, the reaction against Russian brutalities in Poland grew rapidly. In February, at Bar in Polish Ukraine, a new confederation was called by disillusioned nobles and outraged Catholics which started a civil war the Russians were unable to stamp out for nearly four years. This war generated an idealism, a questioning of fundamental principles that had not occurred in Poland for generations, and was to form the base of modern Polish nationalism. Polish forces were taken in the rear by a Russian-supported Ukrainian rising, which in the region of Uman left 20,000 butchered landlords, Jews and priests. The formations were dispersed by the royal army under Hetman Branicki and the Russians under Krechetnikov. But in October, came reaction from Turkey. Exasperated by broken Russian promises to withdraw from Poland, it arrested the Russian minister in Constantinople. This was a declaration of war.

Catherine's troubles multiplied fast. Fighting a war against Turkey, she could not spare the troops to crush the risings that sprang up in Cracow, in Wielkopolska and in Lithuania. In 1769 she found that the confederates had set up a "generality" at Biała on the Austrian frontier, assisted by French officers. In 1771, open war broke out again, with the Russian General Suvorov hard pressed to counter the brilliant improvisations of Casimir Pułaski in Poland, and of Hetman Oginski in Lithuania.

Frederick of Prussia was delighted with the turn of events. He waited until the Polish pot was nicely on the boil, before giving it a stir himself. In September, 1768, he produced a plan of partition, supposedly devised by one Count Lynar. On finding that Catherine was not yet ready, he bided his time, hinting all the while that the Empress' treatment of the ungrateful Poles was too indulgent. Had she not guaranteed their "Golden Liberty?" Had she not championed the cause of religious toleration? Had she not suffered enough insults from dangerous republicans and upstart bishops? Catherine, flattered by the neatness of Frederick's solution, but still humiliated by her failure, gradually surrendered to the inevitable.

Surprisingly enough, Catherine's resistance was finally broken by the Austrians, in particular by Maria Theresa's astute adviser Kaunitz, the leading diplomat of the age. In 1769, profiting by the *Rzeczpospolita*'s preoccupations, Austrian troops

marched into Spisz and annexed it. In 1770 they marched on to Nowy Targ and Nowy Sącz which were also annexed. Noises were made in protest against Russian activities in Poland, and in 1771 Austria joined her traditional Turkish enemy in an alliance against Russia. This was just what Frederick needed; he was now able to argue that Poland's weakness had reached the point where the powers should protect her from further depredations, and a legal partition was necessary to end illegal annexations. In the autumn of 1770, Frederick's brother, Prince Henry of Prussia, visited St. Petersburg emphasizing these arguments. In June, 1771, a partition of Poland was agreed upon in principle between Prussia and Russia. In February, 1772, after a decent hesitation, Maria Theresa accepted their invitation to participate in despoiling Poland.

The division of the spoils exercised the minds of the diplomats for barely five months. Frederick, as instigator of the operation, modestly helped himself to Polish Prussia, Kujawy and Chełmno. His relinquishment of Danzig was proof of his moderation. Catherine, still resenting the failure which in her eyes had made the partition necessary, confined herself to Polish Livonia, and the counties of Polock, Witebsk, Mścisław and Homel. She did not include the Duchy of Courland, as this had already been taken as a condition of her earlier treaty with Prussia in 1764. But Maria Theresa, having dallied longest, could afford to raise her price highest. Overcoming her scruples she allowed Kaunitz to insist upon Małopolska, from the Silesian border in the west to the Turkish frontier in the east. In the final reckoning, Prussia took 5 percent of the *Rzeczpospolita*'s territory and a mere 580,000 of its citizens; Russia took 12.7 percent of the territory and 1.3 million people; Austria, for her difficult moral decision, received 11.8 percent of the territory, with no less than 2.13 million souls.

The Poles were now required to submit to their treatment in the most proper way possible. On the initiative of the new Russian ambassador, Staeckelberg, a *Sejm* was called. In the absence of the nation's leading figures, a suitable puppet was found to form yet another confederation, and then another commission to confirm the treaties. The King was persuaded to join, and in the summer of 1773 he signed the necessary documents.

In a world which was not sensible to Poland's fate, the mechanics of the partitions passed almost unnoticed; the platitudes were widely believed; the good intentions of the partitioners rarely questioned; and the faults of the Poles universally recognized. Court apologists from Berlin, St. Petersburg and Vienna stressed the difficulties in which their sovereigns had been placed. In due course, court and state historians expatiated on the Poles' good fortune in receiving the blessings of foreign rule.

The consequences of the first partition were not realized for many years. Not until the mid-nineteenth century, when Polish risings repeatedly drew attention to the iniquities of the European system,

did a few enquiring minds seek the origin of contemporary ills in the wrongs of the past. Only then was it seen how the "legitimate" system and "holy" alliances of the empires was built on banditry.

The more immediate consequence of the first partition was, of course, the second partition; and of the second, the third. Between 1773 and 1793, the scenario of the previous decade was reenacted with only minor variations. At first the partitioners professed their peaceful intentions, and probably half-believed in them. The Russian ambassador and Stanislas Augustus managed Poland as before, with a pretence at reform. The Poles themselves, reacting against the strictures placed upon them, embarked on a program of genuine reform. Frederick's successor, Frederick William, irked by Catherine's opposition to the secession of Danzig, supported the Polish reformers, and in 1788 actually allied with the *Rzeczpospolita*. He made the error which Catherine had committed in 1767—believing that advantage could be mixed with friendship. In 1791–92, when the Russian-backed Confederation of Targowice plunged the *Rzeczpospolita* into civil war once more, to crush a new constitution in the name of "Golden Liberty," Catherine could bait the Prussian with the choice of being punished for impudence or rewarded with Danzig for apostasy. Frederick William chose Danzig, and also took Wielkopolska, the heart of Poland. Catherine contented herself with some 100,000 square miles.

The final performance was mercifully swift. In 1794, Thaddeus Kościuszko led a Polish national rising. Russia and Prussia invaded in the name of "liberty." After an unequal struggle Poland was defeated, and Austria joined Russia and Prussia in the third partition.

By the partitions of 1793 and 1795 the major share of Poland went to Russia. Russia now bordered on Austria and Prussia and thus became a vital member of Europe. The Russian Empire now included not only Russians, but Ukrainians, Byelorussians, Lithuanians, Estonians, Letts and Poles. For the first time in modern history three major European nations deliberately dismembered a fourth. Poland was not to emerge as an independent entity until the twentieth century. NORMAN DAVIES

The Cracow salt mines in the reign of Augustus III whose death afforded Catherine the opportunity to set up a puppet government.

Catherine the Great, who extended the frontiers of Russia.

The Industrial Revolution

In Britain the 1770s were years of innovation in trade, transport and technology. Josiah Wedgwood (1730–95) was developing a pottery business that advanced the division of labor and the techniques of professional salesmanship. His new factory, named "Etruria," was built to profit by another of the decade's innovations, the Grand Trunk Canal (built 1766–77), which linked the Staffordshire potteries to the Mersey River, the Midlands and London, thus solving the problems of transport on appalling roads. 1771 saw a speculating barber, named Richard Arkwright (1732–92), the holder of the water-frame patent, and his partner Jedediah Strutt (1726–97), open a cotton spinning mill in Derbyshire. In 1773, British transport was

Wedgwood vase in basalt, a black porcelain invented by Wedgwood.

further improved by the Turnpike Act, which encouraged road construction and repair, and the completion of the Runcorn Locks on the Bridgewater Canal. In 1774, the ironmaster Matthew Boulton (1728–1809) and the inventor James Watt (1736–1819) set up their epoch-making engine construction partnership. Two years later, 1776, in Lancashire plate glass was first manufactured; a steam engine was used for the first time to facilitate the smelting of iron ore in Shropshire, and an engine was installed in Samuel

"Throwing" room at Etruria.

Whitbread's (d. 1796) King's Head Brewery. Advances crucial to the textile industry were put into motion in the 1770s, and Abraham Darby III (1750–91) built the first iron bridge over the Severn River in Coalbrookdale.

Cotton

Britain was undergoing an industrial revolution set in motion by a rapid sequence of innovations in the production of cotton cloth. Improvements in one area of cotton production sparked off responsive developments elsewhere. In 1733, the inventor John Kay patented the fly-shuttle, a machine that speeded up the weaving of cloth and thus widened the gap between the efficiency of weaving and the cottage-industry slowness of spinning. Then, in the 1760s, James Hargreaves' (d. 1778) spinning jenny increased the number of threads a worker could spin simultaneously from one to as many as twenty-four. The water-frame (patented, though not invented, by Richard Arkwright in 1769) further multiplied this output by a novel combination of rollers and spindles. And by 1779 Samuel Crompton's aptly-named "mule" had been developed to combine the best features of both the jenny and the frame. These inventions in their turn set the stage for new processes in bleaching and dyeing, and of course, even faster weaving than that which first prompted the inventions. This would come in the 1780s, with the application of steam-power to both looms and mules. By then, the raw cotton processed by the British textile industry would rise to twenty-two million pounds per year; in 1760, the annual consumption was a mere two and a half million pounds.

But an inventory of inventions hardly accounts for the changes of the era. In 1714, England was a country of perhaps five and a half million people, most of whom lived in villages and hamlets. By the end of the century the population had nearly doubled, and thirty percent lived in rapidly expanding cities and towns. During the eighteenth century an entirely new form of production, the factory system, had been established. But the conditions which promoted such rapid changes in the nation's economy, technology and demography antedate the eighteenth century.

The scientific revolution of the sixteenth and seventeenth centuries reflected a growing interest in natural phenomena and the systematic solution of problems. A coincident interest and increasing skill in mechanics also characterized this period in Britain. The mining of tons of coal provided industrial energy in areas where guild restrictions on entry into trades had never been established.

Colonially based power

Early successes in international colonization and trade had already made Britain a great maritime nation by 1700. In that year, mercantile ships formed perhaps one tenth of all capital fixed investments (other than real estate) and their hundred thousand seamen constituted nearly the largest group of non-agricultural workers. The navy was Britain's most powerful weapon, and its power grew with victory in the War of the Spanish Succession in 1713. The foundations of maritime supremacy had been

bolstered by the Navigation Acts (1660–63) which gave British shipping a monopoly on the transport of British goods, thus encouraging shipbuilding and the provision of harbor facilities. Britain's colonies and interests would provide both the raw materials and the markets for an industrial age. British shipping was already established.

The seventeenth century saw Britain rid herself of the last vestiges of feudalism. The defeat of the crown in the civil wars (1642–51), the rule of Cromwell (1653–58), and the ineffectual reign of the Restoration monarchs had dealt a death-blow to royal prerogatives. For instance, with the abolition of the Court of Wards in 1660, the monarchy lost its right to the guardianship of the young heirs of royal tenants—and the income from their estates. Now the capital from such inheritances remained in the hands of private investors. The power of the commercial classes, so forthrightly asserted in the civil wars, made real differences to the feudal social system as well. With land no longer the solitary index of wealth, trade became a legitimate path to social status. Merchants such as the East India trader Sir Joshua Child (1630–99) managed to achieve respectability—his daughter even married a duke—through acquired wealth.

The increase in business prospects was supported by new monetary developments; in 1694 the Bank of England was founded. By the end of the next century, it would function as the matrix of a national credit system operating through a hundred country banks.

A print from "Industry and Idleness" by William Hogarth.

feudalism as the commercial classes assert themselves

Agriculture

British agriculture kept pace with these mercantile developments. From the fifteenth century, open fields and common land were steadily enclosed. With enclosure, landowners could independently improve their breeding stock and cultivation practices. The success of such developments can be measured by the change of expectation in harvest yield—from four to one of seed in the Middle Ages to ten to one by the eighteenth century. But the changeover to large-scale agriculture was not without its disadvantages. The agricultural laborer, who formerly might have eked out his meager living by farming his small allotment and grazing his stock on the common lands, was now dispossessed. Furthermore, larger croppage demanded a seasonal influx of labor at planting and harvesting that was unemployable at other times of the year. Rural poverty increased notably—but even this was to benefit future industry. Poor rural families were good candidates for the early eighteenth-century system of domestic industry or "putting out." The whole family could spin or weave at home with materials supplied by a local entrepreneur, and when machines later took over those functions, a lucky few could man them.

With a large work force, a growing population to feed, a large-scale consolidation of land for planting and grazing, and the incentive to profitable production caused by rising land prices, England was prepared for an agrarian revolution in tandem with that in industry.

Continental contracts

In contrast, continental Europe's progress to industrialization was hampered by absolute monarchs, rigid class systems, feudal tax prerogatives which put money in the hands of those least likely to invest it, social prejudice against business careers and high profit margins, internal tariff barriers which discouraged trade, bad transport and communications and the constant threat of war. Only Holland provided social mobility for its thriving commercial classes. In France a bureaucratic career in the service of the monarchy was the single path to social success. A career in business traditionally meant the loss of noble status. In Germany, legal restrictions strengthened barriers between the three classes of citizens—nobles, burghers and peasants. The relatively rapid ascension of the British commercial classes, their high rate of consumption in emulation of the nobility and the general rough-and-tumble of British social intermingling disgusted Europeans. Thus a French visitor to London in 1750 sniffed at seeing "London masters dress like their valets, and duchesses copy after chambermaids."

However, eighteenth-century Europe did experience a considerable expansion of trade. While Venice and the Hanseatic cities declined, French ports and French shipping prospered tremendously. At Le Havre imports of sugar doubled and imports of coffee increased five-fold between 1760 and 1789. By 1787, Sweden had a fleet of twelve hundred merchantmen and Prussia nearly a thousand. Peter the Great's Russia became a

Winding, warping and weaving.

trading nation and Europe's largest supplier of iron. By 1790, 26,000 metric tons would arrive annually in Britain from the Urals. In 1789 Spain could boast that half the goods she traded to South America were home-produced. Banking and insurance facilities increased rapidly on the Continent, and, until the Napoleonic Wars, no city could displace Amsterdam as the money market of the world. In 1777 the Dutch were said to own forty percent of Britain's national debt.

Generally, continental industry expanded with the expansion of trade. Production fell in most of eighteenth-century Germany, Italy, Sweden and Holland, and even in France after 1770; but the textile and mining industries prospered in Belgium (coal exports down the Haine River increased six-fold between 1764 and 1800). France's textile industries grew considerably, as typified by the Lyons silk weavers trebling in number between 1720 and 1788 to 40,000. In 1789 France was producing 130,000 to 140,000 tons of pig-iron per year, double the British rate. Other important textile centers included Bohemia, Spain and Switzerland, with the latter nation second only to Britain in raw cotton imports from America. Yet no nation in Europe could equal the continuously sustained growth rate of Britain, where industrial production trebled between 1700 and 1790.

Though "King Cotton" set the pace for British industry, production in other areas did not lag far behind. The transport revolution would reach its apogee with the nineteenth-century railroad, but there had already been significant changes by the middle of the previous century. Methods of British road building and repair were greatly improved, but even more

important were the canals. In 1761 the Worsley Canal was opened. This connected the Duke of Bridgewater's coal mines with Manchester and halved the average price of coal in the city. In 1767 Manchester was joined to Liverpool by the Bridgewater Canal, a waterway which even in the 1840s would carry twice the tonnage of the railway. Canal transport was far more efficient than road haulage: a horse that could pull two tons on a well-surfaced road could pull fifty tons along a canal towpath. Even river traffic was surpassed by the efficiency of the canal. In 1785 an observer of the traffic at Barton Bridge, where the Bridgewater Canal was carried by an aqueduct over the Irwell wrote of seeing, ". . . seven or eight fellows labouring like slaves to drag a boat slowly up the Irwell, and one horse or mule, or sometimes two men at most, drawing five or six of the Duke's barges, linked together, at great rate upon the canal."

British production was rapidly expanding, as were the industries that provided power. Though France was leading Britain in pig-iron production toward the century's end, Britain used four or five times as much pig-iron per capita. Such progress was made possible by native discoveries in smelting iron, like the substitution of coke for charcoal pioneered by Abraham Darby 1 (1678–1717) at Coalbrookdale in 1709. But coke-smelting was not a dependable process; it needed a stronger blast to produce a metal that could be worked into wrought iron. In 1776 the problem was overcome when John Wilkinson (1728–1808) installed a steam engine in his works in Shropshire. The engine had been invented by James Watt.

Entrance to Worsley Canal tunnel, beginning of the Bridgewater Canal.

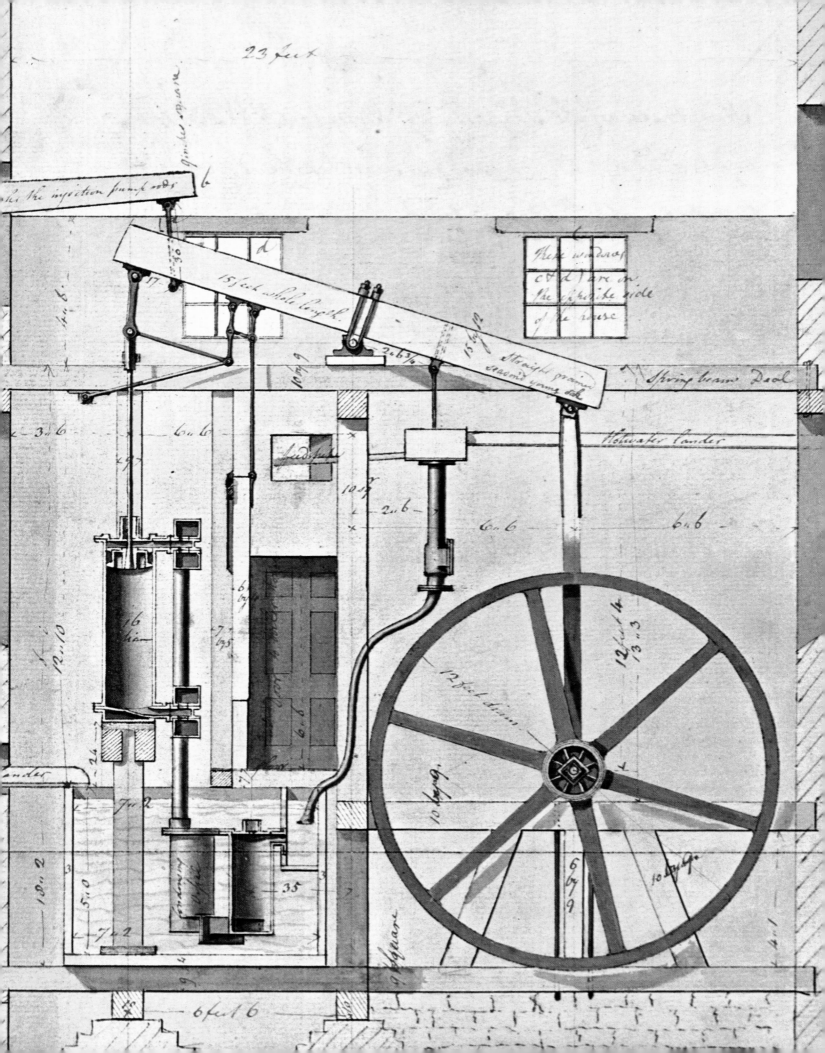

23 feet

shi the injection pump rods

b

d

15 feet whole length.

These windows
c & d are on
the pitside side
of the house

Straight grained
seasond yellow deal

Spring beam Deal

2 by 3 3/4

15 by 12

10 by 9

3 by 6

6 by 6

Hot water lander

feed pipe

10 by 7

2 by 6

6 by 6

6 by 6

16
diam

12 feet la
13 by 3

12 feet diam

10 by 9

lander

7 by 2

6 by 6

condensing cistern

35

6
by
9

10 by 9

7 by 2

18 by 2

5 by 0

square

6 feet 6

Watt Constructs an Efficient Steam Engine

The power of steam had been known as early as the time of the Greeks, but until the seventeenth century, no one had developed the idea. Then a number of crude machines were built, mostly used for pumping out mines. Their fuel consumption was uneconomically high for most purposes, however. It took the genius of James Watt, a sickly instrument maker in Scotland, and the drive of his partner Matthew Boulton to develop a steam engine that was efficient and economical, facilitating the Industrial Revolution and ushering in the Age of Steam.

A story that enchanted Victorian myth-makers was that of a little boy who, watching the lid of his mother's kettle lifting as the water inside boiled, became the first person to notice the inherent power in steam. That little boy was James Watt. However, steam power was known to Hero of Alexandria almost two thousand years before Watt was born. But Hero's knowledge was used only to produce elaborate toys in which steam was employed to make various objects move as if by magic. One contraption, set up in a temple, could open the doors of a tabernacle containing the statue of a god when an altar fire was lit. This, as do all machines using steam power, relied on the fact that the amount of steam created when water is heated is much larger in volume than that of the unheated water. The power to be utilized is that of the steam as it expands, pushing against anything in its way.

But invention needs more stimulus than mere novelty and it was not until the seventeenth century in England that a reasonably efficient steam engine was developed. The machine, built by Thomas Savery, was used mainly to pump water out of mines, such as the Cornwall tin mines, or into small waterworks in the London area. The engine, relying on a system of valves instead of a piston, was relatively primitive and inadequate, until Thomas Newcomen adopted the idea and developed it into a more powerful and useful pump. Newcomen's engine harnessed the power of expanding steam directly to an oscillating beam, pivoted at the center, by means of a piston moving inside a cylinder. The movement of the other end of the beam drew up water through a pipe. The engine was ready for sale by 1720 and was soon in great demand for a wide variety of pumping operations. So at the time James Watt is popularly believed to have been working out the principles of steam power useful, if slow-moving, steam pumps were being installed in many parts of the country. How-

ever, these steam pumps were too cumbersome and wasteful to be economically viable. Watt's refinement of steam power made possible the development of the efficient steam-powered machines that set the Industrial Revolution underway, and brought England—and the world—considerable material benefit.

James Watt was born on January 19, 1736, in Scotland at Greenock on the Clyde River. Son of a successful merchant and shipowner who had in his time turned his hand to many pursuits, including carpentry, building and the making of scientific instruments, James was a weak and sickly child. The only one of a large family to live beyond infancy, he was not strong enough to go to school until ten years old and then was bullied for not playing games. His bad health, however, was more than compensated for by a talent for mathematics, which showed itself when he began to attend the local grammar school at Greenock. As a boy he was also attracted to that side of his father's business concerned with the manufacture of scientific instruments. It was Watt's ability to produce delicate and accurate work of this kind after years of practice in his father's workshop that made him decide, upon leaving school, to set up as an instrument maker. After a short apprenticeship in London and with the help of a school friend whose brother was a professor at Glasgow University, Watt, at age twenty-one, became scientific instrument maker to the University.

Working at Glasgow meant much to the young mathematician; he associated with many of the most eminent scientists of the day, in particular Joseph Black, the discoverer of latent heat. Black had pointed out that the temperature of a substance is not always an indication of the amount of heat applied to it. For example, considerable heat must be applied to a volume of water to turn it to steam, but the temperature of the water as it boils does not

James Watt, whose development of the steam engine ushered in the Age of Steam.

Opposite Steam engine belonging to the Duke of Devonshire, attributed to James Watt.

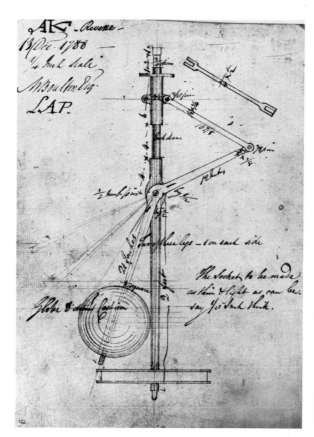

change. Knowledge of Black's discovery was to help Watt when, in 1763, he was asked by the University to mend their model of Newcomen's engine, which had already been examined by a more experienced London craftsman who had been unable to repair it.

For two years Watt had been working on experiments to show the properties of steam, but he appears not to have seen details of Newcomen's machine. His examination of the model was to have far reaching consequences; Watt was not only able to repair it, but in doing so he set himself the task of making it more efficient. His improved engine was to bring him a fortune and provide a new source of power for the growing industries of the country. Watt did not discover the power of steam; that, and ways of making use of it, were established facts before he was born, but it was his economical use of fuel which provided the base of England's industrial progress. Newcomen's engine, to work at all, had to be built on a massive scale—part of the reason for the inadequate performance of the engine was its size. It also used far too much fuel to compare favorably with older forms of power, such as the water mill or windmill. Watt's achievement was to see why so much fuel was wasted and to eliminate that wastage.

Newcomen's engine derived its power from the steam produced by boiling water being let into a cylinder; as it expands, it pushes a piston to the end of the cylinder. Cold water is then poured into the cylinder, condensing the steam and causing a partial vacuum as the steam turns back to water. The state of vacuum pulls the piston back into the cylinder ready to be pushed out again by a new injection of steam. This principle works well enough, but has one serious bar to efficiency: the cylinder must be at boiling point to hold the steam, then a moment later be as cold as 30°c while the steam condenses. This means that the boiler must provide enough heat to raise the temperature of the cylinder from 30°c to 100°c several times a minute. There, Watt realized, was where the fuel was wasted and from his knowledge of latent heat he knew that more heat was being wasted than even the changes of temperature suggested.

For the next two years Watt considered the problem. Not being an academic and having to earn his livelihood meant he could not devote himself completely to the project. Nevertheless, in 1765, the answer came to him. Watt later recalled the moment in which he found the solution:

It was in the Green of Glasgow. I had gone to take a walk on a fine Sabbath afternoon. I had entered the Green by the gate at the foot of Charlotte Street, had passed the old washing-house. I was thinking upon the engine at the time and had gone as far as the Herd's house when the idea came into my mind, that as steam was an elastic body it would rush into a vacuum, and if a communication was made between the cylinder and an exhausted vessel, it would rush into it, and might be there condensed without cooling the cylinder. . . . I had not walked further than the Golf-house when the whole thing was arranged in my mind.

In other words, instead of wasting fuel by having to reheat the cylinder each time it had been cooled for condensation, Watt incorporated a separate condenser. Thus the cylinder could be kept as near boiling point as possible while the condenser would remain at room temperature.

Having made what was to prove a significant discovery, Watt was unable to follow it up immediately. About the time of his breakthrough, Watt had been introduced to John Roebuck, who owned the Carron ironworks on the Forth River. Roebuck was interested in the potentialities of Watt's machine and offered to pay off the debts that Watt's experiments had brought upon him. In return Watt agreed that Roebuck should have two-thirds of any profit gained from the development of the engine. Nevertheless, it was not until 1769 that Watt patented his machine and, even then, the patent was drawn up in so unprofessional a way that in later years it was the cause of much dispute. Roebuck built an engine to Watt's design, but little use was made of it and Watt spent the next years working as a surveyor for canal and harbor projects. Roebuck, having secured for himself an interest in the most significant innovation of the century, was unable to capitalize on it and, by 1772, was in serious financial difficulties.

James Watt had never grown out of his childhood ill-health and sickliness; in addition, or perhaps in consequence, he had a nervous, rather self-effacing character, and lived under the constant worry that his health would fail and his finances collapse. He was the kind of man who, in areas other than his own profession, needed constant reassurance. It was singularly fortunate, therefore, that Roebuck's failure cleared the way for Watt's partnership with a man whose qualities were in many ways the perfect complement to his own.

Watt had met Matthew Boulton in 1768 and the two seem to have become firm friends almost immediately. Boulton was a shrewd but humane businessman who had married a wealthy heiress but still preferred to spend his time working hard at running the Soho Manufactory at Birmingham. He had built this model factory in an effort to change Birmingham's reputation as a producer of shoddy goods and also to prove that it was possible for an industrialist to be a success and treat his work force with consideration. His money and determination were exactly what was required to overcome Watt's hesitant character. He later wrote to Watt: "I cannot help recommending to you to pray morning and evening, after the manner of your countrymen ['The Lord grant us gude conceit of ourselves'], for you want nothing but a good opinion and confidence in yourself and good health."

At the time Boulton and Watt first met, the Soho works derived their power from a nearby stream, which dried up in the summer, leaving Boulton to keep the machinery going with water flowing from a reservoir. Watt's steam engine, if it could be developed efficiently, would give Boulton's factory more power all the year round. If anyone could ensure that Watt's steam engine be developed to its full potential, Matthew Boulton was the man to do so. When he heard of Roebuck's difficulties, he offered to forget debts of £1,200 owed him by Roebuck, in return for his share in the steam engine. While negotiations were underway, he wrote to Watt:

I was excited by two motives to offer you my assistance which were the love of you and love of a money-getting ingenious project. I presumed that your engine would require money, very accurate workmanship and extensive correspondence to make it turn out to the best advantage, and that the best means of keeping up the reputation and doing the invention justice would be to keep the executive part out of the hands of the multitude of empirical engineers, who from ignorance, want of experience and want of necessary convenience, would be very liable to produce bad and inaccurate workmanship; all of which deficiencies would affect the reputation of the invention. To remedy which and produce the most profit, my idea was to settle a manufactory near to my own by the side of our canal where I would erect all conveniences necessary for the completion of engines, and from which manufactory we would

The Soho Manufactory at Birmingham that Boulton had developed into a model factory.

Newcomen's engine. When given a model of the engine to repair, Watt's interest was aroused and he determined to modernize it.

serve all the world with engines of all sizes. By these means and your assistance we could engage and instruct some excellent workmen (with more excellent tools than would be worth any man's while to procure for one single engine), could execute the invention twenty per cent cheaper than it would be otherwise executed, and with as great a difference of accuracy as there is between the blacksmith and the mathematical instrument maker. It would not be worth my while to make for three counties only, but I find it very well worth my while to make for all the world.

Boulton took over Watt's engine in 1772 and, in 1774, Watt, caring little for his work as surveyor, moved to Birmingham, becoming Boulton's partner the following year.

The engine which had been built by Roehampton was brought to the Soho Works and set up as a demonstration model. Soon many of the improved engines of Watt and Boulton were being sold, mainly for pumping out mines. The attraction, of course, was the economy of fuel and the partners always based their fee on the amount the purchaser would save.

Many improvements followed; Watt's ingenuity and Boulton's perfectionism combined with the high standard of accurate workmanship at the Soho works to produce more sophisticated machines. Then, in 1781, Watt filed a patent for an engine which would convert the oscillating motion of the beam into a rotary motion. The idea was not a new one; the patent for Watt's earliest steam engine had contained vague proposals for a rotary engine. Before that, steam pumps had been used to create a stream that would turn a water-wheel, but the possibility of turning a wheel by the powerful action of an efficient engine had wide implications. Improved machines, even whole factories, could be driven by steam, increasing efficiency and production to an

extent that had only been dreamed of in the past.

A rival, working from information supplied by an ex-employee of Watt, filed an earlier patent using a crank—the most obvious method—to obtain rotary motion. Nevertheless, Watt devised an alternative system which was built into a double acting engine that used steam to push the piston both ways along the cylinder. It was this engine that was sold in large numbers by the firm of Boulton and Watt; by 1800 almost five hundred engines had been supplied to the growing industries of the Industrial Revolution, including cotton and woollen mills, iron and steel works, and different branches of mining.

The story of the steam engine did not of course end with Watt; after his retirement in 1800, his invention was taken up by other engineers and its efficiency was improved further. Whereas Watt's original engine was at least twice as efficient as the best model of the Newcomen engine, by 1850 Watt engines had been designed that were eight times as efficient. By harnessing cheap power in this way, Watt provided one of the principal ingredients of the Industrial Revolution. Much greater output could be achieved with the same amount of fuel and a minimum of human effort. While water power had provided the principal motive force in the early stages of industrial growth, it was almost completely eclipsed by the use of steam power in the course of the nineteenth century. Thus by 1850 over ninety percent of cotton and woollen mills were powered by steam—a pattern reflected in almost all other industries.

The changeover from water power to steam had a dramatic effect upon the location of industry. Coal became the most important determinant in siting factories because it was required in large quantities to drive the steam engines. As a result industry tended to move to the coalfields; in the case of the cotton and woollen industries, the centers of production shifted from the narrow Pennine valleys, with their fast-flowing streams suitable for water power, to the coalfields at the foot of the valleys. The textile industry centered upon towns such as Manchester, Bolton, Leeds and Bradford where coal and land to build factories were readily available. The development of steam power ac-

celerated the growth of factory production, for the efficient utilization of steam driven machinery demanded the concentration of production in factories. This transformation of industry also favored areas with readily accessible supplies of coal, so that industrial areas dependent upon water power and far from the coalfields fought a steadily losing battle with the North and the Midlands. Nowhere was the impact of steam more decisive than in the woollen industry, traditionally centered upon the Cotswolds, East Anglia and the West Riding. The rise of steam power led to the irreversible decline of those areas dependent upon water power and far from coal supplies, the Cotswolds and East Anglia, and to the dominance of the West Riding.

These far-reaching consequences of Watt's inventive genius were only part of the impact steam made upon the face of Britain. At the time of Watt's death in 1819 at Heathfield Hall near Birmingham —in spite of persistent fears for his own health he survived to age eighty-three—new epoch-making applications of steam power were being investigated. Experiments were conducted by men such as Trevithick with "high-pressure" steam engines and their application to traction. Before Watt's death the first locomotives and steamships had been built and given successful, although limited, trials. The railway age was to give Watt's work a new dimension and significance, creating a true "steam age."

Today it is fashionable for historians to see the Industrial Revolution as a continuous and complex process, in which the "heroic" inventors played a less important part than was once thought. We now know that Watt's work took place in the context of the considerable scientific work carried out at Glasgow University and among Watt's contacts in the Birmingham Lunar Society. It also depended upon the parallel developments in metallurgy and

precision engineering which were taking place at this time. Moreover Watt's long legal battles to acquire patents showed that he was often not very far ahead of rival inventors. Nonetheless, Watt's place as a great inventor is more assured than most. The range and power of his work was much greater than many other inventors; for Watt was not only an inspired mechanic, but also a considerable scientist—he is recognized as a discoverer of the composition of water. His friend Professor Robison said that he "was a person of truly philosophical mind, eminently conversant with all branches of natural knowledge." He was on close terms with many eminent scientists and professors, and his work was closely based upon scientific experiment and observation. The famous tea-kettle was, in fact, used as a primitive boiler in a series of laboratory experiments into the properties of steam. A great deal of his work was based upon theoretical as well as practical knowledge. His work extended beyond steam engines to include the discovery of chlorine bleaching, a form of duplication, and other important additions to existing knowledge.

Moreover, unlike many other inventors, Watt not only invented an important device, but was also involved in the protracted technical, financial and managerial problems of developing it. He saw his invention through from the drawing-board to its practical application in industry. In the final analysis Watt must stand as *the* great pioneer in the Industrial Revolution, for the invention he made had an immense impact on the structure of industry and society, not only in England but all over the world. Even if the Industrial Revolution was not merely a "wave of gadgets," Watt was instrumental in harnessing the power that sustained that revolution and carried it forward to new heights.

JOHN STEVENSON

Above Watt's garret work-shop at Heathfield Hall near Birmingham where he spent the latter part of his life still devoted to mechanical pursuits.

Above left Gentleman and miner with a specimen of copper ore. Watt's engine was immediately used for pumping in the Cornish copper mines, many of which were in danger of abandonment owing to the difficulty of dealing with large amounts of water.

America before the Revolution

Europe's colonial wars of the eighteenth century had not left America untouched. The treaties of Utrecht (1713) and Aix-la-Chapelle (1748) had been mere truces in the continuing competition for territory between France and Britain. More decisive was the Treaty of Paris in 1763; this recognized Britain's success by breaking up the huge French colony of Louisiana. All the area east of the Mississippi River (Wisconsin, Michigan, Illinois, Indiana, Ohio, Kentucky, Tennessee, Mississippi and Alabama) passed to Britain, as did Canada, Nova Scotia and Cape Breton, while Britain gained Florida from Spain. The new colonies of Florida, Quebec, Nova Scotia and Newfoundland (1774) were administered separately from the thirteen colonies.

The emphasis that Britain had placed on America during the Seven Years War continued after the Peace of Paris. The regular soldiers who had fought the French remained in North America. The value of taxation from the now much enlarged colonies in North America was increasingly recognized by the British government. The thirteen colonies were different from most of Britain's other overseas possessions in that most of the population was of British descent. The native Indian population had been driven westward, and labor was provided either by the colonists or by black slaves imported from Africa. But although the Indians could be driven out of properly colonialized areas, they had to be controlled and prevented from raiding these settlements. Fear of further white settlement led to a widespread Indian rising in 1763 under Pontiac (c. 1720–69), in which most of the forts in the western territory fell. As a result the British government banned further settlement west of the Alleghenies and declared the western territory a separate crown colony reserved for the Indians. The colonists, however, determined to settle more land, simply ignored the boundary and attempted to found settlements and farm the land. Inevitably this exacerbated the troubles with the Indians.

Constitutional problems

Far more serious than the troubles with the Indians was the lack of contact and cooperation between the colonies and the breakdown in the relationship between the colonies and the government in London. The former was to remain a divisive factor even after the Revolution, and could occasionally flare up into open disagreement. The latter, however, was a more immediate problem. Despite the close cultural relationship between the American colonies and Britain— many members of the Royal Society, for example, were resident in America—and a common constitutional heritage, there were widespread differences in outlook between the colonists and the British government. An increasingly large proportion of the colonial population had been born and bred in America, although immigration was still steadily growing. During the years immediately after the Treaty of Paris these disagreements came to a head.

Ostensibly, taxation was the main problem. In 1764 Parliament amended the 1734 Molasses Act into the Sugar Act in order to gain increased taxation from the American colonies. At the same time it was proposed to raise the number of British regular soldiers in the colonies to ten thousand in order to protect the new frontier efficiently, and to give the colonies the responsibility for maintaining the troops. The colonists did not object to the protection, but could not understand why they should be expected to pay for it. In 1765 the Stamp Act was passed in an attempt to raise about £150,000 a year by placing stamp duty on legal contracts and newspapers. There were protests in several of the colonial assemblies, most notably in Massachusetts and Virginia, where Patrick Henry (1736–99) led the opposition to the Act.

It was by now apparent that there was a deep and fundamental difference of opinion between the government and the assemblies. In London the colonists were regarded as treacherous—they had continued to trade with France and Spain during the Seven Years War—and irresponsible—their greed for land made war with the Indians almost continuous. The government wanted to raise taxation in America to a level comparable with, although not as high as, that in Britain. The colonial assemblies were often obstructive in voting on taxation and always ineffectual in their attempts to collect it. On the other hand, to the colonists, whose right to tax themselves was enshrined in their charters, it seemed that "if taxes are laid upon us in any shape without having a legal representation where they are laid, are we not reduced from free subjects to the miserable state of tributary slaves?" Rather than be reduced to that undesirable state, the colonists held a Stamp Act Congress in New York in 1765, at which nine of the colonies were officially represented. Some of the delegates favored the election of American members of Parliament to sit in the House of Commons in London. The majority, however, preferred simply to reiterate that the right of taxation lay not with Parliament but with the colonial assemblies. Meanwhile many east-coast merchants were refusing to import British goods, thereby causing a fall of over fifteen percent in the value of imports from Britain.

The electoral defeat of George Grenville (1712–70) in 1766 led to a slight change in British policy. Under the new Prime Minister, the Marquess of Rockingham (1730–82), the government arranged for the repeal of the Stamp Act. The motion succeeded by 275 votes to 161, but the government went on to secure the principle of its right to tax the American colonies by passing a declaratory act. The dismissal of Rockingham later that same year and his replacement as Prime Minister by William Pitt did not improve the situation. The new Chancellor of the Exchequer, Charles Townshend (1725–67), imposed taxes on the importation of tea, glass and paper in an attempt to increase the government's revenues by £40,000 a year. The appointment of Lord North (1732–92) as Chancellor after Townshend's death led to a further hardening of the British government's attitude, and the assemblies of New York, Virginia and Massachusetts were dissolved on the

"The Bostonians in Distress";
after the Boston Tea Party the British closed the port.

defiance of British rule

MAGNA *Britannia; her Colonies* REDUC'D

Britannia dismembered; her ships have brooms tied to them indicating lack of trade.

orders of the British government.

The center of disaffection was Boston, where British naval and military units were stationed to ensure order. Elsewhere the merchants readopted the policy of nonimportation, which had proved so successful, and imports from Britain, which had never returned to the level of 1764, dropped by over thirty-five percent (from £2,160,000 in 1768 to £1,340,000 in 1769). As a result the government received less rather than more in taxation, and one of Lord North's first actions after becoming Prime Minister in 1770 was the repeal of most of Townshend's taxes, although tea continued to be taxed in order to uphold the government's right to impose taxation.

During the next few years only a few isolated incidents—the Boston Massacre, the Golden Hill riot in Manhattan, the raid on the *Gaspee*, a coastguard vessel near Providence, R.I., and the Boston Tea Party—disturbed the peace. But the calm was deceptive. Several of the colonial assemblies set up committees to undertake joint action against the British, and in 1774 the British replied with a series of harsh laws, including the Quebec Act, a measure that gave control of much of the western territory to the Quebec governor and council—who being directly appointed by the crown were more susceptible to its influence.

However, by now the government had effectively lost its freedom of action. In September, 1774, the first Continental Congress was held in Philadelphia. Fifty-six delegates attended, and only Georgia was entirely unrepresented. The Congress put forward a declaration of rights condemning the new laws.

The outbreak of war

This act of open defiance left the British government divided on what course of action it should follow. Chatham favored conciliation, King George III declared that "We must either master them or leave them totally to themselves as aliens," but the House of Commons favored repression. Meanwhile in Massachusetts an illegal provincial congress was set up to organize defense against the British garrison in Boston, and in Virginia a citizen militia was formed. On April 19, 1775, there was fighting at Lexington, Massachusetts, between British soldiers and the Massachusetts militia, which resulted in the death of 273 redcoats. Soon Boston was besieged and other British outposts, such as Fort Ticonderoga and Crown Point, taken. Around Boston, however, the British were able to strengthen their position as a result of their success in the Battle of Bunker Hill. In addition an American attempt to invade Canada was soon defeated.

The second Continental Congress held, like the first, at Philadelphia, was rapidly accepted as the effective governing body of the rebels. Although it had no statutory power, its orders to the various colonies were almost always carried out. George Washington (1732–99), a delegate to both the Continental Congresses who had proved himself a highly capable officer in the Indian wars, was appointed as commander-in-chief of the American forces. The besiegers of Boston, mostly from Massachusetts, although there were a few small units from some of the other colonies, were given the title of the Continental Army, and precise regulations regarding pay and promotion were formulated.

Effective British administration, except in a few large towns with British garrisons, collapsed. By a process of attrition, the main British force, the Boston garrison, had been reduced from twenty-five hundred men to about a thousand. The British, anxious to use their strongest weapon, naval power, to its full advantage, began to plan a move from Boston to New York City, which was not only strategic-

ally more important, but had the additional advantage of being farther south. The capture by the rebels of Dorchester Heights, overlooking Boston, forced the British to advance their plans. After withdrawing their troops temporarily to Halifax they attacked New York. Although the city was defended by nine thousand volunteers, led by Washington, the British captured it, making it their headquarters.

Meanwhile the Continental Congress was continuing its deliberations in Philadelphia. The Congress had in practice become a government. It opened negotiations with

European Possessions in North America

HUDSON'S BAY COMPANY
NEWFOUNDLAND
NEW FRANCE
NOVA SCOTIA
NEW ENGLAND
VIRGINIA
CAROLINA
FLORIDA
NEW SPAIN
LOUISIANA
NEW GRANADA

English territory
French territory
Spanish territory
Independent territory

HUDSON'S BAY COMPANY
NEWFOUNDLAND
NOVA SCOTIA
QUEBEC
UNITED STATES
LOUISIANA
TEXAS
FLORIDA
NEW SPAIN
CALIFORNIA
NEW GRANADA

France, always ready to take advantage of any sign of British weakness. It opened its ports to ships of all countries. Even more important, it was becoming clear to the delegates that they must become a separate state—linked together through a federal constitution. There could be no going back to loyalty to Britain. Urged on by Richard Henry Lee (1732–94) of Virginia, the Congress made a declaration of independence.

JOIN, or DIE.

Cartoon by Benjamin Franklin of his plan of union which the colonies rejected (1754).

The Declaration of Independence

The angular and garrulous delegate from Virginia seemed an unlikely candidate for the vital task of drafting the Second Continental Congress' proclamation of independence. At thirty-three, Thomas Jefferson was one of the youngest of the representatives who had gathered in Philadelphia —and he was a notoriously ineffective public speaker. Yet Jefferson single-handedly drafted a declaration that not only evoked patriotic fervor in American readers but voiced the rebellious colonies' grievances with consummate diplomatic skill. So artfully worded was Jefferson's document that even the supremely autocratic King of France was able to support it. Ignoring the lanky Virginian's declaration that "governments derive their just powers from the consent of the governed," Louis XVI openly assisted the colonists—and in so doing, ensured the spread of the revolutionary spirit that toppled his own government twelve years later.

The Declaration of Independence, unlike the United States constitution and most other such famous documents of history, is the work of one man. John Adams of Massachusetts and Benjamin Franklin of Pennsylvania suggested a few changes in the wording, but the responsibility for phrasing the sentiments expressed in that momentous manifesto fell to Thomas Jefferson, a gentleman from Virginia who possessed, to a greater degree than any of his colleagues, what John Adams termed "a happy talent of composition."

Jefferson had arrived in Philadelphia in June, 1775, as one of Virginia's delegates to the Second Continental Congress. The Second Congress was far more radical than the First, which had met in Philadelphia from September 5 to October 6, 1774, to protest Britain's colonial policy. The First Congress had sent several petitions of grievances to King George III, and it had formed the "Continental Association" to boycott British imports into the colonies and bar colonial exports to the Empire. But although the First Congress called for a thorough revamping of the Empire, few of its members contemplated a complete break with England when the Congress was adjourned.

By the time the Second Congress convened in May, 1775, however, England had rejected the petitions of the First Congress and had decided to end the rebellion with force. Armed skirmishes between colonial militia and British troops already had broken out at Lexington and Concord, and as the radicals in the Congress gained support, the delegates adopted measures that moved them inexorably toward the final break with the mother country. A Continental Army was formed; diplomatic feelers were sent to France; American ports were opened to foreign shipping; and finally, in June, 1776, a committee was appointed to draft a formal declaration of independence from Great Britain. The committee was composed of Adams, Franklin, Roger Sherman of Connecticut, Robert Livingston of New York and Jefferson.

Tall, sandy-haired, loose-jointed, Jefferson had not made a good first impression upon his arrival in Philadelphia. He seemed awkward. His clothes were ill-fitting and his talk was as loose and rambling as his gait. At a time when the ability to sway an audience counted heavily, he revealed himself as an ineffective public speaker. Fortunately for the cause of independence, he was blessed with other qualities. If he did not shine in public debate, he did show himself to be well informed, outspoken and incisive in committee work. Obviously the reputation he had made for himself in the House of Burgesses at Williamsburg was well earned.

Intellectually and physically the thirty-three-year-old delegate, one of the youngest men in the Congress, was a curious blend of the Old World and the New. Although he had grown up on the fringe of western settlement—which accounted for his fierce opposition to a government that fostered rank and privilege—he inherited from his mother, Jane Randolph, a member of one of the most distinguished families in the province, a taste for the good things of life. A lover of good books, good music and good wine, and at the same time an accomplished linguist, architect, farmer, naturalist and administrator, the extraordinarily versatile Jefferson could have made a name for himself in any one of half a dozen different professions.

There may have been a grain of truth in the wry comment of one critic that Thomas Jefferson was "a martyr to the disease of omniscience." But if like so many men of varied talents he flitted too easily over too many fields of knowledge, for at least once in his life—in the month of June, 1776—he was utterly and

A five shilling stamp of 1765. The Stamp Act of 1765, requiring almost every paper document to have an official stamp, created anger among all sections of the community.

Opposite Thomas Jefferson, author of the Declaration of Independence and third President of the United States.

George III. He unnecessarily alienated his colonial subjects.

Lord North, British Prime Minister from 1770 to 1782. He tried to limit the freedom of the colonists and thus provoked them to oppose British authority by force.

exclusively engrossed in the task that had been assigned to him. Robert Livingston and Roger Sherman agreed with Adams and Franklin that the wording of the Declaration had better be left to the young delegate from Virginia. Jefferson retired to his lodging on Market Street and was not seen again until June 28, when he emerged with his first draft.

As he sharpened his quill, he may well have reminded himself that the primary purpose of the document over which he was laboring was not so much to declare independence as to proclaim to the world the reasons for declaring it. Jefferson's colleague, Richard Henry Lee, already had submitted a resolution to the Continental Congress on behalf of the Virginia delegation, declaring that "these United Colonies are, and of a right ought to be, free and independent States, that they are absolved from all allegiance to the British crown, and that all political connection between them and the state of Great Britain is, and ought to be, totally dissolved." But before Congress would pass Lee's resolution, it had appointed the drafting committee to prepare a justification for independence.

Conscious that he was addressing not just the people of England and America but the whole civilized world, Jefferson began his justification with a lofty statement of purpose:

When, in the course of human events, it becomes necessary for one people to dissolve the political bands which have connected them with one another, and to assume among the powers of the earth the separate and equal station to which the laws of nature and of nature's God entitle them, a decent respect to the opinions of mankind requires that they should declare the causes which impel them to the separation.

There is nothing of the passionate rebel in this statement; indeed Jefferson would have denied that the colonists were rebels at all. On the contrary, they were a free people maintaining long-established rights against a usurping king.

Jefferson was writing with one eye on France, from whom it was essential that the colonists should get supplies if they were to make good their assertion of independence. For if the colonists seemed to be rebelling against rightful authority, no state in Europe would deal with them. Jefferson therefore had to persuade readers of the Declaration that the act of separation was legitimate—and more than that, he had to excite sympathy for a downtrodden people who had submitted for many years to the oppression of an unnatural tyrant. Sympathy for the downtrodden and indignation against the oppressor would, he hoped, culminate in active French support of the American cause. While it was too much to expect a king of France to smile upon the strange theory that "governments derive their just powers from the consent of the governed," it was possible that Louis XVI and his ministers might ignore what they did not like in the Declaration in view of the pleasing prospect of taking a hand in the disruption of the British Empire.

In the second paragraph of the Declaration, Jefferson set out to formulate a general political philosophy upon which to rest his case:

We hold these truths to be self-evident: that all men are created equal; that they are endowed by their Creator with certain inalienable rights; that among these are life, liberty, and the pursuit of happiness; that to secure these rights, governments are instituted among men, deriving their just powers from the consent of the governed; that whenever any form of government becomes destructive of those ends, it is the right of the people to alter or to abolish it, and to institute new government, laying its foundations on such principles, and organizing its powers in such form, as to them shall seem most likely to effect their safety and happiness.

The reader of the Declaration of Independence must even now be on guard against the haunting cadences with which Jefferson beguiled his readers. The truths that he called self-evident were not self-evident at all, either to his contemporaries or to later generations. As for the notion that all men are created equal, posterity is still wondering just what Jefferson meant by those words. Certainly men are equal in the eyes of God and in the eyes of English common law, but in every other way they are obviously and distressingly unequal. Even assuming that Jefferson did not include Negroes as men, he would have done better to have adopted the phrase used by his friend George Mason in the Virginia Bill of Rights—"all men are born equally free."

Yet, while it is easy to cavil over certain statements in the Declaration, we must remember that Jefferson was inspired by an ideal that he believed could be attained, for the first time in history, by the people for whom he was speaking. He was trying to harmonize the conduct of human affairs with what he believed to be the laws of the moral universe. However, like all great statesmen he was at the same time a shrewd, practical politician. The Declaration must also be regarded in another light, therefore, as a propaganda document whose purpose was to invigorate the rebellion. Its utterances must be viewed not only as a noble affirmation of the rights of man, but also as a political platform. Taken together they represented an ideal to which the writer and his party aspired.

Having affirmed the right of revolution under certain conditions, and having set forth the theory upon which the colonies would base their republican government, Jefferson moved from the abstract to a specific justification for exercising the rights enumerated in the first part of the document. Namely, he set forth a long list of grievances—not against Parliament, as might have been expected, since the dispute between the colonies and the mother country had

Above The Boston Massacre. This incident was exaggerated to arouse the colonists' discontent.

Below The attack on Bunker Hill and the burning of Charlestown in 1775.

The Declaration of Independence, signed by delegates from the thirteen colonies.

A satire on the Boston Port Act of 1773, by which the port of Boston was closed as a result of the Boston Tea Party: in the picture Lord North pours tea into the mouth of America.

always centered on the question of parliamentary authority—but against the King. The reason for transposing the odium from Parliament to the King was that Congress had decided that Parliament was the legislative body only of Great Britain.

Jefferson cited the King's interference with representative government in the colonies, the harshness with which he administered colonial affairs, his restrictions on civil rights, his stationing of troops in the colonies and his restrictive tax and trade policies. The list also included some grievances that were not very serious, and others that were untrue—in particular the charge that George III had encouraged the slave trade against the wishes of the colonies.

Congress was only too happy to blame King George for every sin in the calendar, but considering that the slave trade was carried on by New England shipowners and supported by Southern purchasers, it would have seemed better not to mention it in the Declaration. John Adams, who acted as Jefferson's spokesman on the floor of Congress, fought hard for the retention of the passage on slavery, but Congress decided against him and the offending passage was struck out. The word "slavery" therefore does not occur in the final text. There was perhaps an indirect reference to it in the charge that the King had deliberately fomented domestic insurrection in America—a charge that might have been taken as referring either to Indians or to Negroes. To have been more specific would have been embarrassing. Slavery was not a topic to be discussed in a document whose keynote was human freedom.

It was especially curious that Jefferson had inserted the section on slavery in light of his own attitude toward the institution. He never denied that slavery was a great evil, as harmful to the white man as to the Negro, but there was a vein of complacent optimism in Jefferson that allowed him to think that slavery would die a natural death. It was already dying out in the North, and in God's good time it would disappear in the Southern states as well. That he owned from one hundred to two hundred slaves, while at the same time maintaining as a self-evident truth that all men are created equal, does not seem to have disturbed him. He was a kind master, and his slaves were devoted to him, which may explain why he was so unconcerned by the equivocal role he continued to play, from July 4, 1776, to the day of his death exactly fifty years later, as a slaveholding devotee of freedom.

The debate in Congress over the provisions of the Declaration was an agonizing ordeal for the author. His committee had been very complimentary; they made only a few changes, which Jefferson promptly incorporated into a new draft. But the other members of Congress were not so easily satisfied. They cut out a quarter of what he had written, altered about two dozen words, and made two insertions in the peroration—references to a "Supreme Judge" and a "Divine Providence." Jefferson had already mentioned the Deity twice, but Congress wanted God in the peroration as well.

Lee's resolution of independence was approved on July 2, but the debate over the wording of the Declaration lasted another two days. Jefferson himself said nothing—he was busy making notes on the weather and on his current expenses. On July 3, the temperature was 76 degrees Fahrenheit—not a hot afternoon for Philadelphia in July. On that same day Jefferson spent 103 shillings, most of which went toward a thermometer. He also bought seven pairs of women's gloves and gave one shilling and sixpence "in charity." On the evening of July 4, the debate was closed, and all the members present with the exception of John Dickinson of Pennsylvania signed the Declaration. The thirteen colonies now became thirteen independent states.

Jefferson had succeeded in imparting a quality of timelessness and universality to what might otherwise have been merely a national document. His colleagues in Congress sensed they were doing far more than repudiating a king: they were founding a new order of society that had as its cornerstone the rights of free individuals. Jefferson had based his ideal of government on the philosophy of natural rights. According to that philosophy, man originally lived in a state of nature without benefit of civil authority. Possessing the right of life, liberty, property, and the pursuit of happiness, each man enforced those rights as best he could. Since the strong often took advantage of the weak, the time came when men were glad to surrender the state of nature for the civil state. In other words they acknowledged their inability to enforce their natural rights themselves, but in so doing they did not surrender them to anybody else. Those precious rights, frequently identified with God's will, no ruler could take from them. Implicit in this contract theory of the origins of civil authority were the doctrines of the consent of the governed and the right of revolution.

American colonists maintained that their philosophy was part of their inheritance, that it had come down to them in the writings of John Milton and John Locke. So obvious was that line of reasoning to the Founding Fathers that John Adams, who as he grew older was sometimes irritated by the eulogies that Fourth of July orators lavished on Jefferson, complained that there was not an idea in the Declaration "but what had been hackneyed in Congress for two years before." Jefferson did not deny it. He was not aiming at originality of principle or sentiment. The essential thing, he said, was "to place before mankind the common sense of the subject in terms so plain and firm as to command their assent, and to justify ourselves in the independent stand we are compelled to take."

Above A notice calling a meeting which resulted in the famous Boston Tea Party, when all the tea aboard the East India Company tea ships was dumped into Boston harbor.

Below Thomas Paine, author of *The Rights of Man*. In 1774 he went to America and took up the cause of the colonists.

Left Messengers ride through the thirteen states in July, 1776, reading the Declaration of Independence to the colonists.

John Adams, delegate from Massachusetts, appointed a member of the committee to draft the Declaration of Independence.

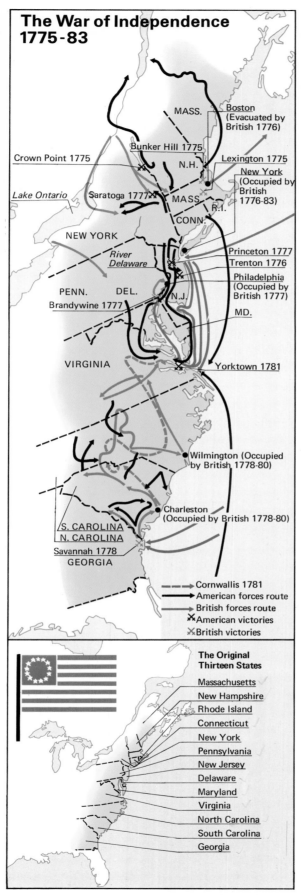

The War of Independence 1775-83

Boston (Evacuated by British 1776)

MASS.

Crown Point 1775

Bunker Hill 1775

Lexington 1775

N.H.

New York (Occupied by British 1776-83)

Lake Ontario

Saratoga 1777

MASS.

R.I.

CONN.

NEW YORK

River Delaware

Princeton 1777

Trenton 1776

Philadelphia (Occupied by British 1777)

PENN.   DEL.

N.J.

Brandywine 1777

MD.

VIRGINIA

Yorktown 1781

Wilmington (Occupied by British 1778-80)

Charleston (Occupied by British 1778-80)

S. CAROLINA

N. CAROLINA

Savannah 1778

GEORGIA

→ Cornwallis 1781
→ American forces route
→ British forces route
✗ American victories
✗ British victories

The Original Thirteen States

Massachusetts
New Hampshire
Rhode Island
Connecticut
New York
Pennsylvania
New Jersey
Delaware
Maryland
Virginia
North Carolina
South Carolina
Georgia

While Jefferson was right in insisting that the chief merit of the Declaration lay in its expression of commonly shared beliefs, both he and John Adams were wrong in assuming that the Declaration did nothing more than state what everyone was thinking, in the tone and spirit called for by the occasion. Even those who agreed with Jefferson—and there were many who did not—must have been aware that the truths he proclaimed as self-evident were far from being as axiomatic as he supposed. In substituting "life, liberty, and the pursuit of happiness" for the familiar formula, "life, liberty, and property," he made a significant departure from John Locke and all the other philosophers from whom he is said to have borrowed. No other state paper had ever suggested that one of the essential functions of government is to make men happy, or that one of man's natural rights is the pursuit of happiness. That was indeed a revolutionary doctrine.

It may be argued that the "pursuit of happiness," whatever it may be meant to include, is already implicit in "liberty." If a man is secure in life and liberty he can pursue anything he pleases. To many of Jefferson's contemporaries, the pursuit of happiness may well have seemed too cheap a thing to mention in a proclamation of human rights. As Aldous Huxley once put it, "happiness is like coke—something you get as a by-product in the process of making something else." Evidently Jefferson did not think of happiness as a by-product, but whether we agree with him or not, there is no question but that in specifying the pursuit of happiness as one of man's inalienable rights he launched America on uncharted seas. Today young people, not only in America but all over the world, are taking Jefferson's dictum more seriously than he may have intended.

In at least one other respect the Declaration was startlingly original, not in what it said but in what it omitted. It made no mention of the rights of British subjects. This was a significant omission, since throughout the entire controversy between the colonies and the mother country, beginning with the imposition of the Stamp Tax in 1764, those rights had been the mainstay of the American case. "No taxation without representation"; Parliament had no right to tax British subjects without their consent. While his colleagues were still fighting it out along that line, Jefferson had shifted his ground. In his diatribe against George III he pointed out that the King had committed a worse crime than violating the rights of his subjects. He had violated the rights of man. Jefferson was now appealing to a higher court. Mankind in general might not be vitally interested in a controversy between Great Britain and her colonies involving intricate questions of constitutional law. There must be a more inflammable issue than that, and it was part of Jefferson's genius to identify it and present it as he did.

Possibly he was influenced by Thomas Paine, an Englishman recently arrived in America who had taken up the cause of the colonists with all the ardor of a convert. In his pamphlet *Common Sense*, Paine had pointed out that "the cause of America is in a

great measure the cause of all mankind." Many were won over by his eloquence, but Paine was in many ways a rabble-rouser, while Jefferson, of course, was not.

The argument that Jefferson made before the bar of world opinion has been attacked again and again, either in anger or contempt, by friends as well as enemies of the American Revolution. The critics have in general agreed with Rufus Choate, one of the great lawyer-statesmen of the nineteenth century, that the famous Declaration was after all nothing but a series of "glittering generalities." Jefferson's champions have been no less insistent and no less vocal than his critics. Perhaps the most famous is Abraham Lincoln. In 1861, on his way to Washington to take up the Presidency, Lincoln said:

I have never had a feeling politically that did not spring from the sentiments embodied in the Declaration of Independence. . . . Something in that Declaration giving liberty, not only to the people of this country, but hope for the world for all future time. . . . And that all should have an equal chance.

In those words, spoken in Independence Hall, Philadelphia, where the Declaration was signed, Lincoln suggests why it is that all leaders of nationalistic movements and all champions of liberal reform inevitably hark back to the Declaration of Independence. To them it stands for hope:

"till hope creates
From its own wreck the thing it contemplates."

Jefferson may have been overoptimistic when, in his old age, he wrote to John Adams that "the flames kindled on the fourth of July, 1776, have spread over too much of the globe to be extinguished by the feeble engines of despotism; on the contrary, they will consume those engines and all who work them. . . ." Unfortunately, the "engines of despotism" and those who work them have not yet been consumed, but wherever they still exist, and wherever they may appear in the future, they will always have to withstand the challenge of Jefferson's devastating rhetoric.

ARNOLD WHITRIDGE

The Battle of Yorktown, 1781. Britain's defeat at this battle made it finally clear that she must accept America's independence.

All Europe trembles as revolutionary

The American Revolution

Apart from the British success in taking New York the advantage in the war during 1776 lay mainly with the Americans. The extra confidence given to the rebels by the Declaration of Independence combined with military victory over Britain's German mercenaries at Trenton to reduce British morale. The following year did nothing to restore Britain's lost self-confidence; although the British general Sir William Howe (1729–1814) defeated Nathanael Greene (1742–86) at Brandywine and Washington at Germantown, and also captured Philadelphia and secured control of Delaware, a second British army under John Burgoyne (1722–92) was less successful, and after two defeats at Bemis Heights was forced to surrender at Saratoga. Britain's enemies were quick to take advantage of the war. A force of French volunteers under the nineteen-year-old Marquis de Lafayette (1757–1834) arrived in America.

Inevitably the war between Britain and her American colonies had been welcomed in France. Louis XVI's foreign minister, Charles Gravier Vergennes (1717–87), hoped that the struggle would reverse the advantages that England had gained from the French and Indian War and provide a fitting retort to the Treaty of Paris. By the time that Burgoyne surrendered to General Horatio Gates (c. 1728–1806) on October 17, 1777, the French were already supplying the Americans with muskets and gunpowder. The following

Burgoyne surrendering to General Horatio Gates at Saratoga. By the time of his surrender France was supplying America with arms.

year France signed an offensive and defensive alliance with the Americans; once again Britain and France found themselves at war.

The British fared better over the next two years. Much of the south was recaptured, partly because of the support of the many loyalists in Georgia and South Carolina. But the needs of the British army in the north, where the fighting was going less well, meant that the British commander in the south, General Lord Cornwallis (1738–1805), was left with only four thousand men. Although he had little difficulty in dealing with the imperfectly-trained volunteers in pitched battle, as at Camden in 1780 and Guildford Courthouse and Eutaw in 1781, he was constantly harried by guerrilla action. After being trapped at Yorktown between Washington's larger forces on land and a French fleet at sea, he surrendered.

The widening war

The surrender of Cornwallis signaled the end of British hopes in the thirteen colonies. But elsewhere the war continued. The League of Armed Neutrality—established in 1780 to prevent British ships from searching neutral vessels for contra-

Nelson at the Battle of Cape St. Vincent, 1797.

band of war—eventually included Russia, Sweden, Austria, Prussia, Denmark, Spain and Holland, as well as France. And of those powers Spain and Holland actively joined in the hostilities against their traditional rival. Spain declared war on England in June, 1779, (after obtaining guarantees of French assistance in recovering Gibraltar and Florida) and immediately laid siege to Gibraltar. England declared war in November, 1780, in a vain attempt to prevent Spain from joining the League.

The British navy—faced with the problem of relieving Gibraltar, supplying the army in America, fighting the French in the West Indies and guarding the Channel—was strained to the limits of its considerable resources. The Caribbean island of St. Vincent fell to the French on June 20, 1779, (two days after Spain declared war on England) and Grenada capitulated a fortnight later. In January, 1780, Admiral George Rodney (1719–92) defeated a Spanish squadron off Cape St. Vincent, temporarily relieving Gibraltar and offering the British some respite. But later that year the British fought three indecisive naval engagements with the French in the West Indies, and in 1781 the French under the Marquis de Grasse-Tilly (1722–88) captured Tobago. A French fleet commanded by Admiral Pierre André de Suffren St. Tropez prevented England from seizing the Dutch post at the Cape of Good Hope, and later captured a Ceylonese port that the Dutch had only shortly before surrendered to the British. In July, 1781, the Spaniards captured Pensacola in Florida.

By February, 1782, the British seemed to be almost on the verge of collapse. The Spanish followed up their victory in Florida by capturing Minorca on February 5, and a week later the French captured the island of St. Christopher in the West Indies. On February 22, a parliamentary motion, harshly critical of the continuing war in America, was defeated by only one vote—and a month later the Prime Minister, Lord North, handed in his resignation.

Back from disaster

Late in 1782, however, the tide began to turn. Admiral Rodney defeated the French in the Battle of The Saints, April 12, captured

The Battle of Tobago (1781), won by the French.

excitement mounts

de Grasse and saved the West Indies. Seven months later, Admiral Lord Howe (1726–99) relieved Gibraltar. Within a year, Benjamin Franklin (1706–90), the American minister in Paris, John Jay (1745–1829), who was to become Secretary for Foreign Affairs in 1784, and John Adams (1735–1826), the future President of the United

Signing the preliminary articles to the Peace of Versailles, 1783.

States, were all in Paris to help negotiate a peace settlement.

By the Peace of Versailles signed in January, 1783, England recovered her West Indian possessions and was able to retain Gibraltar. France, while saving her trading posts agreed to abandon her other ambitions in India. In the West Indies she retrieved St. Lucia and retained Tobago. In Africa she gained Senegal and Gorée and acquired valuable fishing rights in Newfoundland. Spain regained Florida and Minorca. Holland, under the terms of a separate treaty, retrieved all her former possessions, including the Ceylonese port of Trincomalee, but in return granted the British the right of navigation among the Dutch spice islands.

In addition to the concessions made by Britain to her European enemies, the Treaty of Versailles recognized the independence of the American republic and attacked colonization of the American mainland. Sir William Petty, the Earl of Shelburne (1737–1805), whose position as England's Prime Minister had made him responsible for the negotiations, had been anxious to keep the newly liberated

American Republic within the English sphere of influence. Shelburne hoped to see Britain and America become partners in Atlantic commerce, with America assuming the expensive responsibilities of governing North America and Britain becoming the accepted link between America and the European Continent. He had consequently striven to obtain the goodwill of the Americans and to provide them with an extensive market for British goods by conceding all the territory they wanted. Such largesse angered the Prime Minister's critics, who entirely failed to understand its far-reaching economic implications. Shelburne countered their attacks by pointing to the relatively small concessions that he had made to England's other enemies at the end of the recent war—and considering the country's fortunes in that war and the exhausted state in which it had left her, these concessions did indeed seem slight.

Revolution

The American Revolution served as an example for revolutionary ideas in Europe, but it had little in common with its French counterpart. The American Revolution was primarily the result of the inadequately formulated relationship between the British government and the colonies. In Europe the problems of social and economic discontent went far deeper, and were less susceptible to simple solutions; no European government had a dual system of control such as the American colonies, with their uneasy relationship between locally elected legislatures and officials nominated by the British government.

That the American Revolution cannot be seen in the same terms as the French and other European revolutions is shown by the fact that America itself was not immune from revolution. In 1786 a Continental Army veteran, Daniel Shays (1747–1825), led a rebellion against the United States government. Shays' Rebellion found widespread support among the people of Massachusetts, who were dismayed by the evident incapacity of both the state and federal governments to deal with the economic ills of the territory and to lessen the crippling burden of taxation. In September, Shays, with roughly a thousand followers,

converged on Springfield to prevent the Supreme Court from convening, and the insurrection was only quelled when the governor raised a force of 4,400 men. Washington refused to allow the rebels to be executed, calling to mind "the dangers of entirely alienating the affections of a people from a government."

The years before the French Revolution of 1789 were years of frequent risings throughout Europe. In 1775 there was a serious peasant uprising in Bohemia. In 1780 London experienced the worst riots in English history when Lord George Gordon (1751–93), the unbalanced and vehemently Protestant son of the Duke of Gordon, led an angry mob of some 50,000 men to the House of Commons to protest against a recently passed act that provided some minor relief to Roman Catholics. In several days of wild rioting at least seven hundred people lost their lives, and the damage done to property was never calculated. Many of the targets of the mob's fury were Irish immigrants, but the outbreak was essentially a revolt of the poor against authority, and it is possible to detect in the riots the first symptoms of the quasi-revolutionary movement that was to end the political system of George III.

Nor were other apparently stable European countries immune from trouble. In Holland the objects of resentment were the weak and unpopular Prince of Orange and his wife, the intensely disliked Frederika Wilhelmina of Prussia. Holland's commerce, which had in any case been steadily declining,

had been further weakened by the war against England, and the peace that followed greatly strengthened the influence of the anti-Orange or Patriot Party. The insulting attitude of the Patriot Party toward the Prince and Princess, whose position by 1787 had become intolerable, induced the Princess' uncle the King of Prussia to invade Holland, to place William V firmly back on the throne and to dissolve the Patriot Party.

There was trouble, too, to the south of Holland, in the Austrian Netherlands, where there was passionate opposition to the Austrian Emperor's high-handed attempts to reform the Church and the administration without reference to the susceptibilities of the Flemings and the Walloons, and to his contempt for the "antedeluvian rubbish" of the people's treasured rights and privileges. In 1787 their feelings erupted into violent riots that forced the Emperor to give way. In 1789, Belgium declared that it was independent of Austria, a move that brought immediate international support. But because of the difficulties caused by the French Revolution, Belgium's real independence was to be delayed.

Similarly in Sweden there were upheavals in 1789 because Gustavus III, who was becoming increasingly autocratic, tried to establish a new constitution by the Act of Unity and Security (February 17, 1789) thus granting to himself almost absolute powers.

But it was in France in the summer of 1789 that the revolution for which all Europe had been waiting began.

Riots outside London's Newgate prison.

123

"Liberté, Egalité, Fraternité"

In the decades following its conversion into a prison, the crenelated confines of the Bastille served the political whims of four French kings. In the process, the fourteenth-century fortress became the detested symbol of France's arrogant and arbitrary autocracy. Its unfortunate inmates were arrested on lettres de cachet *issued by the King, spirited through the streets of Paris in closed carriages and incarcerated without trial. Not illogically, the ancient fortress became the focal point of anti-royalist ire during the popular risings of July, 1789—and when the fort's entire garrison surrendered to a mob of armed Parisians on July 14, the profound weakness of Louis XVI's government was at last revealed. The King had lost the support of his army—which would not fire upon the citizens—and from that moment, both he and his dynasty were doomed.*

Detail of *Marie-Antoinette à la rose*, by Marie Vigée Lebrun.

Opposite The attack on the Bastille. The prison was thought of as the main bastion of injustice.

Sunday, July 12, 1789. The best of summer was still to come. The day was fine but showery with a hint of coolness in the air. In Paris huge crowds were making their way to the bridges of the Seine. People were saying that Necker—who had been the commoners' favorite minister from the time he persuaded Louis XVI to double the number of deputies representing the Third Estate in the Estates-General—had been dismissed. What was going to happen next? Already there was a shortage of corn and the price of bread was higher than it had ever been within living memory. Did the enemies of the people—the aristocrats—want to starve French citizens in order to force them to give in? Or was the state on the verge of bankruptcy? Would the Estates-General, which had been convened on May 5, be dissolved before it even had a chance to debate the situation?

Instinctively, the crowd hurried to the Palais-Royal, a favorite meeting place for eighteenth-century Parisians. Inside, in the gardens, there were so many people crushed together that it was almost impossible to move. Self-appointed orators were standing on the tables, haranguing the crowds with inflammatory speeches. In order to hear the speakers, some of the onlookers had perched themselves precariously on the branches of chestnut trees.

In spite of his stammer, one particular orator seemed to be holding the attention of the crowd, and he had attracted a large group of interested listeners:

Do you realize that, although the Nation demanded that Necker should be kept on as a minister, they threw him out all the same! How much more insolently can they defy our wishes? They will stop at nothing after such behavior! Who knows whether they may not even be planning, arranging, at this very moment, a new Saint Bartholomew's Eve for all patriotic citizens! To arms! Let us all wear the green cockade, the symbol of hope. No doubt, the wretched police are present among us here! Well, let them watch me, listen to me,

observe me carefully, for it is I who proudly urge my brothers to seek their liberty!

At this point, the orator—an unemployed lawyer named Camille Desmoulins whose name was being whispered by everyone in the crowd—drew a pistol from his pocket and shouted: "At least, they will never take me alive! I shall die a glorious death! My one fear is to see France become enslaved!"

Chanting "To arms, to arms!" the crowd swarmed out of the Palais-Royal. A huge procession surged through the streets of Paris to the theaters, and demonstrators went inside and stopped the performances. Joined by the theater audiences, the crowd pressed on to the Musée Curtius, where waxwork figures of the most famous personalities of the age were exhibited. Some of the demonstrators went inside, only to emerge shortly afterward carrying the busts of Necker and the Duke of Orleans.

They continued on to the Tuileries gardens, where an enormous, frenzied crowd was shouting "Long live Necker!" and "To arms!" Suddenly there was pandemonium. People ran off in all directions, shouting that the "Royal Allemand" cavalry regiment had entered the gardens and was charging the crowd. At that moment it became obvious that if the people were to defend themselves, they had to be armed. It was rumored that a militia was to be formed, and that the district committees in Paris would be distributing arms and ammunition on the following day. The militia would be able to force the King and his evil counselors to recall Necker.

Very early the next morning, Jean-Baptiste Humbert—a watchmaker who eventually recorded his experiences during the turbulent days of July, 1789—went to his district committee headquarters in the parish of Saint-André-des-Arts, only to find that the group had already distributed the small quantity of firearms at its disposal. Nevertheless, Jean-Baptiste volunteered to join the citizens' militia

The opening of the Estates-General in 1789. Popular feeling was expressed at the Assembly that led to outbreaks of revolt.

that was being formed. The "electors"—men chosen by each district assembly to elect the deputies representing Paris in the Estates-General—had decided that every district of the city should raise two hundred men. According to their plan, a total force of 12,000 men could be recruited from the sixty districts of Paris. Those men were badly needed, for news had just come that during the previous night the majority of the customs posts at the gateways to the city had been pillaged and burned down.

It was vital to prevent any repetition of such scenes, and the unarmed watchmaker spent the whole day patrolling the streets of his district. In the evening, the local committee received orders to recruit an additional six hundred men. The anxious electors had decided that the citizens' militia must be increased to 48,000 men. But how were they going to arm all these volunteers? Where could they find the firearms and ammunition?

When daybreak came at last, Humbert and the other exhausted members of his patrol returned to the Assembly. After a short rest, Humbert rose and went out into the street, where he learned that firearms were being distributed at the Invalides. He

immediately rushed off to find Monsieur Poirier, the commander of the local militia, and asked him to lead the members of his group to the Invalides. Poirier, pestered with thousands of questions, seemed in no hurry to leave. Impatiently, Humbert seized him by the arm and, followed by five or six other citizens, escorted the reluctant commander to the Invalides.

An enormous crowd had collected on the parade ground in front of the building, and it proved impossible to remain together. Humbert soon found himself separated from his companions, and he entered the huge building by himself. Following the surging crowd through the corridors, he eventually reached the cellars where the weapons and ammunition were stored. As he gained the bottom of the staircase, Humbert caught sight of a man holding two muskets. He seized one of them and turned to the stairs—only to find that it was impossible to move. The crowd had become so dense that anyone trying to climb up the stairs was pushed down again. It became almost impossible to breathe and terrible shrieks and cries could be heard above the tumult. In desperation, some of those who had obtained

A revolutionary committee meeting during the Terror. Until Napoleon restored firm central government, France was in danger of sliding into anarchy.

muskets advanced with fixed bayonets on the others, forcing those who still had no arms to clear a passage.

Humbert lost sight of his companions in the chaos. He left the Invalides on his own and returned to the Hôtel de Ville, where powder was purportedly being dispensed to the citizens. The watchmaker succeeded in obtaining a quarter of a pound of powder but no musket balls. The clock struck three. Suddenly, the sound of shooting was heard coming from an easterly direction. "They must be fighting at the Bastille," someone said. Humbert rushed into a nearby grocer's shop and bought some little nails, which he planned to use as projectiles in his musket. As he emerged from the shop, a citizen announced that the Hôtel de Ville had finally received a supply of ammunition. Humbert therefore turned back, and was given six pellets of buckshot. Equipped with ammunition, he hurried off to the Bastille.

It was half-past three by the time that Humbert arrived. The outer drawbridge had already been pulled down by the attackers, who were now trying to drag two cannon into the outer courtyard. Humbert gave them a hand and soon found himself in the front of the crowd. Cannon were placed in position at the main gate of the fortress, the drawbridge was raised and the firing began. Humbert fired six rounds of ammunition. As he did so, a hand appeared through a small oval opening on one side of the gate, waving a piece of paper. One of the citizens fetched a wooden beam from a nearby carpenter and placed it across the moat. A man began to walk across the plank but lost his balance and fell. Another man followed him, grasped the paper and read it out loud: "We have about twenty thousand pounds of gunpowder, and we intend to blow up the garrison and the whole district if you do not capitulate. The Bastille, 5 p.m., July 14, 1789."

The note, which was signed by de Launay, the commander of the fortress, did not produce the desired effect. On the contrary, it provoked unanimous shouts of "Lower the drawbridges! We shall never give in!" The citizens began to reload the cannon, and they were on the point of firing when the drawbridge was suddenly lowered. (Later on it was learned that the Invalides soldiers, who formed part of the garrison in the Bastille, had forced the commander to open the gates.) The crowd poured into the fortress; Humbert was in the vanguard. Nine hundred and fifty-four craftsmen, shopkeepers and common citizens, all of whom lived in Paris but many of whom had come from the provinces, earned themselves the title of "conquerors of the Bastille."

The building of the Bastille had been started in 1370, during the reign of Charles V. By the seventeenth century, the fortress had lost most of its importance as a citadel of defense, and Cardinal Richelieu, the chief minister of Louis XIII, had converted it into a prison. The Bastille was no ordinary

The fall of the Bastille on July 14, 1789. The event was seen by many as a symbol of liberty.

The trial of Marie-Antoinette. Although her life had estranged her from the people, many were impressed by her courage during the trial.

prison, however—it was a state prison. The old fort's unfortunate inmates were not being held for crimes or offenses committed under the common law. They had—without exception—been summarily arrested on *lettres de cachet*—in other words, at the direct and arbitrary order of the King.

In Richelieu's time the Bastille housed as many as fifty-three prisoners, but the number of arrests made by *lettres de cachet* had decreased, and under the reign of Louis XVI the prison held an average of only sixteen prisoners a year. Indeed, on July 14, 1789, the day the Bastille was captured, the victorious citizens found only seven prisoners inside. Moreover, these prisoners had a fairly easy time of it. A prisoner with private means was allowed to send for his own furniture, servants and meals. Poorer prisoners received enough money to provide themselves with the necessities of life. In the eighteenth century the cells were furnished by the state, although prisoners were allowed to add their own personal articles. The food, supplied by the prison, was good, and on occasions prisoners were invited to dine with the warden. It is true that there were some damp, unhealthy dun-geons underground—as well as prison cells exposed to bitter cold in winter and the heat of summer, located at the top of the towers of the fortress—but none of them had been used since 1776.

Nevertheless, the Bastille remained an object of great hatred. It symbolized the absolutist authority of the King in its most despotic form. Moreover, its operation was shrouded in secrecy. Prisoners were arrested clandestinely and driven to the Bastille in closed carriages. The soldiers on guard duty were obliged to stand with their faces to the wall, and the prison warders were forbidden to have any conversation whatsoever with the prisoners. Moreover, the latter were not interrogated when they were arrested and never knew how long they were going to be imprisoned in the Bastille. They might be released several weeks, several months or even several years after they were arrested, upon receipt of another *lettre de cachet* from the King.

By the end of the eighteenth century, most of the prisoners in the Bastille were writers who had publicly denounced various corrupt practices of the regime. Voltaire spent a year in the Bastille in 1717–18, and was incarcerated for another twelve days in 1726. The Abbé Morellet, one of the leaders of the *Parti Philosophique*, was imprisoned for six weeks in 1760. The journalist Linguet remained there from 1780 to 1782, and during that time he wrote *Mémoires sur la Bastille*, which he published upon his release from prison. For those who believed in free speech, free thinking and free writing, therefore, the Bastille represented everything that was shameful in the *ancien régime*.

Those reasons do not fully explain why the storming of the Bastille should have brought about the capitulation of the monarchy and the victory of the French Revolution. For an explanation of why the government toppled, one must examine a remarkable result of the capture of the old fort. The fall of the Bastille served to illustrate—better than any other event during that stormy period—a fact that was both obvious and almost incredible: the army did not want to fight against the revolutionaries. On June 24, two companies of *Gardes Françaises* had refused to go on duty. They were followed on June 28 by other companies of soldiers, who laid down their firearms and ammunition and joined the people assembled in the Palais-Royal, assuring the crowds of citizens that they would never fight against the Parisians. Fourteen grenadiers, believed to be the ringleaders, were put in prison, only to be released by the demonstrators. Seventy-five members of the Swiss regiment of Salis-Samade deserted to the citizens' side during the first fortnight in July.

The army's reluctance to fight was graphically demonstrated on the morning of July 14, when the crowd attacked the Invalides and seized the 40,000 muskets that were stored there. Five thousand well-armed soldiers were encamped some four hundred yards from the Invalides at the time. Their commander, the Swiss general Besenval, intended to defend the Invalides. In fact, as soon as he received word that the rioters had arrived, he sent for his

The march to Versailles in October, 1789. Officers of the Royal Guard who tried to prevent the march were decapitated and their heads carried on pikes by the marchers.

Louis XVI is separated from his family. The royal family were accused of conspiring with foreign countries against the French people.

corps commanders—who informed the general that they could not rely on the cooperation of their men. According to one witness, the Count of Salmour, "from that moment onwards, the generals were agreed that it was impossible to subdue Paris and that the only prudent course of action was to withdraw." Thus, when de Launay surrendered the Bastille, he did so for two reasons: first, because the Swiss soldiers who garrisoned the Bastille refused to fight, and second, because he knew that he could expect no help from the army outside the fortress. In truth, the fall of the Bastille was due far more to the defection of the troops stationed in Paris than to the enthusiasm and bravery of the attackers. If the 30,000 troops that Louis XVI had concentrated in and around the capital had made the slightest attempt to stop the citizens from attacking, the Bastille would never have been taken. But the defection of the soldiers and their fraternization with the revolutionaries was a clear indication that they too were infected with revolutionary zeal. From that day on, the French monarchy, deserted by its defenders, had no choice but to capitulate.

The fall of the Bastille served as the perfect symbol of royal surrender. The Duke of Dorset, British ambassador to Paris, wrote to the British foreign secretary on July 16: "So, My Lord, the greatest revolution ever known in the history of mankind has just taken place and, relatively speaking, taking into consideration the results as a whole, it has cost very little in the way of bloodshed. At this moment we can consider France as a free country, the King as a monarch whose powers are restricted and the nobles as being reduced to the level of the rest of the nation." In explaining the situation to President Washington, Gouverneur Morris, the new United States ambassador to Paris, noted: "You may now consider the revolution to be over since the authority of the King and the nobles has been utterly destroyed."

The consequences of the fall of the Bastille soon made themselves felt. On July 17, Louis XVI visited Paris in person and was forced to recognize the Permanent Committee, or new revolutionary muni-cipal council, as well as the citizens' militia known as the National Guard. Before July 14, revolutionary municipal councils and citizens' militias had been formed in some of the provincial towns of France. After the fall of the Bastille, this revolutionary movement spread like wildfire. In the country, the peasants attacked the chateaux and destroyed the ancient charters that recorded the peasants' feudal obligations to their masters. In the towns, the bourgeois seized power from the King's representatives and formed National Guard companies to defend themselves. In order to keep the people calm and under control, the Estates-General, which had become the constituent national assembly, proclaimed the abolition of the "feudal regime." On August 26 they published a "Declaration of the Rights of Man and of the Citizen" that laid the foundations for the new regime: liberty, equality and the sanctity of property.

The movement grew in violence, and soon reached the point of no return. On October 5 the citizens of Paris, fearing fresh counterrevolutionary action on the part of the King, marched on Versailles and took Louis XVI and his family prisoner. The constituent assembly gave France a new constitution and new institutions, based on the rational ideas and beliefs that the French *philosophes* had been developing since the beginning of the century.

The revolutionary fervor soon spread to other countries, including the United States, Great Britain, the Netherlands, Germany, Switzerland, Italy, Hungary and Poland. At the same time, the forces of reaction and conservatism began to organize a counterrevolutionary movement. The clash between revolution and counterrevolution proved disastrous for Europe. From April 20, 1792, onward, that clash took the form of an international war—one that was to last for twenty-three years almost without a break. The counterrevolution's apparent triumph at Waterloo in 1815 proved to be an illusion. In reality, revolutionary ideas, principles and institutions had taken firm root not only in France but in all Europe, and in North, Central and South America.

JACQUES GODECHOT

129

France

The arrest of the King left the Paris mob in control of government in France. But the mob was not united in its ideas. Royalist supporters, realizing that the King was a puppet in the hands of the mob, fled abroad, where they found support for their counterrevolutionary views from governments that were already terrified that they would be overtaken by the fate of the Bourbons.

Meanwhile the National Assembly set about reforming French institutions; Church property was nationalized and monasteries suppressed, new administrative districts were established in the country (although they were not properly financed for their work) and the municipality of Paris was reorganized. The main task that the Assembly set itself was, however, to draw up a written constitution, which was passed in 1791. Its attempt to create a constitutional monarchy failed; a contemporary observed: "The constitution was a veritable monster: there was too much republic for a monarchy and too much monarchy for a republic." In reality the constitution was highly conservative, making no attacks on the property rights of the rich and enfranchising only a minority of male citizens.

The relations between revolutionary France and the other states of Europe were already poor. In 1791 Austria and Prussia—usually enemies—made a joint declaration at Pilnitz that they would intervene in French affairs in support of the King, and Gustavus III of Sweden saw himself as the leader of a European crusade to restore Louis XVI to his full powers. The papacy had been antagonized by the Civil Constitution of the Clergy in 1790, which gave the electorate the right to choose bishops and parish clergy. In 1791 Pope Pius VI (1717–99) condemned the Civil Constitution, and the French government annexed the huge papal possessions, Avignon and the Venaissin, that remained in the south of France, despite an energetic defense by the papal garrison. Corsica was also brought within the French kingdom and the small German enclaves in Alsace and Lorraine were simply treated as French territory.

France at war

France's lack of success in the wars of the eighteenth century had helped create an enormous feeling of resentment against the government of the *ancien régime* and jealousy of France's neighbors. Although there was little real danger from Austria, Prussia or Sweden—particularly after the assassination of Gustavus III in March, 1792—and none from England, where William Pitt the Younger (1759–1806) was busy pursuing a policy of peace and retrenchment, the declaration of Pilnitz helped to fan the flames of xenophobia. A militant group in the new Legislative Assembly, which replaced the National Assembly in 1791, found a leader in Jacques Pierre Brissot (1754–93), who demanded that France's neighbors expel the *émigré* nobles, and interpreted their refusal to do so as a threat to French independence.

One of Brissot's supporters advocated a true revolutionary war—"a war of peoples against kings."

In April, 1792, the Legislative Assembly, carried away by war fever, voted almost unanimously for a declaration of war against Austria. Three months later war was declared against Prussia too. At first the war went disastrously for the French. The army had been neglected as a result of the Revolution; a majority of army officers had either joined the *émigrés* or deserted, and the army was not equipped to fight a full-scale war. It was more by chance than by skill—an inexperienced French general refused to withdraw despite the probability that his lines of communications would be cut—that the Prussian army under the Duke of Brunswick (1735–1806) was forced to retreat from France. As a result the route to the Austrian Netherlands (Belgium), which was already in revolt against the Emperor, lay open. The Austrian army, largely made up of Belgians, showed little stomach for fighting. By December most of Belgium had been occupied, and it appeared that Brissot and the advocates of revolutionary war had been proved right; the people of Belgium had shown little loyalty to their Austrian ruler. Elsewhere, too, military failure turned into success. Nice and Savoy were occupied and the French army invaded Germany.

Economic and social difficulties

The early years of the Revolution had been aided by the confiscation of Church lands. The severe financial problems of the French government, which had been one of the major difficulties of the royal administration, were bypassed. Church and monastic lands provided a large revenue, and the sale of many Church estates offered—as a short-term measure—still more. Paper money—*assignats*—was introduced, and, in an attempt to prevent inflation, the old currency was gradually withdrawn. The attempt was unsuccessful and the *assignats* fell in value, but it gave the revolutionary government a valuable breathing space.

Far more dangerous than economic instability was the volatility of opinion among the Paris mob, which was easily swayed by capable demagogues whatever their stand. Within the Legislative Assembly

Cartoon by Gillray on the Parisians learning of Louis XVI's flight and (*below*) their joy at his arrest.

Jacques Pierre Brissot, French revolutionary leader and political writer.

of the monarchy—and condemns the King to death

The new paper money—*assignats*. The continued issue of *assignats* led to inflation.

Meeting in one of the political clubs established during the early years of the Revolution.

there were enormous differences on policy, and many members of the Assembly relied for support on one or other of the dozens of political clubs established during the early years of the Revolution. The clubs were not merely social or educational, but were organizations designed to influence the opinion of both the public and members of the Assembly. Most of the clubs were more radical than the Assembly, demanding a wider franchise and attacking property rights. About half the 745 members of the Assembly were moderate in their views, but among the rest of the members royalists outnumbered the supporters of the left-wing clubs. But despite their relatively small numbers and their own disagreements, it was the 136 "left-wingers," of whom the most effective were Brissot and Maximilien Robespierre (1758–94), who could rely on popular support.

The growth of republicanism

The incident that provided the republicans with the ammunition that they needed was the attempted flight of the King in June, 1791. Louis had found his position as a virtual prisoner of the revolutionaries increasingly difficult. He tried to join an army stationed at Metz on whose general he could depend. At the village of Varennes he and his family were recognized. They were escorted back to Paris by members of the National Guard. It immediately became clear that the country could be run without a king and that the loyalty of the royal family to the Revolution could

not be relied upon. Although the Assembly acquitted the King, there were riots in Paris, suppressed only with great difficulty by the National Guard. From that time on republican ideas won increasing popular support, at least in Paris. The Assembly, however, resolutely ignored popular demands for the deposition of the King.

In July, 1791, Robespierre won the leadership of the left, when, speaking at the Jacobin Club he gave an impassioned plea for the abolition of the monarchy and the election of a National Convention by universal suffrage. Two weeks later a Paris mob invaded the

Palace of the Tuileries, massacred the Swiss Guard, and imprisoned the King. The mob organized a Paris commune and the National Assembly agreed to Robespierre's suggestion for a National Convention and the suspension of the King's powers. The Convention, which met on September 20, 1792, was firmly republican in sympathy. Two days after the Convention opened France formally became a republic and a new revolutionary

calendar was adopted to show that the break with the past was complete. The Convention showed that its revolutionary sympathies were not confined to France; it offered assistance to all peoples who rose against their governments—Geneva promptly responded as her people overthrew their rulers and asked France for help. In France the Convention had decided to show its republican fervor by executing the King.

The Paris mob invading the Tuileries and massacring the Swiss Guard.

The Execution of Louis XVI

Captured while trying to flee France, and returned to Paris, Louis XVI and his family were imprisoned in the "Temple," virtually a walled town within Paris. There they awaited the outcome of the debates in the Convention between the moderate "Girondin" and the more fiery "Mountain" factions. In sealing the fate of the King, the Convention totally repudiated the past and established the sovereignty not of the King but of the nation.

On July 17, 1789, three days after the fall of the Bastille, King Louis XVI of France made his will and went from Versailles to Paris—to be bewildered by the warmth of the welcome that awaited him. Some men literally wept for joy at what they believed to be the true union of the King with his people and Louis, hailed as "The Father of the French, the King of a Free People," took and wore the tricolor in which the red and blue of Paris were wedded to the white of the House of Bourbon.

Two years later to the day, the capital was the scene of the "Massacre of the Champ de Mars." Flying from Paris toward the frontier on June 20, 1791, Louis and his family had been ignominiously recaptured at Varennes the next day, and republican agitation had since grown. On July 17, a considerable crowd assembled on the Champ de Mars to sign a petition demanding that the National Assembly should recognize the King's "crime" as an act of abdication, and then "convene a new constituent assembly to proceed in a truly national manner to the trial of the culprit and, above all, to his replacement and the organization of a new executive power." This petition being technically illegal, the municipal authorities attempted to disperse the crowd; the National Guard opened fire and some fifty people died.

As these events indicate, the early hope that the ancient monarchy of France might be happily reconciled with the Revolution had become increasingly remote. The absolutism of the old order had indeed been abandoned at an early stage by all but the most intransigent royalists, most of whom went into exile. Moreover Louis himself, essentially a well-meaning and kindly man, had willingly offered in 1789 to initiate extensive reforms in cooperation with a properly constituted assembly, and on various occasions during the next two years he had formally promised to honor and uphold the constitution that finally came into full effect in

September, 1791. Long before that, however, men had become deeply suspicious of his sincerity. Twice in 1789 it had seemed that Louis was about to use the army to crush the Revolution, and the "Flight to Varennes" in 1791 was commonly regarded as conclusive proof of the King's determination to reestablish his power by some combination of civil war and foreign intervention. More important, when war with Austria and Prussia broke out in 1792, the King's evident reluctance to approve and expedite emergency measures was seen as tantamount to treachery. As the danger of an invasion increased, many came to believe that the Tuileries Palace was both a center of counterrevolutionary activity and an enemy outpost in the heart of Paris. Had they known that the King had long been urging the other sovereigns of Europe to assemble forces great enough to overawe the revolutionaries, and that his Queen, Marie-Antoinette, had not hesitated to reveal French military plans to the enemy, they would have been angrier, but not greatly surprised.

This is not to say that Louis alone was at fault. As a king he undoubtedly had serious deficiencies, being naturally indolent and indecisive; but it could be argued that only a man of outstanding character and ability would have succeeded in keeping the Revolution within reasonable bounds. Confronted from 1789 with the claim that the sovereign authority of the nation superseded all existing laws and even the most sacred of traditional rights, Louis was quickly pushed into the position of defending particular groups against those who called themselves the exponents of the general will. As he wrote in a private letter dated August, 1789: "I will never consent to the spoliation of my clergy and of my nobility. I will not sanction decrees by which they are despoiled." In short, the King's very awareness of his responsibilities compelled him to oppose apparently progressive measures which were often essentially arbitrary; and it was the

Louis XVI and his son, while they were in prison.

Opposite The execution of Louis XVI. At the base of the painting are Louis' last words to his people: "I die innocent of the crimes of which I am accused. I have only desired the happiness of my people, and my last wishes are that Heaven may forgive them my death."

more unfortunate that the constitution he was compelled to accept deprived him of all independent authority, leaving him no real power save that of the veto. Finally alienated by the revolutionaries' drastic reorganization of the Church, which he and approximately half the clergy of France regarded as incompatible with their faith as Catholics, he naturally resorted to evasion, procrastination and even deceit.

Once war had been declared, such obstruction soon seemed intolerable. Most of the deputies clung to the constitution of 1791 until the last possible moment, alternately threatening the King and imploring him to show himself a true defender of the Revolution. To the more uncompromising, as to the militants who met in the Jacobin Club and the *sans-culottes* who spoke for the people in the streets, the issue was nevertheless sufficiently simple: by his use of the veto, Louis, one man alone, was frustrating the will of twenty-five million; by favoring the cause of the tyrannical kings of Europe, he was showing himself to be essentially a tyrant. In July and August, 1792, demands that the Assembly depose him were gradually gathered into a formal ultimatum which, on August 3, was presented to the deputies by the mayor and the sections (or wards) of Paris in the name of the sovereign people. When that expired at eleven o'clock on the night of August 9, open insurrection began.

On August 10, the Tuileries Palace was assaulted by a host of armed men—citizen-soldiers from as far off as Marseilles and Brittany as well as Parisians. As the King's guards and many loyal gentlemen fought desperately to defend the doorway and the great staircase of the palace, Louis and his family—

his Queen, his sister and his two children—crossed the gardens to take refuge in the Assembly. The deputies, however, were themselves beleaguered by angry demonstrators. They afforded the fugitives some shelter behind the iron grille of their tiny press-box, but finally they had to declare that the King was provisionally suspended from office and that a new national convention would be convened to decide what should be done "to assure the sovereignty of the people and the reign of liberty and equality." Although the deputies had hoped to have the royal party housed in the Luxembourg Palace, they had also to submit to the will of the new revolutionary municipality of Paris, the "Commune of the Insurrection," which was determined to have custody of the King. On August 13, therefore, the officers of the Commune took the royal family from the Assembly to imprison them in the great tower of the Temple.

Thus began a long and unhappy story of increasingly stringent confinement. The Temple, once the headquarters of the powerful Order of the Knights Templar, was nothing less than a walled town within Paris. The King at first supposed he would live in its palace, formerly the home of his youngest brother, the Count of Artois. In fact, until the massive medieval keep could be made habitable, the royal family was kept in a smaller tower that abutted it; at the same time a new encircling wall and ditch were constructed round both buildings. Roughly partitioned into separate rooms, the second floor was allocated to the King and the one above it to the ladies. At first, all were allowed to be together by day and gradually a simple routine of life was established. After an hour at prayer each morning, the King would join his family and teach

Below right An anti-clerical cartoon that expresses the revolutionaries' abhorrence of Christianity as the defender of reactionary politics.

Below Louis accepts the red bonnet with the tricolor cocade. Though the King finally signed the constitution his flight to Varennes had convinced the revolutionaries that he was plotting against the new regime.

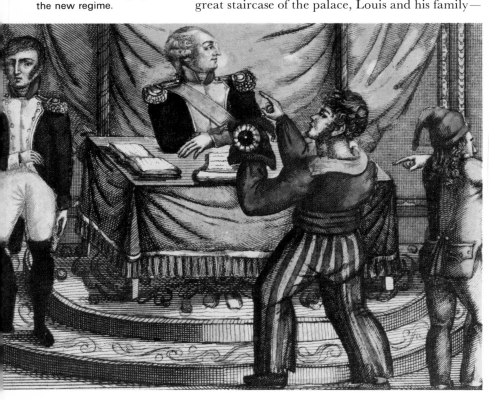

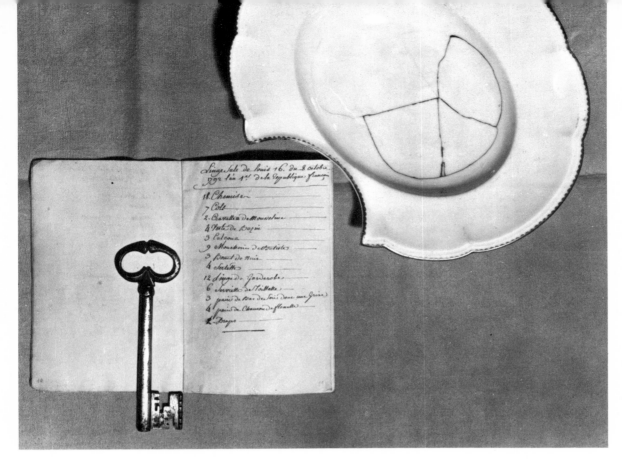

his seven-year-old son until it was time for them to walk, and be seen by their guards, in the grounds; then dinner, followed by games like backgammon, by reading, embroidery and further lessons until supper and retirement to bed. Although the prisoners were soon deprived of their attendants—notably the Queen's ladies, the Princess de Lamballe and Madame de Tourzel—they were allowed ample money, servants and books; and the devotion of men like the waiter, Turgy, and the King's valet, Cléry, both of whom voluntarily submitted to imprisonment to serve their master, helped them feel they were not wholly alone.

Their situation was nevertheless a terrible one. Enclosed by walls nine feet thick, with blocked or heavily barred embrasures, they were also plagued by perpetual supervision. The Commune, fearful lest its captives should either kill themselves or be rescued by royalists, daily appointed two of its members to observe their every action, and even to taste each dish set before them. As equality demanded, the King, now "Citizen Capet," was deprived of all his personal decorations, and in the name of security his sword, and many minor articles like scissors and toothpicks were taken away. Then there were the guards, some of whom regularly made themselves obnoxious by coarse familiarities and crude reminders that the guillotine was waiting. Although all endured these trials with dignity, Louis in particular remaining unruffled, horror was never far from them. Early in September, when the Prussians had taken Verdun and Paris itself was in real peril, all those supposed to be royalists in the city's prisons were systematically slaughtered, and one insensate crowd deliberately paraded round the Temple the impaled head of the Queen's friend,

the Princess de Lamballe—a sight officials kept from the Queen's eyes, though the fact could not be kept from her knowledge. Worse still, perhaps, there came with the passing days a growing conviction that the King at least was a man marked for execution.

Meeting formally for the first time on September 20, the very day the Prussian advance was stayed by the Battle of Valmy, the new National Convention began its debates next day and at once unanimously approved a decree declaring royalty to be abolished in France. Thus the first French Republic was founded; and there, in all probability, most of the deputies would have been content to leave the question of what was to be done with the King. Inactivity, however, proved impossible. If in 1791 the republicans on the Champ de Mars had demanded that the King be brought to trial, that demand was far more general in 1792, when he was held responsible for the actual invasion. Moreover, by a curious inversion of thought, the King was particularly blamed for resisting the insurrection that had overthrown him. By reinforcing his guard, men believed, he had made the rising imperative to prevent a coup d'état, and by firing on the people his soldiers had made him a murderer. Tragically, Louis had failed to countermand his orders to the guards when he first left the palace on August 10; still more tragically, the command that he wrote as soon as he heard firing, instructing the guard to lay down its arms and retire to barracks, was not delivered until heavy fighting had taken place; then the attempt to implement it led only to the massacre of the soldiers. So intense, indeed, was the public anger in Paris that the Commune feared that the royal prisoners would be massacred

RESTATION, DU ROI ET·DE·SA·FAMILLE A VARENNE LE 22 JUIN 1791 ·

rrestation du Roi a eu lieu a Varennes, a cinq lieues de France, vers une heure après
nuit, au moment où l'on venait d'en être prévenu par M. Drouet, maître de poste de
inte-Menehould, qui a rendu un service essentiel à la France, qu'elle surprise pour les
iiifs de se voir arrêtés au milieu de la nuit, par deux braves gardes nationaux

LA RÉCOMPENCE ACORDÉE A Mᴿ
DROUET EST DE 30 MILLE LIVRE
ET A Mᴿ SAUCE 20 MILLE LIVRE

qui ont bravé les menaces d'un détachement de-hussards, qui avoit été commandé pa
traître Bouillé ! M. Sauce, Procureur de la Commune, a invité le Roi d'entrer
lui et de s'y reposer lui et sa famille Le généreux citoyen de Varennes n'a p
accepté les offres du Roi, disant qu'il devoit tout à sa patrie.

The arrest of the royal family at Varennes in 1791. The failure of Louis' attempt to escape showed the revolutionary government that he could not be trusted and led to his execution.

A caricature of the Prince of Condé (center) reviewing his troops. Condé had fled to Germany where he organized a counterrevolutionary army made up of *émigrés* and Austrians.

if judicial proceedings were not opened very soon.

The Convention nevertheless moved only reluctantly. On November 6, a report upon the mass of papers that had been found in the Tuileries furnished convincing evidence that Louis had long been playing a double game, and the next day preliminary consideration of the constitutional position began a debate that was to occupy the Assembly almost without interruption for eight weeks. This debate was generally serious, for most of the deputies were men of the law and, whatever their personal sympathies may have been, they were much concerned about the perversion of legal process that was inevitably implicit in the trial of a king. Since Louis had been constitutionally inviolable before he was deposed, arguments in favor of judicial action against him usually bore some taint of retrospective law. Although all were sure that no body other than the Convention was sufficiently representative of the sovereignty of the nation to conduct the trial, many disliked initiating proceedings in which they would be both prosecutors and judges. These issues, however, were

increasingly overshadowed by political passions, for the Convention had soon split into two bitterly hostile parties, the "Girondins"—so called because the leading members came from Bordeaux, the department of the Gironde—and the "Mountain" —so called because they occupied a "mountain" of high seats in the Convention. As the latter became identified with the preeminence of Paris and ardor for continuing the Revolution, they became convinced that their more cautious opponents were in reality royalists determined to save the King's life by some legal expedient.

In these circumstances the fact that there was a trial at all was something of a success for moderation, for to Robespierre and some other men of the Mountain no more than a political decision was involved. Since the people had shown by insurrection that they had judged and convicted the King, all the Convention had to do was condemn him. On December 11, however, Louis was brought before the bar of the House to hear and answer a detailed indictment. Unlike Charles I of England, he did not deny the competence of the supposed court, but answered the charges with simple dignity, usually professing his innocence or his ignorance of what had been done in his name. Only the accusation that he had "caused the blood of Frenchmen to flow" moved him to an emphatic denial. Subsequently counsel pleaded his cause, a task made more difficult by the discovery in November of further incriminating papers in a secret safe in the Tuileries, and from January 14 to 19, 1793, the deputies, sitting in continuous session, cast the critical votes.

Four questions were before them, and on each in succession every man was required to pronounce his opinion publicly. To the first question, whether the King was guilty, nearly everybody answered

"Yes." The second question, whether the deputies' decision be submitted to the people for ratification, was far more critical, for this proposal was in part a move by the moderates to thwart the Mountain, and its rejection—by 425 to 286 voices—boded ill for them as well as for the King. The vital third question, what penalty should be inflicted, was nevertheless voted upon through hours of rising tension. Descriptions of scenes in which exhausted deputies slept on the benches while the people in the galleries ate and drank and gambled on the voting, and women in loose attire lounged at one end of the hall, are no doubt exaggerated; but the building was certainly crammed to capacity, and the result long in doubt. Many spoke in favor of temporary or permanent imprisonment or exile, reminding the Assembly that greater severity might well lead to civil war and the extension of the war in Europe. Others favored a symbolic sentence of death, to be followed immediately by a reprieve, and others again voted simply for the death penalty. Among these last, it should be said, was the King's own cousin, the Duke of Orleans, who had thrown in his lot with the Revolution, being known as "Citizen Equality." Only when the votes of twenty-six of the men who had spoken for a reprieve were finally established to be primarily votes for death was it found that the King had been condemned to execution by 387 votes to 334, a majority of fifty-three. When the final question, whether a reprieve should be granted, was answered in the negative by 380 votes to 310, the King's fate was sealed.

Efficient in such matters, the Revolution granted its victim only twenty-four hours to take leave of his family and the world. At half-past eight on the bitterly cold morning of January 21, 1793, Louis left the Temple for the last time. Traveling in a closed carriage with a priest of his own choice, he was taken slowly across Paris; his guards were so numerous, and the beating of their drums so persistent, that an attempt by a handful of loyalists to save him passed almost unnoticed. On the Place de la Révolution, now called the Place de la Concorde, a great multitude of soldiers and spectators surrounded the scaffold, and again the rolling of the drums drowned almost all the few words Louis sought to say in affirmation of his innocence and forgiveness of his enemies. Only recoiling briefly when he found that his arms would have to be bound, he confronted the guillotine courageously, as a Christian and a king; a moment later, as the soldiers shouted "Vive la Nation!" the executioner was displaying the severed head to the people.

The consequences of this deed were momentous. There followed inexorably the still more somber executions of the Queen and of the King's sister, as well as the brutal treatment which killed the young prince in 1795. Politically, the outcome of the trial was the first major triumph of the Mountain, which was afterward able to brand all who had failed to record truly revolutionary votes as avowed or potential enemies of the people; and this contributed in no small measure to the victors' ability to

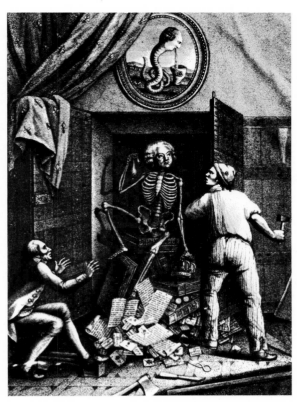

Louis as a skeleton in the cupboard. The discoveries of Louis' secret papers in the Tuileries confirmed his counterrevolutionary activites.

seize power and establish the Terror later in the year 1793. Moreover, as foreseen, the killing of the King fostered both royalist rebellion and further foreign wars. Now wholly convinced that the counterrevolution could only be accomplished by violence, the royalists recognized Louis' exiled brother and found a base for action in western France, which from March, 1793, became the scene of savage and protracted civil war. The news of the execution, which was received with revulsion throughout Europe, also led directly to war between France and Spain, and it undoubtedly helped rally the British people to the great struggle against French expansion that began in February, 1793, to end only when Napoleon Bonaparte fled from the field of Waterloo.

The importance of the execution of Louis XVI is, however, hardly to be measured by its more or less immediate repercussions alone. Even more than their opponents in the Convention, the regicides of 1793 remained marked men for the rest of their lives, and that same mark was stamped indelibly upon the republic they established. Nor was this inappropriate, for in the hour of decision each one of them had made a choice that implied total acceptance of the Revolution and total repudiation of the past. Ultimately Louis XVI died because, as Saint-Just said, he was "guilty of the crime of being a king," and because, as Danton cried, the French Republic was ready "to hurl at the feet of its enemies, as a gage of battle, the head of a king." Superseding all other laws, national and international, human or divine, the new doctrine of the sovereignty of the nation had—and perhaps still has—to be accepted in its entirety or not at all.

M. J. SYDENHAM

Poland

Like France, Poland was at war in 1793. Reduced by the partition of 1772 to a third of her former size, Poland rose bravely in revolt against her oppressors. Under the leadership of General Kościuszko, the Poles won several battles against the Russians and recaptured large tracts of territory. Warsaw and Vilna were liberated and Kościuszko was proclaimed dictator. Prussia then joined the Russians in suppressing the patriots; and after Kościuszko's defeat at Maciejowice and the fall of Cracow and Warsaw the last Polish field unit surrendered in November, 1794. The final partition of Poland came in 1795. Russia moved still further west, occupying what remained of Lithuania; Austria moved farther north, beyond Cracow, as far as the Bug River; Prussia took the rest, including Warsaw. Poland had ceased to exist as a nation, but for generations remained an area of dispute between Prussia, Russia and Austria.

Sweden

Frederick the Great and Catherine of Russia planned to partition Sweden as well as Poland. When Gustavus III succeeded to the throne in 1771, Sweden was close to anarchy. The previous fifty years had been a period of remarkable artistic and scientific achievement. Societies of science, sculpture and painting flourished; the great botanist Carl von Linné, or Linnaeus (1707–78), published his *Species Plantarum* in 1753; Anders Celsius (1701–44), professor of astronomy at the University of Uppsala for fifteen years, invented a thermometer; Emanuel Swedenborg (1688–1772), the Swedish philosopher, inventor, scientist and mystic, also studied and conducted research at Uppsala. But this great intellectual activity coincided with ruinous party political rivalry. In a forceful but bloodless coup d'état, Gustavus III arrested the council, dissolved the Diet and promulgated his new constitution of 1789. He pushed forward reforms in

Gustavus III, King of Sweden, who built up Sweden's strength to avoid Poland's fate.

agriculture, commerce, administration and law, encouraged the development of scientific research and built up a powerful and well equipped navy and army. Gustavus thus demonstrated to Prussia and Russia that Sweden would not submit passively to Poland's fate.

By 1787 Gustavus' forces were strong enough for a full-scale war. Suspecting that Catherine was subsidizing his enemies, he attacked her while the Russian army was heavily engaged in the Second Turkish War. Gustavus' navy did

Constitutional change in America

Although the American Revolution cannot be seen as a democratic uprising, it necessitated substantial constitutional change. Some of the leading rebels had a broadly democratic or populist view. Thomas Jefferson (1743–1826), for example, contrasted the "old aristocratical interest" with the "plebeian interest," which he believed would prevail. But such views did not triumph easily; two of the colonies, Rhode Island and Connecticut, did not even abandon their old colonial charters, and in practice, except where they had been open loyalists, members of the old assemblies were usually reelected to the new assemblies.

Most of the new constitutions for the states did, however, make three changes; property qualifications for voting were reduced or abolished, the legislatures were made bicameral and their powers were strengthened while those of the governors were reduced. In addition, the Revolution had drastically altered the balance of property ownership in some of the states. The British royal family and the descendants of the original proprietors of some of the colonies, particularly the Calverts (Baltimore) and the Penns, had previously held millions of acres; other leading landowners, too, were among the loyalists. As a result of their support for the losing side in the war, many of the leading loyalists, perhaps as many as fifty thousand, emigrated either to Canada or England. Their land was either confiscated or compulsorily sold at low prices.

The United States

It was inevitable that there would be pressure to give the former colonies some political coherence. Success against the British would certainly not have been possible without united action, and during the war years the Continental Congress had provided the necessary leadership. But it was several years before all the states could be persuaded to sign the Articles of Confederation that had been adopted by the Continental Congress. A powerful federation was regarded with little less suspicion than had been the British government. It

General Kościuszko, the Polish patriot, who strove until his death in 1817 to gain Poland's freedom.

Emanuel Swedenborg, Swedish scientist, philosopher and religious writer.

well, and his army was preparing to march on St. Petersburg when an attack by Denmark, from which Gustavus wished to wrest Norway, forced him to withdraw his forces to defend Göteborg. Peace was finally achieved through the mediation of Prussia and England, both of whom had reason to fear the growing power of Russia in the Baltic.

Russia and Prussia

was not until March 1, 1781, that Maryland, the most reluctant of the states, signed the Articles and the Confederation of the United States of America became a reality. The individual states retained their sovereignty, but foreign affairs, defense and economic management were mostly delegated to a congress. It very soon emerged, however, that the Congress had been given too little power to operate effectively; it was unable to raise taxation and could only pass legislation with the consent of at least nine of the thirteen states. Only in the western territory had Congress any far-reaching powers, and even there it was unable to govern effectively as the Continental Army had been disbanded for financial reasons. The Congress was, however, able to persuade the states to abandon their claims to land in the western territory; as the population in the west increased, parts of the territory would become states, equal in every way to the original colonies.

A Constitutional Convention, under George Washington's presidency, was held in 1787, and a new constitution was drawn up, despite disagreements on fundamental matters of representation between the larger and the smaller states. Eventually a compromise situation was agreed: there was to be a congress of two chambers, the House of Representatives, whose membership was based on a state's population, and a Senate, to which each state sent two members. A president was to be elected by an electoral college, but in their fear of monarchical power, the members of the Convention decided that the exercise of presidential authority should be controlled by an elaborate system of checks and balances, a system that was to remain unchallenged by either the legislature, the executive or the courts for nearly two centuries. The powers of Congress were increased so that it could raise taxation and had control of military and some commercial matters. In addition it was to legislate "for the general welfare of the United States."

As in England, party alignments had developed in the American colonies during the early years of the eighteenth century, but it was only over the issue of the constitution that party loyalties really polarized, and in the state legislatures federalists and anti-federalists quarreled for months before the ratification of the necessary

nine states was obtained. Washington became President in 1789 and John Adams, former envoy to Great Britain, was elected Vice President.

The United States in 1790

The new constitution necessitated regular censuses so that the electoral system could function properly, and the first federal decennial census was taken in 1790. Philadelphia, with a population of forty-five thousand, was by far the largest city and the obvious capital of the

A merchants' counting house in Philadelphia, America's largest city.

United States and seat of the federal government. New York had 33,000 inhabitants, and only four other cities had a population of over 8,000. Unlike the countries of Western Europe, which were already fairly heavily urbanized, the United States was still a predominantly rural and agricultural country, with only about three percent of the population living in the six large cities concentrated on the eastern coastal strip; no inland town had a population of over four thousand. The typical American family lived on a small farm, probably owned freehold.

In the South, however, larger plantations were common. Labor on these was provided by slaves. The population of Virginia totaled about three-quarters of a million, of whom 300,000 (forty percent) were slaves. In Georgia and the Carolinas the percentage of slaves was even higher. In the North there were far fewer slaves, less

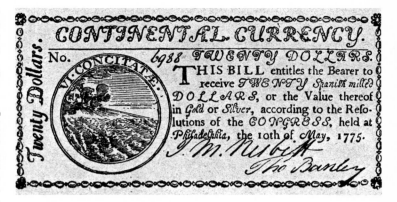

An American twenty-dollar bill. In 1785 the dollar was adopted as the money unit of the United States.

than four percent of the population. There was increasing opposition to slavery, although by an agreement made in 1787 the importation of slaves was not to be interfered with by Congress until 1808 at the earliest. Despite efforts to change the law, Congress insisted that slavery should be banned in the northwest territories from the beginning.

During the last few years of the century, the western territory, although thinly populated, was developing rapidly. As the population of Kentucky, Tennessee and Ohio passed the 60,000 mark (1792–1803) they became independent states. Treaties with Spain and with Britain in the 1790s helped solve territorial disagreements and the United States was free to expand westward.

Economic development

America experienced pressures similar to those that were leading Britain and the rest of Europe to rapid industrial development; the results, too, were similar. Both America and Europe had a high birthrate—the average colonial family had between seven and eight children—and because of continuing immigration, the population (both black and white) grew rapidly. In 1776 there were probably about two and a half million people, excluding Indians; by 1790 there were over four million. The growth was particularly noticeable in the cities; despite the tiny percentage of city-dwellers in 1790, Philadelphia and New York were growing far faster than the population as a whole. By the end of the century the United States had a higher population than many Euro-

pean countries—for example, the Netherlands, Portugal, Ireland and Scandinavia.

It soon became necessary to mint more money. Until the Revolution the coinage had been made up largely of Spanish and British money, but by the 1780s there was an extreme shortage of coins, particularly of the lower denominations. In 1785 the Congress adopted the dollar—a term already widely used —as the money unit of the United States, and in 1787 the right of the states to issue coinage—a right hardly exercised—was withdrawn. Copper cents were issued from 1787, and after the Coinage Act of 1792 a mint was established in Philadelphia, which began to issue silver dollars in 1794.

American industry was growing rapidly after the economic difficulties caused by the breach with Britain, America's traditional trading partner. Both America and Britain saw the advantage of rebuilding trade contacts. Initially this was more to Britain's advantage than to the United States', as the latter was still dependent on Europe for many necessities. In 1784 Britain imported under $4 million-worth from the United States, but exported four and a half times as much. American exports, not only to Britain but also to other European countries, were beginning to rise rapidly; between 1790 and 1807 they rose from $20 million to $108 million. This growth was largely due to the development of the cotton industry, made possible by various technological improvements. Power-driven machinery for spinning cotton was successfully applied in 1791, taken to date the beginning of America's industrial revolution. But of most significance was Eli Whitney's cotton gin.

Eli Whitney Invents the Cotton Gin

Eli Whitney's invention of the cotton gin allowed the planters of the American South to clean cotton fast and cheaply and dramatically increased the amount they could sell, encouraging them to grow more. By importing more slaves—to tend the new crops—the planters exacerbated relations between North and South. Whitney, deprived of any profit from his invention, returned North and devised a system of making muskets and other small arms with interchangeable parts— an innovation that tipped the scales in favor of the North when the Civil War, hastened perhaps by Whitney's earlier invention, eventually broke out.

After the Revolution gave the United States its separate existence, free from the distant rule of Britain, the new nation had to face a host of severe economic and defense problems. Many saw the United States as a limb torn from the parent body, unlikely to maintain the supplies necessary to survive long.

The total population was no more than four and a half million, spread over a vast land. These people had been obliged to depend on the industries of Britain for most of their manufactured goods and did not seem capable of building up their own production facilities with such a shortage of labor. The Southern states were in a particularly difficult situation. Crops such as rice had been halved as a result of war damage and, without the special import favors previously offered by Britain, other sources of income, such as indigo and tobacco, were failing. In the South there was therefore a desperate need for a crop that could find a ready market at good prices across the Atlantic.

Seeing the dynamic expansion of the Lancashire cotton industry, the Southern plantation owners hurried to experiment with cotton, but to their dismay discovered that only some coastal areas were suitable for growing it commercially. The one variety that would flourish on the uplands, remote from the coast, was "green seed cotton." This produced a boll with very short staple (fibers) and worse, the boll contained a seed covered in a velvet-like fur that clung tenaciously to the fibers so that no more than about one pound of cleaned cotton could be gathered daily by a Negro slave. The cotton that came from areas such as the West Indies, Brazil and India, had a smooth, black seed that slipped out graciously when the bolls were put through a machine that resembled a mangle, with fluted grooves running the full length of the rollers. The raised edges of the grooves gripped the fibers firmly and pulled them through the machine, leaving the seeds to fall in a heap on the other side.

This machine was a cotton gin, the name presumably derived from the way workers in India pronounced the word "engine." American farmers tried putting their cotton through an Indian gin, but the only result was a mess of wet, unusable fibers as the rollers crushed the green seeds—about the size of an olive stone—which refused to be parted from the staple. Meanwhile, in Britain, the inventions of Arkwright, Hargreaves and Cartwright had created a need for more cotton than the existing producing countries could supply, to feed the increasing number of power-driven spinning and weaving machines. The farmers in the Southern states had grown, in 1792, over two million pounds of the short staple cotton, only to find it unsalable because of the cleaning difficulty. By chance, the following year Eli Whitney arrived in Georgia. His quick brain and interest in machines would enable him to solve the cotton-cleaning problem and give the United States its financial salvation.

Eli Whitney was born in Westborough, Massachusetts, on December 8, 1765. His father was a New England farmer who also had a small workshop for the repair of his own agricultural equipment. As a boy, Whitney was apparently more interested in the workshop than in the farm, and at age fourteen had run a profitable sideline manufacturing nails and hatpins, even employing the services of a laborer in his forge. It took all his determination to convince his father and stepmother (his mother died when he was eleven) that he would benefit from a college education. He eventually succeeded in going to Yale where he earned a considerable part of his expenses through his mechanical ability. When he graduated he was already twenty-eight years old and was obliged to face a future that was suddenly dull, if not bleak. An appointment as schoolteacher in New York fell through at the last minute and only the post of private tutor to the

Short staple or "green seed cotton," the only cotton seed that would flourish inland.

Opposite Eli Whitney, whose cotton gin revolutionized the economy of the United States and made possible the unimpeded growth of the British cotton industry.

Whitney's cotton gin from the original model. A cylinder bearing rows of wire teeth rotated so that the teeth first passed through a hopper and then through very narrow slats in a wooden breastplate. Underneath the slats was a set of brushes rotating at a faster rate and in the opposite direction to the toothed cylinder.

children of a Major Dupont in a remote rural area of South Carolina at a salary of eighty guineas (£84) a year was open to him.

Reluctantly he accepted the offer; he was particularly apprehensive about the unhealthy climate and the incidence of disease in the South. No one could have had a less promising start to a career. The boat that was to take him from New Haven to New York to start his journey south was shipwrecked at night, while Whitney lay groaning with seasickness. With some other passengers he hired a horse-drawn coach to New York and then, immediately on his arrival there, met an old acquaintance who shook him by the hand to congratulate him on his survival of the shipwreck. The acquaintance had smallpox.

Whitney had only a mild infection, but it delayed his journey for several weeks. For part of the time he was nursed by a new acquaintance, Catherine Greene, the forty-year-old widow of the national hero General Nathanael Greene, who had been George Washington's Quartermaster-General as well as a commander in the field. Catherine had a large estate, Mulberry Grove, in Savannah, Georgia. Her estate manager, Phineas Miller, had offered Whitney the post of tutor on behalf of Major Dupont. Whitney was planning to travel south with Miller and Catherine, and so had joined them in New York.

Catherine Greene was a captivating companion, and a very fond attachment that lasted all their lives developed between the general's widow and the young graduate. Whitney's letters show that when Catherine married Phineas Miller in May, 1796, his spirits dropped to a particularly low ebb and it is perhaps significant that Whitney himself did not marry until he was fifty-two, in 1817, three years after Catherine's death.

Catherine was exuberant, sparkling and hospitable and Whitney readily accepted her invitation to stay a while at Mulberry Grove when their ship from New York docked at Savannah. Mulberry Grove became even more desirable a residence when Whitney discovered that the salary for the position in South Carolina was not eighty, but only forty guineas a year—about ten guineas less than

he had hoped to save from his income. Whitney's construction of several ingenious household devises prompted Catherine to introduce him to neighboring plantation owners who were discussing the necessity of a machine to separate the short staple cotton from its seeds. Whitney suggested that he might be able to design an appropriate machine and, with Catherine and Phineas' encouragement, applied himself to the task.

On June 1, 1793, only ten days after setting to work, Whitney demonstrated a small model of the gin that would revolutionize the whole economy of the United States and would make possible the unimpeded growth of the British cotton industry. The model was manually operated but could clean cotton of its green seeds at ten times the rate of the best Negro worker. When the bigger, power-operated machines came into operation, they could gin cotton a thousand times more rapidly than a man and produce cotton cleaner than by hand.

The impact of Whitney's invention on the American economy can be illustrated by statistics:

	British imports of cotton, per annum	British imports of US cotton
Before 1793	28 million pounds	Almost nil
1812	63 million pounds	30 million pounds
1825*	228 million pounds	170 million pounds

*year of Whitney's death

In the thirty-two years between Whitney's invention and his death, imports of cotton into Britain from non-American sources rose by 30 million pounds, while imports of the short staple cotton from America went up by 170 million pounds. Simultaneously, the price of cotton increased on the world market.

So great and sudden was the prosperity that flowed into the Southern states, and so frantic was the drive to grow more cotton now that it could be ginned by machine and exported so profitably, that there was a major shortage of labor to pick the cotton and tend the fields. The Negro slave became a vital factor in the economy of the South and slavery was maintained by the planters at all costs for a further three generations—until the Civil War.

Whitney's gin consisted of a cylinder bearing rows of wire teeth which rotated so that the teeth first passed through a hopper and then through very narrow slats in a wooden breastwork. In this way, cotton bolls containing seeds were collected from the hopper but only the fine cotton fibers could pass through the slats; the seeds were trapped and fell back out of the machine. The wire teeth were able to tear the staple away from the velvety fur of the seeds without damaging the seeds. Underneath the slats was a "clearer"—a set of stiff brushes. These rotated at a faster rate than the toothed cylinder and in the opposite direction, so that the cotton staple was brushed off and fell into a collection bin.

Upon showing his invention, Whitney was immediately offered one hundred guineas for the sole rights. He refused and went into partnership with Miller, taking the trade name Miller & Whitney. Phineas, with Catherine Greene's help, was to finance the production of big, power-driven or horse-driven gins and offer a ginning service to the plantations. Whitney was to perfect the design and manufacture the gins in the North—the partners built their factory at New Haven—where industrial labor and materials were more easily available.

A patent was granted to Miller & Whitney by President Jefferson on March 14, 1794. Because of the simplicity of Whitney's gin the design could be easily described and copied, and soon pirate machines were constructed and put into use before Miller & Whitney could profit from their exclusive invention. The partners planned not to sell the machines but to offer them on loan, partly because it would take too long to construct enough, and partly to encourage farmers to plant cotton extensively, knowing that they could have the cotton ginned without incurring great costs. To meet the deadline for planting cotton in 1794, Miller advertised the ginning service before the patent had been confirmed. The terms for ginning would be:

> For every five pounds delivered him in the seed, he will return one pound of clean cotton for the market. For the encouragement of cotton planters he will also mention that ginning machines to clean the green seed cotton on the above terms will actually be erected in different parts of the country before the harvest of the ensuing crops.
>
> (*Gazette of the State of Georgia*, March 6, 1794).

Hence, the cleaned cotton would be shared out on the basis of three-fifths to the planter and two-fifths to the ginners, having taken into account the weight of the removed seeds.

Rather than be held to ransom at this price by exclusive service, the planters set up their own gins secretly or patronized copies built by others. Worse for Miller & Whitney was the rumor circulated by their competitors that Miller & Whitney machines (and no others) spoiled the cotton by breaking the seeds. Buyers in England refused to purchase cotton from the partners. Yet another disaster for

Miller & Whitney was the fire that destroyed their first factory in March, 1795.

Nor did the partnership benefit initially from the exhausting, time-consuming and financially crippling series of lawsuits (sixty in the state of Georgia alone between 1798 and 1806) to settle the validity of the patent. The most serious setback for Miller & Whitney was the judgment, declared against them in May, 1797, of the case they brought against Edward Lyon. The judgment was in Lyon's favor purely because of a tiny error in the wording of the recently revised patent law of the United States. "And" was unwittingly used instead of "or," losing the partners hundreds of thousands of dollars, and thereby contributing to a breakdown in Whitney's health and the financial ruin of Catherine and Phineas Miller, who had mortgaged their estate to fight for the patent rights. The law stated that for a person to be found guilty it had to be proved that he had devised, made, constructed, used, employed

Model of Whitney's cotton gin.

Loading cotton at St. Louis. In the years between Whitney's invention and his death American cotton exports to Britain rose by 170 million pounds.

143

and vended the patented machine. It was not
constructing *or* selling that was illegal, but the
combination, and Lyon had simply sold the
machines. They had been built for him by others.
It was only when the law was later corrected that
the partners had a chance to regain some of their
lost license revenues; they had to wait until 1807
for the validity of their patent to be settled.

An earlier defeat in the legal battle was the
patent—later annulled—granted to Hodgen Holmes
in May, 1796, for what he claimed was his own
design of a cotton gin. This differed from the
Whitney design merely in the use of a row of
circular saws in place of wire teeth on a cylinder,
so that the teeth of the saws rotated through the
hopper and the slats in the breastwork. The principle
was otherwise identical, but Whitney's patent had
been broken before any money had been earned
by it.

Miller died in December, 1803, at the height of
the legal and financial troubles. No cleaned green
seed cotton had been salable prior to Whitney's
invention of the gin in 1793; in 1795 American
output was 8 million pounds and 35 million pounds
in 1807, with a price increase on the market from
36 to 44 cents per pound. America became rich
while Miller & Whitney faced bankruptcy. The
partners had not even sufficient funds for Whitney
to travel to England to prove to the importers that
his cotton was useable.

The hostility of the plantation owners had made
Eli Whitney turn to another industrial pursuit to
make his fortune. On May 1, 1798, the year
following the loss of his lawsuit against Edward
Lyon, Whitney wrote to Oliver Wolcott, Secretary

of the Treasury under President Adams, offering to
manufacture 10,000 "stands of arms"—sets of
muskets, bayonets, ramrods—in a very short time
and at reasonable cost. He explained:

> I am persuaded that machinery moved by water
> adapted to this business would greatly diminish the
> labor and facilitate the manufacture of this article.
> Machines for forging, rolling, floating, boring, grind-
> ing, polishing, etc., may all be made use of to advantage.

Wolcott, with testimonials to Whitney's ability as
a manufacturer and designer, could not fail to be
interested. France was making warlike noises and,
in the middle of the Napoleonic Wars, no help
could be expected from any other European nation.
The United States official armories could not turn
out more than a few hundred stands of arms each
year. At the time gun-making was an art; the
individual components of any one musket were not
interchangeable.

Whitney's plan was to produce standardized
parts of firearms in quantity, each identical with
others of the same kind which could be rapidly
assembled by unskilled workers and not craftsmen
as formerly. This was the principle of interchangeable manufacture that became known as the
"American System." The following century Henry
Ford mechanized and speeded up the assembly end
of production. By introducing division of labor in
his firearms factory near New Haven—the spot is
now called Whitneyville—Whitney had mechanized
manufacture of individual components. This system
had been previously tried in one or two establish-
ments in France and the United States, but only on
a small scale. The system had never been widely
advertised or adopted because either the work was

carried on in secret to safeguard the ideas or the results were too inaccurate. Whitney convinced the United States government that he could use the technique effectively to solve the dire shortage of home-manufactured arms.

In a contract signed shortly after he wrote to Wolcott, Whitney guaranteed to produce 10,000 stands of arms for a total cost of $134,000. Signed in May, 1798, the contract stipulated delivery of the first 4,000 sets before September 30, 1799, and the remainder by September 30, 1800. At that time Whitney had not even looked for a site for his factory. He could not know that unreliable sub-suppliers, difficult government inspectors, yellow fever quarantine periods and severe winters would so delay his plans that the terms of the contract would not finally be met until January, 1809. It transpired, therefore, that while the Miller & Whitney court battles dragged out in the South, in the North Whitney was overwhelmed by severe difficulties in the manufacture of the muskets for the government. He was even forced, on occasion, to commute, by rough road and coach, from Connecticut to Savannah.

The advantage accruing to Whitney from the government contract was an advance of funds to set up production. "By this contract," he wrote to a friend, "I obtained some thousands of dollars in advance which has saved me from ruin." Whitney maintained the confidence of the government in his methods and in his integrity and they in turn appreciated the extent to which the country as a whole would be rewarded in return for the invest-ment of more time and money in Whitney's plans. Elizur Goodrich, the Congressman for Whitney's district of Connecticut, wrote:

> All judges and inspectors unite in a declaration that they are superior to any [arms] which the artists of this country or importation have brought into the arsenals of the United States—and all men of all parties agree that his talents are of immense importance and must be exclusively secured by and devoted to the means of defense.

Because Whitney was making muskets for the government and his methods and products were scrutinized by the highest men in the country his ideas gained wide recognition and support. The interchangeable system of manufacture spread rapidly. The United States could build up a machinery industry, the most powerful in the world, even though there was a shortage of labor. Whitney's techniques could be used to reproduce the original work of a craftsman in large numbers and more faithfully than the craftsman himself. On this principle the whole of modern industrial production has been founded.

Eli Whitney died at age fifty-nine on January 8, 1825, to his dying day a dedicated inventor. Only in the last eight years of his life, when his health was already very poor, was he able to live the married life, with children and without financial burdens, that had been his life's ambition.

Whitney was not to know that by 1861 his country would be divided against itself, with the industrially rich North waging war against the cotton-rich South. By his invention of the cotton gin he had, unwittingly, provided a cause of dissension. For after the French Revolution many Southerners had agreed with Northerners on the abolition of slavery. The growth of the cotton industry, however, with its increased demand for slave labor, gradually changed Southern sentiment, and the antagonism between North and South developed into war. Both sides fought with American arms, the mass production of which Whitney had also initiated. But the positive aspect of Whitney's contribution to technology cannot be underestimated: he brought the United States wealth and introduced the "American System," which became the basis of the mass production characteristic of the growing American industry during the late eighteenth and nineteenth centuries. SYDNEY PAULDEN

Cotton picking. The need for more labor to tend the fields necessitated the continuance of slavery in the South.

William Pitt and England

The long reign of George III, which lasted from 1760 to 1820, was disturbed by revolution in America and Ireland, by almost total military isolation from the rest of the world during the Napoleonic Wars and by social difficulties caused by the rapid industrialization begun in the 1760s. Yet by the death of George III England had by far the

William Pitt the Younger; a political prodigy, he was regarded England's greatest Prime Minister.

most advanced economy in the world and outside Europe had established a political dominance with which no other nation could compete. This achievement was in no way due to the King; George was a man of very limited intelligence. He was unstable and immature, sometimes easily influenced and at other times obstinate to the point of unreason. As he grew older he became increasingly liable to attacks of insanity, which made him incapable of ruling. His belief that the power of the crown should be increased had been instilled in him by his tutor, the Earl of Bute (1713–92), who was made Prime Minister soon after the King's accession.

The real architect of British success was William Pitt the Younger (1759–1806), the second son of the Earl of Chatham. A political prodigy, Pitt became Chancellor of the Exchequer when he was twenty-three, and in 1783, at age twenty-four, Prime Minister. He remained in office until his death, with only one three-year interval (1801–04). His achievements were outstanding. Deeply influenced by the economic theories

of Adam Smith (1723–90), he was largely responsible for the introduction of free-trade ideas into British politics; he increased the power of the British government in India; he allowed the British colony of Canada a measure of self-government; he was responsible for bringing about the Union between Britain and Ireland; he introduced a variety of social measures, and sought to introduce many more—because the King refused to accept the principle of immediate Roman Catholic emancipation Pitt resigned from the premiership in 1801. He gave Britain the confidence she had lost by strengthening her economy and army and navy. It was this new-found military prowess that ensured Britain's success in the French revolutionary wars.

Pitt's achievements are the more remarkable in that he could not rely on consistent support from the unbalanced King and at the same time had to withstand energetic parliamentary opposition, particularly from the supporters of Charles James Fox (1749–1806). Fox, a brilliant man, became the leading parliamentary exponent of radical ideas, praising the French for attacking the Bastille and later demanding that peace be made with revolutionary France. Pitt, by astute parliamentary maneuvers, was able to retain control, and Fox, although he had a widespread popular following, was without influence in government circles.

Ireland: the 1798 and the Union

One of the major problems that faced Pitt was Ireland. The long-term effect of the Glorious Revolution of 1688 had been to strengthen the Anglican and Presbyterian ascendancy in the country. Roman Catholics had been penalized, both by law—they were deprived of the right to vote in 1727 —and by the discriminatory attitude of most of the Anglo-Irish establishment. The economic effect of English domination in the country was no less marked than its social and religious effect, and no less serious; Ireland had never developed any substantial industry apart from the wool trade, and the government succeeded in virtually destroying this by high taxation in order to protect the English wool traders. The linen trade and brewing, both of which had a chance of

Charles James Fox taking part in an election meeting; Fox's radical ideas had little parliamentary impact.

developing into substantial industries, were also heavily taxed in order to prevent their doing so. Even agriculture was unable to flourish as most of the land belonged to English landlords, who were in the main non-resident and took little interest in their Irish estates. They were foreigners whose religion, culture and economic interests differed from their tenants'. Often their title to the land was based on no more than conquest or illegal seizure. They had little incentive to invest money in improvements as most of the land was rackrented. The high level of rents and the widespread use of Irish pensions to pay for English office-holders was a serious and continuing drain on the economy.

Although the Irish Houses of Parliament continued to exist, in practice they had little power, and even their theoretical powers were largely ignored. The electorate was tiny; only Anglicans, who formed under ten percent of the population, could be elected to the House of Commons; and well over half the members of Parliament were returned by "pocket boroughs" controlled by peers, spiritual or secular. The House of Lords was no more representative, as the government could almost always rely on the support of the bishops.

The American Revolution produced a change of attitude in the British government toward Ireland. It was feared that Ireland might emulate the American colonies.

Massacre at Scullabogne during the 1798 rising.

revolutions Ireland attempts to throw off British rule

The fear was well based. Troops had been taken from Ireland to fight in America. The threat of invasion from France had been met by the setting up of volunteer forces who in turn demanded self-government. As a result the government reduced the restrictions against the linen trade, and Irish ships were permitted to fish off Newfoundland. But the loss of American trade so seriously affected Ireland's economy that even these relaxations could not help her. In 1779 the government withdrew much of the penal legislation against Roman Catholics, and Poynings' Law of 1494, which had made the Dublin Parliament dependent on Westminster, was virtually repealed in 1783. Ireland's only direct link with England was that George III was King of both countries. It was largely through the efforts of Henry Grattan (1746–1820) that this liberalization was brought about, but Grattan's further attempts to win the vote for Roman Catholics were unsuccessful.

The independence of the Irish Parliament, however, did very little to help solve the country's fundamental problems—the plight of the peasantry, who were largely subsistence farmers, and the discrimination against the Roman Catholic majority. Although the government passed further reforming legislation in an attempt to disarm opposition, it failed to satisfy radical opinion. In 1791, a Society of United Irishmen, whose aim was to establish an independent, non-sectarian Irish republic, was founded in Dublin by an Anglican barrister, Wolfe Tone (1763–98). Over the next few years political discontent continued to grow steadily, encouraged by the French Revolution. The government refused even to discuss the question of Roman Catholic membership of Parliament, and tried instead to buy the support of the majority by setting up and financing a huge Roman Catholic seminary at Maynooth. Sectarian rioting became common, and the United Irishmen—who at first had wanted to win support by constitutional means—began to advocate rebellion. In 1798 a widespread rising broke out, backed by promises of French help. Although the rebellion was in large measure a war against landlords and Protestants, most of the effective leadership of the rebel forces was provided by Anglican landlords, such as Beauchamp

Bagenal Harvey (1745–98). The French were too slow in sending aid and the rebellion was put down.

The British reaction to the "ninety-eight" was to suppress the Irish Parliament altogether, and to stop making further concessions to the Roman Catholics (despite the efforts of Pitt). Britain and Ireland were united under the Parliament at Westminster.

For over a century, from the passing of the Act of Union in 1801, Ireland became part of Britain—and an almost continuous source of trouble to the government. Many of the most vexing problems for British politicians in the nineteenth century were caused by the Union.

France

The death of the King sealed the fate of constitutional government in France. The government ordered a total mobilization and set up a Committee of Public Safety to enforce laws against monarchists and other counterrevolutionaries. The machinery that the Convention had set up was to become the means by which many of its members fell. Most of the Brissotin members of the Convention were tried and executed. The reign of terror—a product of France's need to fight an all-out war for the success of the Revolution, a war against both internal and external enemies—began. Robespierre and his supporters, of whom the ruthless Louis de St. Just (1767–94) was the most

notable, were able to dominate the Committee of Public Safety, which quickly became the real government of France.

Perhaps as many as forty thousand people were executed for a variety of real or imagined crimes, and ten times that number were arrested and questioned. Under the influence of the Paris mob, Christianity was formally abolished by the government and replaced by the secular cult of Liberty. Under pressure from some to extend the terror and from others to reduce it, the Committee turned with an even but heavyhanded injustice on both groups, claiming that they had been plotting together with foreign governments to overthrow the Revolution. Politically isolated as it now was, the Committee could only govern by the continued use of terror.

But, despite its uses as a political weapon, terror proved to be the cause of Robespierre's fall. The Convention still preserved a nominal authority, and its members, who were convinced that it was only a matter of time before they too were arrested and sent to the guillotine, voted that Robespierre and his allies should be executed. After a brief counter-terror, order was restored. A five-man Directory and two assemblies ruled in place of the Committee of Public Safety and the Convention. A new constitution, which restricted the vote to a wealthy minority, was introduced in 1795. The Revolution was over, and although the monarchy was not

restored, the Directory was a conservative body. Those, like François (Gracchus) Babeuf (1760–97), founder of a "conspiracy for equality," who advocated radical measures were still in danger of execution.

Napoleon defeats the Turks at Abukir Bay.

War and the rise of Napoleon

The execution of Louis XVI resulted in a coalition of Europe's major powers to destroy the Revolution. In 1793, the Allies were at first successful, but the full-scale mobilization of France produced an army of 650,000 men which managed to recover most of the ground that had been lost. By the end of 1794 both Spain and Holland had been invaded by the French. One of the causes of the widespread discontent with Robespierre was that the success of the war made people feel that the need for terror had gone, while the cost of the war was to prove a constant source of embarrassment and difficulty to the Directory. Many of the countries of the coalition were little less exhausted—Prussia, Britain and Spain all agreed to end the fighting.

As a result, from 1796 the war was largely confined to Italy, where Austria and Sardinia still fought on. A twenty-seven-year-old Corsican, Napoleon Bonaparte, was placed in command of the French army in Italy. He was brilliantly successful. Sardinia was forced to make a humiliating treaty with France, and the Austrians were hard put to avoid complete defeat. In the Mediterranean, as well, Napoleon enjoyed a brilliant run of successes, and was only prevented from capturing Egypt by Britain's control of the sea, demonstrated by her navy's success at the Battle of the Nile in 1798.

Military force made Napoleon a power to be reckoned with in French domestic politics, too, and in 1799 he took control of the government.

Irish House of Commons; after the 1798 rising it was united to the Westminster Parliament.

BONAPARTE

Napoleon Bonaparte Becomes First Consul

By 1799, the Directory that ruled France had lost whatever popular support it may have had and its overthrow was widely expected. One of the five Directors, the Abbé Siéyès, teamed with the popular General Bonaparte to accomplish this. The first steps were carried out with precision, but then lack of planning led to near chaos and the peaceful coup d'état was marred by the necessity of calling in soldiers. Order was maintained, and out of the confusion Bonaparte finally emerged as First Consul, with powers that were virtually dictatorial.

The coup d'état of Brumaire 18–19 (November, 9–10, 1799), by which Napoleon Bonaparte acquired power in France, has always been recognized as a turning point in history. Its interpretation nevertheless remains highly controversial. To some, Bonaparte is the hero who came forward amid universal acclaim to save a republic so rotten that society itself was in danger of dissolution; to others, he is an unscrupulous adventurer, able but inordinately ambitious, who unnecessarily destroyed a nascent republic in order to establish his own military dictatorship. Whatever truth there may be in either of these interpretations, the course of events during and immediately after the coup scarcely supports the underlying assumption they have in common—that all was premeditated and practically predetermined.

The coup certainly began in accordance with a plan, some part of which must have been made known to Bonaparte by the man principally responsible for it, Emmanuel Siéyès, at the time one of the five executive Directors of the French Republic. Early in the morning of November 9, special messengers went around Paris summoning members of the upper house of the legislature, the Council of the Elders, to an immediate meeting in the Tuileries. Significantly, however, not all were called; those men who were known to be "democratic," or "Jacobin," in their sympathies were left undisturbed in their beds. At seven in the morning, when sufficient Elders were assembled, they were told of the discovery of a frightful Jacobin plot to reestablish the Terror of 1793, and they were urged to exercise their constitutional right to move the legislature away from Paris. The Elders accordingly ordered the removal of both councils—their own, and that of the lower house, the Five Hundred—to St. Cloud, where both were required to reassemble at noon the next day. As this made any further debate in Paris illegal, latecomers found

that their right to protest had been taken away.

By the same decree, but by an extension of their authority, the Elders appointed General Bonaparte to command all military forces in Paris and its vicinity, and made him responsible for the safety of the legislature. The General, who had deferred various reviews until this same day, already had adequate forces available in the Champs Elysées; and on the pretext of a sudden journey, he had assembled a considerable number of high-ranking officers at his home in the Rue de la Victoire. As soon as word of his appointment reached him, he led a brilliant cavalcade through the streets to the Tuileries. There, by declaiming generally, he was able to evade the usual oath of allegiance, simply swearing that he would defend "a republic founded upon true freedom."

At the same time, the old government was craftily dismantled. Of the five Directors, two, the Abbé Siéyès and his henchman Ducos, resigned by arrangement, and two others, Gohier and Moulins, the Jacobin minority of the Directory, were left in their official residence, the Luxembourg Palace, in ignorance of what was afoot. The fifth Director, the corrupt but formidable Barras, who potentially held the balance of power, was then neatly eliminated. Having been led to suppose that a prominent place would be reserved for him in the new order, he isolated himself in his rooms to await his call. But when the minister Talleyrand, a man as brazen as himself, finally arrived, he came with a detachment of dragoons and a prepared letter of resignation. Having no option, Barras agreed that he would "joyfully resume the simple rank of citizen"; and he promptly left Paris, heavily escorted—and in all probability, heavily bribed. Gohier and Moulins, detained at the Luxembourg for as long as possible by Fouché, the Minister of Police, eventually repudiated his "protection" and made their way to the Tuileries; but by then the govern-

Charles Talleyrand, Napoleon's Minister of Foreign Affairs. He later quarreled with the Emperor and helped restore the Bourbons.

Opposite Napoleon, by Jacques Louis David, as the modern Hannibal crossing the Alps.

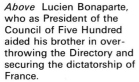

Above Lucien Bonaparte, who as President of the Council of Five Hundred aided his brother in overthrowing the Directory and securing the dictatorship of France.

Above right The morning of 18 Brumaire. Napoleon's officers profess their allegiance to their general.

ment of which they had been members had ceased to exist. Refusing to resign, they returned to the Luxembourg, where General Moreau, one of Bonaparte's principal rivals, isolated them—and himself—until all was over.

Despite the participation of the military, this day's work was essentially a piece of civilian chicanery, skillfully effected by men who had learned their trade in ten years of turmoil. True, troops abounded in Paris, and Siéyès, who had taken riding lessons in preparation for the occasion, was overshadowed and perhaps even publicly reproached by Bonaparte. However, even Bonaparte hardly did more than play out an agreed part. Far from there being any opposition for the soldiers to suppress, the Parisians seemed elated by the sound of martial music and by the appearance of the army on parade at the Tuileries.

The fact of the matter was that a coup, either by the moderates or by the Jacobins had been commonly anticipated. However sound its long-term administrative reforms may now appear, the Directory had practically no public support. It had repeatedly purged the assemblies in order to nullify the results of elections, but it had never won, or even attempted to win, the backing of any substantial section of opinion. Never achieving stability, it had never commanded confidence, and this fundamental failure had aggravated economic evils and contributed considerably to the exhaustion of the Treasury. In these circumstances, and particularly since the approach of more elections in 1800 promised still further instability, the real question of the time was not whether there would be a coup, but by whom it would be directed. Since the Jacobins, who were strong in the Council of Five Hundred, had recently been unwise enough to revive some of the drastic emergency measures of

1793, men not unnaturally feared that their victory would also mean the return of the Revolutionary Tribunal and the extensive use of the guillotine. Siéyès, on the other hand, was still generally regarded as a constitutional genius; and although Bonaparte had not in fact returned to Paris from Egypt until after the armies of the second coalition had been decisively defeated, he was immensely popular with the people as the man who had brought the country victory and peace in 1797, and could be expected to do so again. Not surprisingly, the intervention of these two men in combination was widely welcomed.

The situation of the conspirators was nonetheless precarious, for while it was fairly easy to overthrow a divided and unpopular government, it was much more difficult to replace it legitimately. For that, the two councils had to be confronted; but at a meeting between Bonaparte and the politicians on the evening of November 9, it became apparent that no plans had been prepared for the following day. Both Bonaparte and Siéyès had been primarily concerned with reaching agreement on general principles, and each had presumed that the other had the second stage of the coup well in hand. Worse still, no firm agreement could be reached in the meeting, for Bonaparte refused point-blank to countenance the most obvious course, the immediate arrest of the principal Jacobin deputies. This was certainly partly because he was constantly concerned to ensure that he would not appear to be committed to any single party. Sincerely or insincerely, he steadily maintained that he was acting for the nation as a whole. Earlier, on November 9, he had found that Fouché, following a well-established revolutionary precedent for times of crisis, had closed the gates of Paris, and he had rebuked him angrily: "We are acting with the nation and by its strength alone. Let no one be disturbed, and the triumph of the nation will have nothing in common with the uprisings of minorities." Beyond this, too, there was probably some doubt in his mind about how far the rank and file of the army would be prepared to go. The ordinary soldiers detested the Directory as much as they adored Bonaparte himself; but they were generally ardent republicans, more sympathetic to the bellicose Jacobins than to Siéyès and his associates. What is more, several of the generals, notably Bernadotte, would certainly have preferred to act in conjunction with the Jacobins, and Bonaparte had to avoid giving them an opportunity to intervene.

The second day of the coup was consequently one of haphazard action and protracted uncertainty. During the morning a throng of deputies, officials, military detachments and spectators converged upon St. Cloud; but many prominent people kept their carriages ready for hasty departure if things should go awry. To make matters worse, the accommodation assigned to the councils in the palace was not ready until well into the afternoon, and as the deputies waited on the terrace their conversations soon established the fact that the alleged Jacobin plot was merely a myth, trumped up to cover and excuse some real consolidation of authority. Thus when the councils finally assembled, the Elders were uneasy and the Five Hundred were alarmed and angry. Left on this occasion without any positive lead, the Elders became involved in indecisive debate, while the Five Hundred lost invaluable time by insisting that each of its members should personally swear to uphold the existing constitution of the Republic. Gradually, however, opinion began to harden in both houses, and Lucien Bonaparte, Napoleon's brother, presiding over the Five Hundred, found it increasingly difficult to stave off dangerous motions. At this point the appearance of Generals Jourdan and Augereau, both Jacobin deputies, and the increasing restlessness of Talleyrand, indicated clearly enough that the success of the coup d'état was swaying in the balance.

In these circumstances Bonaparte, whose forces were massed around the building, reluctantly agreed to attempt to win the day by addressing both councils personally. This proceeding, utterly unnatural to him, was almost disastrously unsuccessful. In the Elders, his appeal for support was unconvincing, and when he was interrupted by a reference to the constitution, he ruined the effective part of his reply—that repeated abuse had already stripped the constitution of all sanctity—by threats and bombast: "Remember that I march accompanied by the god of war and the god of victory!" In the Council of Five Hundred, housed in the Orangerie on the other side of the palace, his failure was complete. Appearing ahead of an escort of a few grenadiers, he was immediately assailed by angry cries of "Down with the tyrant!", "No swords in the sanctuary of the laws!" and "Outlawry, outlawry!" ("Hors de la loi!")—the terrible

forerunner of so many revolutionary proscriptions.

Dramatic scenes ensued. Surrounded, jostled and in considerable danger of actual assault, Bonaparte had to be protected by the grenadiers and rescued by Murat and other officers from outside. The situation was saved by Lucien. Severely shaken, Bonaparte left the Five Hundred in disorder, and joined his brother outside the building and appealed to the nearest troops to disperse a factious minority of men who had sought to slay, and were now about to proscribe, their general. For a moment, all remained in doubt, for as the men of the regular army had been kept some way to the rear, those Lucien addressed were the guards of the councils, and they were reluctant to betray their particular trust. Only Lucien's theatrical promise to kill his brother with his own hand if he should ever attack liberty, and the bold example of Murat in advancing toward the hall, made these men move. Once begun, however, all was quickly over; entering the Orangerie with bayonets fixed and drums beating, the guards rapidly cleared the room, many of the deputies shedding their distinctive Roman robes of office and following the spectators ignominiously

Napoleon flanked by Jean Jacques Cambacérès and Charles Lebrun.
Below Emmanuel Siéyès nominates Napoleon as First Consul and Cambacérès and Lebrun as second and third consuls.

Napoleon, assailed by
deputies in the Council of
Five Hundred, is protected by
the grenadiers. His success
and popularity with the army
gave him the military power
from which his political
authority derived.

prepared new constitutional laws. Since the Council
of Five Hundred was dispersed, this order was of
course illegal; but matters were not left there. Later
that night a sufficient number—possibly even a
majority—of the Five Hundred were brought together again to accept the same proposals, save that
there were now to be constitutional commissions
from both houses, and sixty-two deputies of the
Five Hundred were declared deprived of their seats.
Arrangements being thus made for the reestablish-
ment of constitutional rule, at two o'clock in the
morning of November 11, the three provisional
consuls took an oath of loyalty to "the Republic,
one and indivisible" and to "liberty, equality and
the representative system."

Although this completed what is commonly
called the coup d'état of Brumaire, Bonaparte was
still far from being able to exercise dictatorial power.
Nor, indeed, is it certain that he wished to do so.
All that can be said with confidence is that in the
course of the next few days he clearly emerged as
by far the ablest of the provisional consuls, being in
fact the head of the government, and that in the
course of the next few weeks his genius began to
bring new life to France. Although the new government, desperately short of money, lived as best it
could from day to day, Bonaparte continued to
repudiate party. Setting his face against all proscriptions and abrogating revolutionary legislation
as soon as it was possible to do so, he spoke always
of a new order of affairs, of reconciliation and
reconstruction; and to unify the nation he called
all men to its service regardless of their past.

The principal task of the provisional consulate
was, however, that of providing the Republic with
a more stable constitution, and it is in his achievement of this that both Bonaparte's ability and his
innate rascality become apparent. In brief, he
succeeded in confronting the two constitutional
commissions with two alternative constitutions,
one of great complexity drafted by Siéyès, and one,
at once more straightforward and more liberal,
drafted by Daunou. Then, literally wearing out the
fifty commissioners by his own untiring energy, he
was able in a week to persuade them to accept from
each of these drafts those proposals that did most
to concentrate authority in his own hands. On
December 13, 1799, this process culminated in
what amounted to a second coup d'état. In the
first place, the commissioners were suddenly called
upon to sign as completed the new constitution as
it then stood, no vote being taken; and second,
although votes were cast for the election of new
consuls, Bonaparte abruptly set these aside un-
counted, calling instead upon Siéyès to select the
three men he preferred. Siéyès, who seemed to
have lost all interest in the proceedings once the
unity of his original grand design had been shattered,
responded, as had no doubt been arranged, by
nominating Bonaparte as First Consul, and Cambacérès and Lebrun as his colleagues. By the new
constitution the second and third consuls were
to be simply consultative officers, with the right to

through the windows. Thus—unexpectedly—the
legislative councils as well as the executive Directory
perished in the days of Brumaire.

Suitably embellished, the story of these events
was later widely diffused, so that to this day popular
pictures contrast the disciplined unity of the
national army with the tumult and disorder
engendered by parliamentary passions. The truth
is that Bonaparte had played an inglorious role in
an affair that had been sadly mismanaged. Contrary
to their hopes, the conspirators had had to have
recourse to force; the rule of law, the principle of
which, enshrined in the constitution of 1795, had
at least technically been preserved through the
intervening years, had been finally broken. To an
extent which our own more cynical age may well
find almost incredible, all now sought to restore this
breach. Initially the Elders, who were still in session,
were persuaded to approve the establishment of an
interim government, a provisional consulate composed of Siéyès, Ducos and Bonaparte, and to order
an adjournment of their own debates for six weeks
while a commission of twenty-five of their members

record their opinions, but "thereafter the decision of the First Consul shall suffice." As for the Councils of the Elders and the Five Hundred, their adjournment proved perpetual; they were simply superseded by new legislative bodies, the composition and powers of which were much more closely controlled.

When this new constitution came into effect on December 25, 1799, Bonaparte had indeed acquired great power. This situation was not unpopular for, quite apart from his personal merits, everyone was agreed that constitutional revision to strengthen the executive had long been imperative. It would, moreover, be wrong to suppose that the new government was merely a crude military dictatorship. Although Bonaparte had, of course, had strong military backing, there is little in the story of his rise from general to First Consul to suggest that the army was distinct from the rest of the nation, or that he was dependent upon it. Rather, indeed, it would seem that he made every effort to avoid involving the soldiers in the initial coup d'état, and that the subsequent extension of his authority was essentially a consequence of his personal impact in a civil situation. Again, although his power as First Consul was immense, it was not absolute: France remained a constitutional republic, and for the first years of the Consulate, in what was perhaps the finest period in his breathtaking career, Bonaparte was to pride himself upon his observance of the restraints imposed upon him by the constitution.

His advent nevertheless presented France and the world with a form of democracy fundamentally different from that familiar to liberals in Europe and America. When Bonaparte swore loyalty to the representative system, when he assured France that "the constitution is founded upon the true principles of representative government," he placed a singularly literal interpretation upon those terms; in future, it would be the government, not a legislative assembly, that would be the representative of the people. Moreover, since by general assent the people were sovereign, it followed that ultimately the man who exercised sovereignty in the name of the people could legitimately repudiate even constitutional law. Bonaparte's new authority was thus really dictatorial because, as he took good care to ensure, it could always be endorsed, at least in appearance, by a plebiscite. At the opening of 1800, however, no one, not even Bonaparte himself, knew what balance would be struck between freedom and tyranny.

M. J. SYDENHAM

Joachim Murat, the great cavalry commander, whom Napoleon later placed upon the throne of Naples.

Napoleon's seizure of power, a satirical cartoon by Gillray.

Aurangzeb 1618-1707
Mogul Emperor

Antonio Vivaldi c. 1675-1741
Italian violinist and composer

Isaac Newton 1642-1727
Physicist

Sir Robert Walpole 1676-1745
English Whig statesman

Gottfried Leibnitz 1646-1716
German mathematician and philosopher

Stanislas I Leszczynski 1677-1766
King of Poland

Pierre Bayle 1647-1706
French philosopher and critic

Shih-tsung (Yung Cheng) 1678-17
Manchu Emperor

William III (of Orange) 1650-1702
Stadtholder of Holland, King of Great Britain and Ireland

Henry St. John, Viscount Bolingbro
English Tory statesman

John Churchill, Duke of Marlborough 1650-1722
English general and statesman

Georg Philipp Telema
German composer

André Hercule de Fleury 1653-1743
French cardinal and statesman

Charles XII 1682-
King of Sweden

Sheng Tsu (Hsuan-yeh; reign title, K'ang Hsi) 1654-1722
Manchu Emperor

Philip V 1683
King of Spain

Frederick I 1657-1713
First King of Prussia

Domenico
Italian compo

Alessandro Scarlatti 1659-1725
Italian composer

George II 168
King of Great

George I 1660-1727
King of Great Britain and Ireland, Elector of Hanover

Char
Holy

Daniel Defoe c. 1660-1731
English journalist and novelist

Joha
Gern

Mary II 1662-94
Queen of Great Britain and Ireland

Geo
Irish

Anne 1665-1714
Queen of Great Britain and Ireland

Geor
Gern

Victor Amadeus II 1666-1732
Duke of Savoy, King of Sardinia

Jonathan Swift 1667-1745
Irish satirist

Augustus II the Strong 1670-1733
Elector of Saxony, King of Poland

John Law 1671-1729
Scottish financier in France

Peter I the Great 1672-1725
Tsar of Russia

Philip, Duke of Orleans 1674-1723
Regent of France

1713 Twilight of the Sun King – The treaties
of Utrecht and Rastatt curb the Sun King's
territorial ambitions and restore peace to
Europe

1720
The South Sea Bubble – The spectacular
collapse of the South Sea Company ruins
thousands of stock speculators and
topples the English government

Charles de Montesquieu 1689-1755
French political philosopher

Henry Fielding 1707-54
English novelist and playwright

Johann Joachim Winckelmann 1717-68
German archaeologist and art critic

Samuel Richardson 1689-1761
English novelist

Carl von Linné (Linnaeus) 1707-78
Swedish botanist

Maria Theresa 1717-80 *Archduchess of
Austria, Queen of Hungary and Bohemia*

Mir Jafar 1691-1765
Indian general, puppet Nawab of Bengal

Georges Buffon 1707-88
French naturalist

Jean Le Rond d'Alembert c. 1717-83
French mathematician and philosopher

Elizabeth Farnese 1692-1766
Queen of Spain

Francis I (Francis Stephen, Duke of
Lorraine) 1708-65 *Holy Roman Emperor*

Charles Gravier Vergennes 1717-87
French statesman

78-1751

Anna Ivanovna 1693-1740
Empress of Russia

William Pitt the Elder, Earl of Chatham 1708-78
English statesman

81-1767

Thomas Pelham-Holles, Duke of Newcastle 1693-1768
English Whig statesman

Elizabeth Petrovna 1709-62
Empress of Russia

18

François Marie Voltaire 1694-1778
French philosopher

Samuel Johnson 1709-84
English writer and conversationalist

46

Maurice de Saxe 1696-1750
French marshal

Louis XV 1710-74
King of France

arlatti 1683-1757

Augustus III 1696-1763
Elector of Saxony, King of Poland

David Hume 1711-76
Scottish philosopher and historian

60
itain and Ireland, Elector of Hanover

Giambattista Tiepolo 1696-1770
Italian painter

Count Wenzel Anton von Kaunitz 1711-94
Austrian statesman

1685-1740
man Emperor

Charles VII (Charles Albert of Bavaria) 1697-1745
Holy Roman Emperor

Ch'ien-lung 1711-99
Manchu Emperor

bastian Bach 1685-1750
ganist and composer

Joseph François Dupleix 1697-1763
Governor of French East India Company

Louis Joseph, Marquis of Montcalm 1712-59
French general

rkeley 1685-1753
ilosopher and bishop

William Hogarth 1697-1764
English painter and engraver

Jean Jacques Rousseau 1712-78
French philosopher and author

ederick Handel 1685-1759
nglish composer

Antonio Canaletto 1697-1768
Italian painter

Frederick II the Great 1712-86
King of Prussia

Frederick William I 1688-1740
King of Prussia

Sebastian Pombal 1699-1782
Portuguese statesman

Denis Diderot 1713-84
French encyclopedist and philosopher

Alexander Pope 1688-1744
English poet and satirist

Anders Celsius 1701-44
Swedish astronomer and inventor

John Stuart, Earl of Bute 1713-92
British statesman

Nadir Shah 1688-1747
Turcoman Shah of Persia

Charles Emmanuel III 1701-73
Duke of Savoy, King of Sardinia

George Whitefield 1714-70
English evangelist

James Francis Edward Stuart, "James III" 1688-1766
The "Old Pretender" to the English throne

François Boucher 1703-70
French painter

Christoph Gluck 1714-87
German composer

Emmanuel Swedenborg 1688-1772
Swedish scientist, philosopher and religious writer

John Wesley 1703-91
English founder of Methodism

Thomas Gray 1716-71
English poet

John V 1689-1750
King of Portugal

Benjamin Franklin 1706-90
American statesman, scientist and philosopher

Charles III 1716-88
King of the Two Sicilies, then of Spain

1700 ●
Battle of Narva: Swedish
victory over Russians

1700-21
Great Northern War
●

1713 Pragmatic Sanction
● reserves Hapsburg
succession to Maria
Theresa

1718
Sicily becomes Austrian
possession: Duke of
Savoy obtains Sardinia in
exchange

1701 ●
Elector of Brandenburg
becomes King of Prussia

Act of Union (with
Scotland) creates Great
Britain ● **1707**

1715-16 ●
Jacobite rebellion in
Scotland

1721 ●
Treaty of Nystadt: Russia
gains control of Baltic
littoral and unofficial
protectorate over Poland

War of the Spanish **1701-14** ●
Succession

Battle of Poltava: Russian
victory over Swedes

1724
China closed to
Westerners: missionaries
expelled

1703 ●
Methuen Treaty between
England and Portugal:
England gains commercial
advantage

1709 ●
Asiento Treaty gives **1713**
Britain monopoly of ●
African slave trade in
South America

1717-20 ●
Rise and fall of John
Law's financial system in
France

● **1721-42**
Rise of Walpole and
establishment of cabinet
government in Britain

1736
Ch'ien-lung Becomes Emperor of China – Greatest Emperor of the Manchu dynasty, Ch'ien-lung forcibly unifies China and establishes a brilliant cultural orthodoxy

1742
First Performance of Handel's *Messiah* – Straitened circumstance compels Handel to compose a work in twenty-four days; the result, the *Messiah*, is the acknowledged classic of English oratorio

1751
An Encyclopedia for the Enlightenment – Hounded by government censors and condemned by the Church, Denis Diderot edits his thirty-five volume encyclopedia

1755
Disaster Strikes Lisbon – When a seri of earth tremors shatter Lisbon, mystics insist that the disaster is Divine Retribution for Portugal's sins

The War of the Austrian Succession – **1740**
Heir to her father's disparate dominions, Maria Theresa is attacked by Prussia in an international war that transforms the Hapsburg Empire

1749
***Tom Jones* Revolutionizes Literature** – Incorporating the precedents of Defoe and Richardson, Henry Fielding launches into prose and provides the first model for the English novel

1759
The Year of Victories – On land and at sea in Europe, West Africa, India and North America the British defeat the French and establish the Empire on which the sun never set

---

Pontiac c. 1720-69
American Indian chief

James Cook 1728-79
English navigator and explorer

Edward Gibbon 1737-94
English historian

Ho-shen 1750-99
Chinese Grand Councillor

James Hargreaves ?-1778
English inventor

Robert Adam 1728-92
Scottish architect

Luigi Galvani 1737-98
Italian scientist

James Madison 1751-1836
American statesman

Charles Edward Stuart, "Bonnie Prince Charlie" 1720-88
Pretender to the English throne

Gottold Ephraim Lessing 1729-81 *German dramatist and critic*

Sir William Petty, Earl of Shelburne 1737-1805
English statesman

Samuel Crompton 1753-1827
English inventor

Emelyan Ivanovich Pugachev ?-1775 *Cossack leader*

Catherine II the Great 1729-96
Empress of Russia

Thomas Paine 1737-1809
Political writer and theorist

Louis XVI 1754-93
King of France

Madame de Pompadour 1721-64 *Mistress to Louis XV*

Edmund Burke 1729-97
British historian and statesman

Lord George Macartney 1737-1806
British diplomat

Jacques Pierre Brissot 1754-
French journalist and

Ferdinand, Duke of Brunswick 1721-92 *Prussian field-marshal*

Josiah Wedgwood 1730-95
English potter

Lord Charles Cornwallis 1738-1805
English general

Charles Maurice de Talleyra
French statesman

John Burgoyne 1722-92
British general in North America

Lord Frederick North 1732-92 *English statesman*

George III 1738-1820
King of Great Britain and Ireland, King of Hanover

Marie–Antoinette
Queen of France

Adam Smith 1723-90
Scottish economist

Sir Richard Arkwright 1732-92
English inventor and manufacturer

Ivan VI 1740-64
Tsar of Russia

Wolfgang Amadeu
Austrian composer

Sir Joshua Reynolds 1723-92
English portrait painter

Richard Henry Lee 1732-94
American revolutionary statesman

Joseph II 1741-90
Holy Roman Emperor

Alexander Hamilt
American statesm

Ahmed Shah 1724-73
Afghan ruler

Stanislas II Augustus Poniatowski 1732-98
King of Poland

Nathanael Greene 1742-86
American revolutionary officer

Antonio Canov
Italian sculptor

Immanuel Kant 1724-1804
German philosopher

George Washington 1732-99
First President of the United States of America

Antoine Lavoisier 1743-94
French chemist

William Blake
English poet an

Robert Clive 1725-74 *English soldier, Founder of British Indian Empire*

Jacques Necker 1732-1804
French banker and statesman

Sir Joseph Banks 1743-1820
British naturalist, promoter of exploration

Marquis de
French statesm

Colonel Sir Eyre Coote 1726-83
British commander-in-chief in India

Jean Honoré Fragonard 1732-1806
French painter and engraver

Thomas Jefferson 1743-1826
American statesman

Maximilie
French

James Wolfe 1727-59
British soldier in Canada

Franz Joseph Haydn 1732-1809
Austrian composer

John Jay 1745-1829
American jurist and statesman

Friedr
Germ

Anne Robert Jacques Turgot 1727-81
French economist and statesman

Warren Hastings 1732-1818
English statesman and colonial administrator

Gustavus III 1746-92
King of Sweden

Willia
Englis

Thomas Gainsborough 1727-88
English painter

Joseph Priestly 1733-1804
English clergyman and chemist

Thaddeus Kościuszko 1746-1817
Polish patriot, general

John Wilkes 1727-97
English political reformer

Karl Wilhelm Ferdinand, Duke of Brunswick 1735-1806 *Prussian general*

Henry Grattan 1746-1820
Irish orator and statesman

Siraj-ud-Daulah c. 1728-57
Nawab of Bengal

John Adams 1735-1826
American statesman

Jacques Louis David 1748-1825
French painter

Peter III 1728-62
Tsar of Russia

Patrick Henry 1736-99
American revolutionary leader

Charles James Fox 1749-1806
English statesman

Oliver Goldsmith 1728-74
British poet, playwright and novelist

James Watt 1736-1819
Scottish mechanical engineer and inventor

Johann Wolfgang von Goethe 1749-1832
German writer

1733-35 War of the Polish Succession

Second Jacobite **1745-46**
Rebellion

1748
Treaty of Aix-la-Chapelle: Spanish gains in Italy; Austrian and Hanoverian successions confirmed; Prussia emerges a great power

1756
The "Black Hole of Calcutta"

1761
Surrender of Pondicherry, end of French influence India

1737
Walpole's Licensing Act: all plays subject to censorship

1744-45
Second Silesian War

1757
Battle of Plassey: British gain control of Bengal

1739-48
Anglo-Spanish War of Jenkins' Ear

1745
Treaty of Dresden: Prussia gains Silesia

1750-77
Pombal institutes administrative reform in Brazil and promotes trade

1759
Battle of Kunersdorf: Russo-Austrian victo over Prussia

Nadir Shah of Persia **1739**
defeats Afghans and sacks Delhi

1747
Afghanistan under Ahmed gains independence from Persia

1756-63
Seven Years War (Third Silesian War), French and Indian War

c. 1750-60
Most notable of Ch'ien-lung's "Ten Great Campaigns"

1740-42
First Silesian War

1770

"Terra Incognita" – Certain that an undiscovered continent lies somewhere in the South Pacific, James Cook sets out in search of the "Great South Land"

1775

Watt Constructs an Efficient Steam Engine – By improving on the uneconomical, crude existing models, Watt's steam engine contributes to the Industrial Revolution and ushers in the Age of Steam

1794

Eli Whitney Invents the Cotton Gin – Whitney's patent stimulates the growth of the cotton industry in the American South, thus entrenching the different social and economic systems that will contribute to the Civil War

The Declaration of Independence – **1776**
Thomas Jefferson drafts the American colonies' proclamation of independence to justify rebellion and win French support

"Liberté, Egalité, Fraternité" – **1789**
The French monarchy is doomed when troops garrisoning the Bastille refuse to open fire upon a mob of armed citizens

1799

Napoleon Bonaparte Becomes First Consul – A bloodless coup dissolves the French Directorate and, carefully observing constitutional form, establishes a Consulate giving Napoleon near-dictatorial power

The First Partition of Poland – **1772**
Russia, Prussia and Austria nurture and exploit the internal weakness of their Polish neighbor in order to dismember that state in an act of political cannibalism

1793

The Execution of Louis XVI – By the trial and execution of their monarch, the French people finally break with the past and establish irreversibly the sovereignty of the nation

Joachim Murat c. 1767-1815
French commander, King of Naples

Napoleon Bonaparte 1769-1821
Emperor of the French

Ludwig van Beethoven 1770-1827
German composer

volutionary leader

754-1838

755–93

ozart 1756-91

757-1804

757-1822

757-1827
tist

fayette 1757-1834
d officer

obespierre 1758-94
volutionary

on Schiller 1759-1805
riter

tt the Younger 1759-1806
atesman

amille Desmoulins 1760-94
ench revolutionary

rançois (Gracchus) Babeuf 1760-97
ench revolutionary conspirator, journalist

Wolfe Tone 1763-98
Irish revolutionary

Jean Baptiste Jules Bernadotte c. 1763-1844
French general, elected King of Sweden

Eli Whitney 1765-1825
American inventor

● **1765-66** Clive's reforms in India

1775-83 American Revolutionary War

● **1783**
Russia annexes Crimea

● **1789**   ● **1792** National Convention declares France a republic

763 Treaty of Paris ends Seven Years and French and Indian Wars

1773-75 ●
Pugachev's revolt in Russia

● **1781**
United States' Articles of Confederation signed

Belgian declaration of independence

1790 Civil Constitution of the Clergy in France

● **1798**
Whitney contracts to standardize arms manufacture

● **1763**

● **1777-81**
Franco-American alliance

● **1787**

1793
●

"Pontiac's War": Indian sing in America

1774 ●
Quebec Act: transfer of much Western American territory to control of Quebec governor

● **1778-79**
War of the Bavarian Succession

1784 ●
Pitt's India Act: East India Company's power transferred to British government

Constitutional Convention under Washington

1801
Act of Unio between Britain and Ireland

1764 British defeat Emperor of Delhi

1780 ●
The League of Armed Neutrality formed against Britain

1791 ●
Constitutional monarchy in France

Committee of Public Safety establishes the Terror

1764 Invention of spinning jenny by James Hargreaves

1774-76 ●
Continental Congress held in Philadelphia

1786 ●
Daniel Shay's rebellion in the United States

● **1794**
Polish national rebellion

1765 ●
Stamp Act Congress asserts right to self-taxation in American colonies

● **1768**
Unrest in Poland: new Confederation called

● **1774-82**
Ch'ien-lung's "literary inquisition"

1783 ●
Treaties of Versailles and Paris: Britain recognizes American independence and French renounce India

1791
Louis XVI's flight to Varennes

1788
Sydney founded as first Australian penal settlement

● **1795**
New French government: the Directory

1773 ●
Boston Tea Party

● **1792**
Beginning of French Revolutionary Wars

● **1798**
Battle of the Nile

Acknowledgments

The authors and publishers wish to thank the following museums and collections by whose kind permission the illustrations are reproduced. Page numbers appear in bold, photographic sources in italics.

12 *Mansell Collection*
13 Marquess of Anglesey
14 (1) *Mansell Collection* (2) Rijksmuseum, Amsterdam
15 (1) *Mansell Collection* (2) National Portrait Gallery, London (3) *Giraudon*
16 British Museum, London: *John R. Freeman*
17 British Museum: *John R. Freeman*
18 (1) Hudson's Bay Company, London
19 (1) *Mansell Collection* (2) *Giraudon* (3) National Portrait Gallery
20 *Mansell Collection*
21 (1) British Museum (2) *A. C. Cooper* (3) National Portrait Gallery (4) British Museum: *John R. Freeman*
22 Guildhall Museum, London
23 National Portrait Gallery
24 (1) National Portrait Gallery (2) *Mary Evans Picture Library*
25 (1) *Mary Evans Picture Library* (2) *Mansell Collection*
26 (1) *John R. Freeman* (2) National Portrait Gallery
27 (1) *Mansell Collection* (2) Victoria and Albert Museum, London: *Michael Holford Library*
28 (1) Museo del Prado, Madrid: *Foto Mas* (2) Svenska Portrattarkivet Nationalmuseum, Stockholm
29 (1, 2) Victoria and Albert Museum
30 British Museum: *R. B. Fleming*
31 Sir Isaac Wolfson Collection: *Michael Holford Library*
32 Victoria and Albert Museum: *A. C. Cooper*
33 Victoria and Albert Museum: *Michael Holford Library*
34 *History Today*
35 (1) *Christie, Manson and Woods Ltd* (2) Percival David Foundation
36 British Museum: *R. B. Fleming*
37 Victoria and Albert Museum: *R. Todd-White*
38 Victoria and Albert Museum
39 (2) *Mary Evans Picture Library* (3) British Museum (4) British Museum: *Michael Holford Library*
40 *Photo Meyer*
41 *Anton Graphic Art*
42 *Archiv Gerstenberg*
43 (1) Staatsbibliothek, Berlin (2) Musée Carnavalet, Paris: *Photo Bulloz*
44 (2) British Museum, Cruikshank Collection: *R. B. Fleming*
45 *Archiv Gerstenberg*

46 (1) By permission of the Trustees of the Wallace Collection (2) National Gallery, London (3) By permission of the Trustees of Sir John Soane's Museum: *Cooper-Bridgeman Library*
47 (1) Mrs. E. L. Green-Armytage (2) National Portrait Gallery
48 National Portrait Gallery
49 G. Coke Collection: *Kenneth Fensom*
50 (1) National Library of Ireland (2) *Mansell Collection*
51 Tate Gallery, London: *John Webb*
52 (1) Thomas Corham Foundation: *Cooper-Bridgeman Library* (2) National Portrait Gallery
53 *John R. Freeman*
54 (1) British Museum (2, 3) *Mansell Collection*
55 (1) Trinity College, Dublin: *Courtauld Institute of Art* (2) University Library, Cambridge: *Phoebus Picture Library* (3) *Radio Times Hulton Picture Library*
56 Birmingham Art Gallery: *Reilly and Constantine*
57 *Mansell Collection*
58 British Museum: *John R. Freeman*
59 (1) British Museum: *John R. Freeman* (2) *Courtauld Institute of Art*
60 (1) National Portrait Gallery (2) *Mansell Collection*
61 (1) British Museum: *R. B. Fleming* (2) *Radio Times Hulton Picture Library*
62 (1) British Museum: *John R. Freeman* (2) *Radio Times Hulton Picture Library* (3) National Portrait Gallery
63 (1) National Portrait Gallery (2) *Radio Times Hulton Picture Library*
64 *Giraudon*
65 Louvre, Paris: *Giraudon*
66 (1, 2) *Mansell Collection*
67 (1, 3) *Mansell Collection* (2) *Radio Times Hulton Picture Library*
68 (1) *Mary Evans Picture Library* (2) Louvre: *Giraudon*
69 (1) *R. B. Fleming* (2) *Mansell Collection*
70 (1) Staatsbibliothek, Berlin (2) *Mansell Collection*
71 (1, 2) British Museum: *John R. Freeman*
72 *Centre Cultural Portugaise*
73 *Lisbon Tourist Board*
74 *Mansell Collection*
75 (1) Bibliothèque Nationale, Paris (2) *Lisbon Tourist Board*
76 *Lisbon Tourist Board*
77 *Lisbon Tourist Board*
78 (1) British Museum: *John R. Freeman* (2) *Mansell Collection*
79 (1, 2) *Mansell Collection*
80 National Army Museum, London
81 *Phoebus Picture Library*
82 British Museum, Cruikshank

Collection: *Marshall Cavendish Picture Library*
83 *Radio Times Hulton Picture Library*
84 (1) National Trust, London: *Phoebus Picture Library* (2) *Snark International*
85 *Snark International*
86 The National Gallery of Canada, Ottawa—Gift of the Duke of Westminster, 1918
87 National Maritime Museum, Greenwich, London: *Marshall Cavendish Picture Library*
88 (1, 2) Staatsbibliothek, Berlin (3, 4) *Mansell Collection*
89 (1) Victoria and Albert Museum (2) *Mansell Collection*
90 Private Collection: *Michael Holford Library*
91 *Mary Evans Picture Library*
92 *Mary Evans Picture Library*
93 National Maritime Museum, Greenwich
94 (1) Private Collection: *Michael Holford Library* (2) National Maritime Museum, Greenwich: *John R. Freeman*
96 (1, 2) *Radio Times Hulton Picture Library*
97 (1) British Museum: *John R. Freeman* (2) *Roger-Viollet* (3) Chester Beatty Library, Dublin
98 *Verlag Aural Bongers, Recklinghausen*
99 *Archiv Gerstenberg*
100 *Radio Times Hulton Picture Library*
101 *Archiv für Kunst und Geschichte*
102 *George Rainbird Ltd*
103 (1) *Archiv für Kunst und Geschichte* (2) Count Bobrinskoy Collection: *Michael Holford Library*
104 (1) Victoria and Albert Museum (2) *Mansell Collection* (3) British Museum: *John R. Freeman*
105 (1, 2) *Mansell Collection*
106 Courtesy of Birmingham Public Libraries, Local Studies Department: *W. G. Belsher*
107 National Portrait Gallery
108 (1) Courtesy of Birmingham Public Libraries, Local Studies Department: *W. G. Belsher* (2) Science Museum, London
109 Science Museum
110 Walker Art Gallery, Liverpool
111 (1) Mrs. J. G. P. Pendarves, on loan to The Royal Institution of Cornwall (2) Science Museum
112 *Orbis Publishing Ltd*
113 (1) Library Company of Philadelphia: *Orbis Publishing Ltd* (2) Historical Society of Pennsylvania: *Orbis Publishing Ltd*
115 Museum of Art, Bowdoin College, Brunswick, Maine: *Radio Times Hulton Picture Library*
116 (1, 2) National Portrait Gallery

117 (1) Metropolitan Museum of Art, New York (2) Parker Gallery, London
118 (1) *Mansell Collection* (2) *Radio Times Hulton Picture Library*
119 (1, 3) *Mansell Collection* (2) *Radio Times Hulton Picture Library*
120 National Gallery of Art, Washington D.C.
121 Musée de Versailles
122 (1) *Courtauld Institute of Art* (2) American Embassy, London (3) *Radio Times Hulton Picture Library*
123 (1) *Radio Times Hulton Picture Library* (2) *Mansell Collection*
124 Musée de Versailles: *Photo Bulloz*
125 Musée de Versailles: *R. B. Fleming*
126 (1) *Mary Evans Picture Library* (2) *Photo Bulloz*
127 (1, 2) *Mansell Collection*
128 British Museum: *R. B. Fleming*
129 British Museum: *R. B. Fleming*
130 (1, 2) *Mansell Collection*
131 (1) Musée Carnavalet: *Photo Bulloz* (2) Musée de Versailles: *Giraudon* (3) Bibliothèque Nationale, Paris: *Photo Bulloz*
132 Musée Carnavalet: *Photo Bulloz*
133 British Museum: *Mansell Collection*
134 (1) Bibliothèque Nationale, Paris: *Photo Bulloz* (2) *Photo Bulloz*
135 (1) Musée Carnavalet: *Editions Robert Laffont*
136 (1) *Mansell Collection* (2) Bibliothèque Nationale, Paris: *Editions Robert Laffont*
137 Bibliothèque Nationale, Paris: *Photo Bulloz*
138 (1) *Archiv für Kunst und Geschichte* (2, 3) *Radio Times Hulton Picture Library*
139 (1) Courtesy of New York Historical Society, New York City (2) *Western Americana*
140 Yale University Art Gallery—Gift of George Hoadly
141 *Radio Times Hulton Picture Library*
142 *Mansell Collection*
143 (1) *Mansell Collection* (2) Science Museum: *R. B. Fleming*
144 Yale University Art Gallery
145 *Mansell Collection*
146 (1) National Portrait Gallery (2) London Museum (3) *Radio Times Hulton Picture Library*
147 (1, 2) *Phoebus Picture Library*
148 Malmaison, Paris: *Photo Bulloz*
149 Musée Carnavalet: *Photo Bulloz*
150 (1) Musée de Versailles: *Photo Bulloz* (2) Bibliothèque Nationale, Paris: *Photo Bulloz*
151 *Photo Bulloz*
152 Musée de Versailles: *Photo Bulloz*
153 (1) Private Collection: *Photo Bulloz* (2) *Photo Bulloz*

Managing Editor *Adrian Brink*
Assistant Editors *Geoffrey Chesler, Francesca Ronan*
Picture Editor *Julia Brown*
Consultant Designer *Tim Higgins*
Art Director *Anthony Cohen*

Index